A Fateful Love

Sport, History and Culture

Edited by

Professor Richard Holt
Professor Matthew Taylor

International Centre for Sports History and Culture
De Montfort University, Leicester

Vol. 10

PETER LANG
Oxford · Bern · Berlin · Bruxelles · New York · Wien

A Fateful Love

Essays on Football in the North-East of England 1880–1930

Gavin Kitching

PETER LANG

Oxford · Bern · Berlin · Bruxelles · New York · Wien

Bibliographic information published by Die Deutsche Nationalbibliothek
Die Deutsche Nationalbibliothek lists this publication in the Deutsche
Nationalbibliografie; detailed bibliographic data is available on the Internet at
http://dnb.d-nb.de.

Library of Congress Cataloging-in-Publication Data

Names: Kitching, G. N., author.
Title: A fateful love : essays on football in the north-east of England 1880-1930
    / Gavin Kitching.
Description: Oxford ; New York : Peter Lang, [2021] | Includes bibliographical
    references and index.
Identifiers: LCCN 2020030742 (print) | LCCN 2020030743 (ebook) |
    ISBN 9781789978346 (paperback) | ISBN 9781789978353 (ebook) | ISBN
    9781789978360 (epub) | ISBN 9781789978377 (mobi)
Subjects: LCSH: Soccer--England, North East--History--19th century. |
    Soccer--Press coverage--England, North East--History--19th century. |
    Professionalism in sports--England--History--20th century. |
    Soccer--Economic aspects.
Classification: LCC GV944.E5 K57 2021 (print) | LCC GV944.E5 (ebook) |
    DDC 796.33409427/09034--dc23
LC record available at https://lccn.loc.gov/2020030742
LC ebook record available at https://lccn.loc.gov/2020030743

Cover image: Thomas Hemy's painting of Sunderland v Aston Villa at SAFC's
Newcastle Road ground, 2nd January, 1895. Reproduced by kind permission of Ryehill
Football (ryehillfootball.co.uk).

ISSN 1664-1906
ISBN 978-1-78997-834-6 (print)   ISBN 978-1-78997-836-0 (ePDF)
ISBN 978-1-78997-835-3 (eBook)   ISBN 978-1-78997-837-7 (MOBI)

© Peter Lang Group AG 2021

Published by Peter Lang Ltd, International Academic Publishers,
52 St Giles, Oxford, OX1 3LU, United Kingdom
oxford@peterlang.com, www.peterlang.com

Gavin Kitching have asserted their right under the Copyright, Designs and Patents Act,
1988, to be identified as Author of this Work.

This publication has been peer reviewed.

*In memory of my beloved father, Norman Kitching, and
for the people of Northumberland and Durham.*

Contents

Foreword

RICHARD HOLT

In writing this Foreword I am breaking the self-imposed editorial silence I have maintained over many years. I always thought it best to let authors introduce themselves, setting out their stall in a Preface or in the introductory chapter. Why change the habit of a lifetime? I have two reasons: one personal and intellectual; the other professional and historical.

On the personal level, as Gavin Kitching generously acknowledges, I bear some responsibility for encouraging him to carry out this research. As friends since postgraduate days – almost fifty years ago – we both discovered we grew up with football. As a boy I occasionally went to Newcastle United with my uncle when he went regularly to Sunderland with his father, whose formative and wise influence is tenderly evoked in the opening pages of the book. Unlike the visceral loathing of the 'Mags' and 'Mackems' of today – I never recall hearing those words then – in our youth the rivalry was fierce but more friendly, fans sometimes attending each other's games, rooted in a shared industrial heritage and the world of organised Labour. Football and the north-east along with the predictable mix of Sixties radical politics and music were the things we found we had in common when we met in the early 1970s at Oxford. Gavin was finishing a doctorate on Tanzanian agriculture and I was writing a thesis on sport in France.

Gavin moved from a successful academic career in African Studies to a second life as a professor of philosophy with major published works on Marx and Wittgenstein and a chair in Politics at the University of New South Wales. Just as he spread his wings – crossing academic disciplines in a way which remains rare – I went the other way, getting more narrowly involved in the new sub-discipline of sports history. He always took a close interest in what I was doing in the history of sport in general and the history of football in particular. This, I now realise, was partly to do with his father, whom he lost at a young age, and partly a product of a profound interest in history. He has a long-standing admiration for the work of Eric Hobsbawn, whose flexible empirically grounded historical materialism and comparative method encompassed all manner of socio-cultural phenomena, including organised sport. I was also an admirer of Hobsbawm's work, especially on the class cultures of urban industrial society which included professional football. Although Gavin's work was predominantly philosophical, we discovered we were both fascinated by the historical moment when the industrial world that had shaped our own childhoods first came into being.

As the author of a general history of British sport, I was familiar with the literature including the excellent work on association football by Tony Mason, Dave Russell and Matthew Taylor amongst many others. But there were still gaps. In particular, scholarly 'bottom up' urban and re-gional studies, which captured the transition to modernity in detail, were still thin on the ground. Doctoral work, which went narrow and deep, had begun at the International Centre for Sports History and Culture at De Montfort University, where I worked and where Gavin became an Honorary Fellow. Other universities – notably in Ireland – followed suit but there was plenty of scope for new research, especially by someone with vast experience and proven research expertise. Hence when Gavin retired and expressed an interest in working on the history of football in the north-east, I was encouraging. As his research progressed, I became increasingly convinced he would make a genuine contribution to the history of the game. He had a fresh pair of eyes combined with a philosopher's clarity of focus and vast experience in posing and answering research questions. He was also fully committed to a grass-roots approach and seemed to relish doing the 'hard yards' in the primary sources.

Gavin came to sports history from a very different place than most of us working in the field. He was first an economist and then a philoso-pher. His philosophical work underpins his approach to writing about the history of sport, especially his interest in both Marx and Wittgenstein. This made him both sensitive to economic forces and to social class but also to the language in which such changes were expressed. In particular, Wittgenstein's insistence that words are understood through their use in language rather than having fixed universal meanings encouraged him to explore the mutability of terms such as 'tradition', 'amateur' and 'professional'. Far from losing the lay reader in abstraction, his philosophical work has made him profoundly sceptical of theory-led social science research. He has even written a book about the danger of basing social science research on canonical texts of social theory. The conclusions he draws come directly from an exhaustive study of primary sources with limited reference to the existing secondary literature.

He was a newcomer to what had become quite a substantial academic literature. There were advantages to being an outsider. He could be an 'enfant terrible' almost without realising it, who could ask the 'Emperor's new clothes' kind of questions. Why did people play these games? How did they play them? Instead of looking at sports through the lens of class, gender or politics, he could simply ask 'why did they expend so much energy or income on it?' 'Pleasure' was the elephant in the room. In a liberal society no one was actually forced to play football or cricket and yet hundreds of thousands of people – mostly but by no means exclusively young men – freely chose to do so. By extension, why did they pay to watch other people doing the same thing? What kinds of satisfaction did they get from it? As he kept saying, sport had to be 'fun' or it would never have happened at all. It was easy for the 'professionals' of sports history to forget this, it took an 'amateur' – albeit an unusually qualified one – to remind them.

His approach was to ask these big questions. Capturing lived experience is the Holy Grail of cultural history. This is especially difficult when working on popular culture where participants rarely wrote about their daily lives or personal feelings. How can we find out more about the sporting lives of those who started to play and to watch 'football'? What were early games of football like? The answer turns out to be partly hidden in plain sight. Reading hundreds and hundreds of match reports in the local press, which he often quotes at some length, turned out to be very revealing. The assumption of most historians, including myself, was that these would be uniformly thin and formulaic. This was wrong. Poring over them, especially those of his favourite reporter, 'Mercutio', revealed detailed descriptions of how the game was being played and by whom; how spectators travelled to the ground, what they found there and how they behaved. This is laborious work. Digital searches can throw up vast swathes of material but only long hours of patient reading can find what is hidden there. This 'panning for gold' is an important achievement in its own right. No-one – least of all someone with such a deep and wide-ranging knowledge of social science as he has – would claim this provides more than a series of snapshots of the sporting past. But in the absence of survey data and personal reminiscence – and crucially in the right hands – match reports and extracts from other press coverage prove most revealing.

He has found his own way to tell this story. His is neither a regional narrative nor a case study of a single community. His approach is episodic, peripatetic and loosely chronological. He shifts from 'traditional' forms of football in the old county town of Alnwick in mid-century to the new versions of the game taking shape in the regional capital, Newcastle, in the 1870s. He then looks at the early professionalisation of the sport in Sunderland in the 1880s and finishes in the 1920s with semi-professional 'amateur' football in the mining communities of the Durham coalfield. As he explains, this work was originally conceived as part of a bigger project to tell the history of the region through football, which he decided not to pursue. However, arbitrary as it may seem, there is a strong case for stopping where does. This is a history of origins and growth, pinpointing moments of change, digging deeply and moving forward, as an entire region was saturated in a single sport from back lane kickabouts to the First Division of the Football League with a myriad of clubs in between.

So much for why this book is distinctive both in conception and method. What has been revealed which we did not already know? It is not my purpose to provide a summary of the book. I simply want to underline some of the ways he challenges received wisdom as well as sometimes confirming it. In an analysis of Shrovetide football in the Northumberland town of Alnwick, he interrogates the long-held binary division between 'traditional' and 'modern'. It turns out there were several forms of the 'traditional' game, each succeeding the other, moving from streets and open fields to written rules and precisely demarcated spaces; from the old conjugal order of married versus bachelor to a parish-based structure. 'Traditional' football was not the unchanging customary practice commonly supposed.

Next he moves to the establishing of the association and rugby football codes in the region. Here he confirms rather than challenges the drift

of recent research away from the specific origins of either code, preferring to stress the flux of early 'football' with Tyne Association FC playing
Northumberland (Rugby) FC and other instances of hybrid games in the
early years. He is fascinated by the game itself, by the process of 'learning
though playing'. Why did the north-east become a stronghold of the association rather than the rugby code? Was it to do with *how* both games
were actually played? The point here is to re-focus our attention on the
pitch and the nature of play itself rather than on the socio-economic structures around it.

As his work is so heavily dependent on the local press, it makes sense
to have a closer look at early sports journalists. Again, with a few exceptions it is surprising historians have not done more of this before. T. W.
Gale, 'Mercutio', is his favourite reporter. Gale's work for the *Newcastle
Daily Leader* from 1885 to 1892 took him from Middlesbrough in the
south to Ashington in the north, commenting as he went not only on the
games he saw but on the state of grounds, the size, age and behaviour of
crowds and the importance of the railway in the thriving new world of
professional football.

In a careful micro study of the 'process' of professionalisation and commercialisation in Sunderland, we see how a club formed by school teachers
playing as amateurs within a decade were changed out of all recognition to
become one of the best teams in England. This story, of course, has been
told before for other clubs such as Preston North End or Blackburn Rovers.
What makes his account new and compelling is the insistence that this was
not part of a predetermined 'process of transformation' in the sense that
it was 'inevitable'. On the contrary, it was a bitter personal feud between
key individuals, which drove the precise course of events in Sunderland.
In passing, he also takes a side swipe at the idea of amateurism as the dominant ideology of Victorian sport. The schism between Sunderland AFC
and the short-lived Sunderland Albion was sparked not by the payment of
players but by the policy of importing them from Scotland.

This indifference to amateur values informs the final chapter on 'The
Crook Town Affair', which explains in forensic detail how a system of
semi-professional football operated within the 'amateur' Durham Football
Association. Using evidence from the FA's investigation of Crook Town

in 1928 after allegations of illegal payments, which were followed by the club's own retaliatory revelations, he meticulously pieces together a story of personal intrigue. This is 'thick description' which tells a story whilst also explaining why neither full professionalism nor genuine amateurism were feasible. Sports history has overlooked the intermediate category of 'semi-professionals' and explains why the FA colluded in getting round their own regulations.

'Small keys can open big doors' was advice that used to be given to doctoral students undertaking local case studies. These essays on the early history of football in the north-east of England are an excellent example of what can be achieved by going 'narrow and deep'. Each chapter, in its own way, refutes, modifies or expands our understanding whilst cumulatively providing a compelling account of how association football took such an unshakable hold in the north-east England during its industrial hey-day.

Newspaper Title Abbreviations Used in this Book

AJ:	*Alnwick Journal*
AM:	*Alnwick Mercury*
DC:	*Durham Chronicle*
DCA:	*Durham County Advertiser*
HC:	*Hexham Courant*
NCh:	*Newcastle Weekly Chronicle*
NC:	*Newcastle Courant*
NDC:	*Newcastle Daily Chronicle*
NDL:	*Newcastle Daily Leader*
EC:	*Newcastle Evening Chronicle*
DG:	*North-Eastern Daily Gazette* (Middlesbrough)
NM:	*North Mail* (Newcastle)
NA:	*Northern Athlete* (Newcastle)
NDE:	*Nottingham Daily Express*
NDM:	*Northern Daily Mail* (Hartlepool)
NE:	*Northern Echo* (Darlington)
NG:	*Northumberland Gazette* (Alnwick)
SDG:	*Shields Daily Gazette*
SDN:	*Shields Daily News*
SDE:	*Sunderland Daily Echo*
SDP:	*Sunderland Daily Post*

Introduction

My Father

My father took me to see my first Sunderland first team match at Roker Park in 1955 or 1956 when I was eight or nine years old. He introduced me to the experience slowly, taking me first to a few reserve matches and seating us safely in the old 'Clock Stand'. As I grew though I was allowed the full first team experience, and to stand with him in his preferred Roker End, a habit which I continued long after he died.

Depending on the match involved, we either travelled to Sunderland by train, (in the days when the Durham to Sunderland branch line ran through our village), or on a blue-and-white 'Philadelphia' bus chartered by Lambton 'D' colliery, the 'pit' in which my dad worked along with many other men in Fencehouses. As far as I remember, we mainly took 'the excursion bus' when there were big matches – a derby game against Newcastle, a match against some big-name opposition club like Manchester United or Arsenal, or for evening fixtures.

My father, like many north-eastern men, considered himself a football connoisseur. On the way home from a match he would regale me, and all friends and acquaintances around, with his opinions on strategy, tactics and player performances – his assessments including opposition as well as Sunderland players. Although a life-time Sunderland fan, he was invariably irritated by forms of partisanship he considered 'stupid'. When Sunderland lost (and then, as now, they lost rather a lot) he would often contrast the performance of some Sunderland player or players unfavourably with their opposition counterparts.

Consistently with his self-identification as an objective observer and unbiased judge, my father's favourite footballer was not even a Sunderland player. He was insistent that 'the best I ever saw' was the Middlesbrough and England inside-forward Wilf Manion, the so-called 'golden boy'.

When, after his retirement from the game, Manion sank into alcoholism and homelessness, my dad was a regular contributor to appeals on his behalf made in the local press. In 1958, some two years before he died, but while already in poor health, he was cajoled into attending a Sunderland v Manchester United match by his oldest and dearest friend. 'They were saying', said his friend, that a young Manchester United inside forward, Bobby Charlton 'was even better than Wilf'. So my dad dragged himself to the match, United won 2–1, and Charlton played a leading role in both goals. My dad was duly impressed. 'Oh he's good, he's very good, the lad' he announced on the bus home, 'but he's not as good as Wilf.'

My father's intolerance of 'stupid' partisanship extended even to his own son. The end of the 1957–8 season, which saw Sunderland's first relegation from the top-flight, also saw me regularly distraught. Opponents' goals (Birmingham City scored six in one match!) were clearly off-side, the referee was obviously biased, 'they' had only won by dirty play, etc. At first my dad was sympathetic to the tearful frustrations of a ten year old, but eventually his patience ran out. 'Gavin, they won because they were the better team,' he said gently but firmly, 'that's how it is sometimes, there's nowt to be done.'

Although I had no inkling of this at the time, only a boy's sense of the unbearable hardness of fate, I have often thought in retrospect that this was my first lesson in the emotional reality of objectivity. To be objective is to acknowledge that something is true that one would prefer – infinitely prefer – were not. And that is why the standard social science conception of objectivity, which sees it simply as the product of, or embodied in, some research 'technique' or 'method' or other, is so impoverished. It entirely fails to grasp objectivity as *a moral virtue* and one closely related to others. For objectivity is impossible without honesty, and sometimes honesty in its hardest form – about self, as well as about the world. In fact, objectivity, when it matters most, is honesty about the world made possible *by* honesty about self. Understanding that, or beginning to understand it, is something I owe to my father, and through him, to football. And though I would not claim that being a football fan is typically an education in objectivity (rather the reverse!), *it was in my case*, and all the more powerful for operating in the teeth of love – the love a fan always has for his or her team.

The Project

Against this background, when my old friend Dick Holt suggested that I might like, late in my career, to write something on the social history of football in the North-East, I was both moved and intrigued, moved by these memories and intrigued by the task. It was a task made all the more difficult by the fact that, when he made the suggestion (in 2008 or so), I was living far away – in Sydney, Australia – and had been for some time. Also, I had no experience of undertaking sports history research – or any kind of research – in Britain, my academic career having been given over entirely to study of the non-European world. As a result, I was not nearly so sanguine as Dick that I would be up to the task, particularly given my novice status as a historian and the marked constraints of distance and thus of time.

But it proved possible to overcome all these obstacles, at least to a degree. In 2009 the University of New South Wales provided me with sabbatical leave to begin the project and provided regular support funding thereafter. Several weeks spent in the summer of 2009 in the British Library newspaper archive, (then based in Colindale, London), got me started. Regular summer visits to the 'Local Studies' sections of Newcastle and Sunderland central libraries, and other north-eastern archives, deepened things immensely. And in the intervals between UK visits, access, in Australia, to the extraordinary, and ever-growing, 'British Newspaper Archive' online, was invaluable. And throughout, my secondary reading in sports history was encouraged and guided by Dick Holt and his colleagues at the International Centre for Sports History and Culture, De Montfort University, Leicester. If he and they have not been able to make me into a good sports historian, they have at least prevented me committing the worst mistakes of a bad one.

The result is this book, which, while narrower in its focus than originally intended (see below), does, I think, make an original contribution to understanding the beginnings and crucial initial development of association football in the North-East.

Neglected Issues

The role played by Victorian Britain in creating 'modern sport' – by converting a number of traditional or folk 'recreations' into codified and bureaucratically organised activities and *calling* them 'sports' as it did so – is a central focus of sports history. But that history has far more general overviews of this transition than detailed, short-period, accounts of the process for particular sports. In the case of soccer, traditional or 'folk' 'foot-ball' (a loosely linked family of games) was first converted into two codified 'amateur' sports called 'association football' and 'rugby', and then – in the case of association football – professionalised at its top or elite levels. All this is well known in general terms. But the detailed implications of these changes for football play; for the organisation and financing of football clubs (both 'amateur' and 'professional'); for the grounds on which the new codified games were played; for the size and composition of the crowds which first came to soccer matches; and for the relationship between soccer clubs and other local institutions, especially the local press – all this is less explored in detail.[1]

Perhaps most interesting and most neglected of all, however, is the issue of *language*. The creation of a new football world was accompanied by, and expressed in, changes in the meaning of football words and phrases. Between the 1860s and the 1890s in England and Scotland, the meaning of terms like 'goal', 'scoring a goal', 'tackling', 'passing', 'dribbling' 'goalkeeper' (and 'goalkeeping'), 'forward', 'defender', 'football club', 'football match' and 'football ground' all changed, as indeed did the meaning of the terms 'football', 'association football' and 'rugby football' themselves.

We are not dealing here with changes in terminology, in the words themselves, but in concepts. The same words denote different concepts by changing their use. They are put into sentences and paragraphs which

---

1   Less explored, but not totally unexplored. As the notes to subsequent chapters will
     show, I am as indebted as all other students of football history to the observations
     of Matt Taylor, Tony Mason, Wray Vamplew, Dave Russell and Steven Tischler on
     all these matters and others, and to the work of Alan Metcalfe and Mike Huggins
     for observations on the history of north-eastern football particularly.

say new things (in this case about football), and their meaning is changed through changing their role in those sentences and paragraphs. And that is precisely the problem for the sports historian. For if inadequate attention is paid to word *use*, it is easy to mistake continuity of words and phrases for continuity in what they *name*, and to be profoundly misled in the process. In the case of mid-Victorian Britain, it is easy to miss the subtle but significant changes in football play and organisation hidden behind continuities in the nouns and noun phrases used in describing both.

On the face of it, it is rather odd that so little attention has been paid to this linguistic issue in the history of sport, because the principal source for that history in the Victorian period is the sporting and popular press. Indeed, as a number of scholars have noted, the history of modern sport is closely intertwined with the emergence of a genuinely popular press in Britain in the second half of the nineteenth century. Sports reporting, and especially sports betting, helped to build mass readerships for papers, and, in the case of football in particular, ever larger crowds for matches were stimulated by newspaper publicity.[2] Despite this, almost no detailed attention has been given to precisely how press reports described football play or the broader organisation of the game, or how such descriptions changed over the last four decades of the nineteenth century. Yet there is a lot to be gleaned by a detailed analysis of such matters. I hope this book shows just how much and will encourage further research along these lines.[3]

2   See Chapters 3 and 4 for the symbiosis between the local press and football clubs, a symbiosis that can sometimes make the former an unreliable source for the history of the latter. For more general accounts of the symbiosis Tony Mason, 'Sporting News 1860–1914' in Michael Harris and Alan Lee (eds) *The Press in English Society from the Seventeenth to Nineteenth Centuries* (London: Associated University Presses, 1986), 168–86, and Andrew Walker, 'Reporting Play: The Local Newspaper and Sports Journalism c.1870–1914', *Journalism Studies*, 7 (3), 2006, pp. 452–62. For the effect of the creation of a popular press on Victorian politics generally, Alan J. Lee, *The Origins of the Popular Press in England, 1855–1914* (London: Croom Helm, 1980), and for a fascinating but all too brief account of direct ownership and other links between the press and football clubs in the late Victorian and Edwardian period, Steven Tischler, *Footballers and Businessmen: The Origins of Professional Soccer in England* (New York: Holmes and Meier, 1981), 79–81.

3   The Victorian press has been the object of academic 'content analysis' of both a quantitative and qualitative sort. The aim of the former has been to provide word

All these neglected issues are addressed, to varying degrees, in the chapters which follow. With the partial exception of Chapter 1 (on the traditional Shrovetide 'foot-ball' match in Alnwick, Northumberland), all are set in the period 1880–1930, and all deal with these issues in reference to north-eastern soccer clubs in general and the Newcastle and Sunderland clubs in particular.

Limitations of the Project

However, although, taken together, the chapters below throw genuinely new – or at least sharper, more penetrating – light on all these neglected issues, they constitute only a small part of the research project as I originally conceived it. When I began work in 2009, I hoped to write a series of essays tracing the relationship between north-eastern soccer and the entire modern economic history of the region. I wanted to show how the game began in a period of regional industrial growth and ascendency, how it was affected (and not affected) by subsequent economic troubles, especially the 1930s depression, and how it was changed (and not changed) by the post-war 'de-industrialisation' of the North-East.

None of these broader aims have I accomplished, for two reasons. Firstly, as I should have known, the amount of time required to undertake

---

counts and percentages of different kinds of content and their changes over time. The aim of the latter has been to determine how and in what way, newspapers tried to mould the views and preferences (especially the political views and preferences) of their readerships. (For an overview, see Virginia Berridge, 'Content Analysis and Historical Research on Newspapers" in Harris and Lee (eds) *op cit*, pp. 201–18.) However, my type of content analysis is rather different from this. I am not concerned with what press football reportage was consciously 'designed' to do – whether to sell newspapers or attract spectators to matches – but with how, in its changing use of language, it quite *unconsciously* reflected and moulded the way football was played and perceived in the last four decades of the nineteenth century.

a research project of that scale was well beyond what I could make available, living 11,000 miles away from Britain. But secondly, I found that my interest waned markedly once the North-East became recognisably the football region in which I had grown up. I was absolutely fascinated by the arrival of association football in the region and the multi-sided process of its commercialisation and professionalisation. I was utterly intrigued by being cast back into an 1870s North-East in which even the word 'football' was hardly to be found in the local press, and then watching an astonishingly rapid transformation unfold. For by 1895 or so, the North-East was already the 'duopoly-dominated' (i.e. Sunderland and Newcastle United dominated) football region which my father knew and introduced me to. But once that transition had occurred, I found my enthusiasm for my project waning rapidly.

In this book's concluding chapter, I reflect at length on why that was. But in a phrase, I think it just one expression of my distinctly ambiguous attitude to the commodification of football, an ambiguity which is shared by many, though probably not most, contemporary football fans.[4] By 1895 football in the North-East was completely commercialised and professionalised at its elite levels and commercialised and quasi-professionalised at some lower levels. (See Chapter 5 on the 'Crook Town Affair' for the latter.) And that pattern, once set, changed little. In writing this book I have discovered how distinctly contradictory are my feelings about that. Football as a professionalised and commercialised sport has entrancing virtues and repulsive vices, and as this book's concluding chapter argues at length, the commodification of clubs and players is at the root of both.

---

4   See Matthew Taylor, *The Association Game: A History of Football* (Harlow: Pearson Education, 2008), 426 for the suggestion that this ambiguity *is* more broadly shared. See also, and more especially, the 'Against Modern Football' movement of football fans, described at <https://www.goal.com/en-au/news/against-modern-football-what-grassroots-campaign/1s6qqrxn1xv7013v4z208i5vr6> and contactable through its home page, <https://www.facebook.com/Against-Modern-Football-247030311967/>. I am grateful to Tony Collins for bringing the movement to my attention.

History, Methodology and Philosophy

One final point by way of introduction. All the chapters below contain not just sports history, but philosophical and methodological reflections on that history, and indeed on the writing of history generally. I know this is unusual. Sports history is not normally a stimulus to, or a focus of, reflections on the philosophy and methodology of history. But there is no reason why it should not be, for it poses as many issues of this kind as any other sort of history. But whether unusual or not, these reflections emerge from my strong interest in philosophy in general and in the philosophy of history in particular. Moreover, far from distracting from, or intruding upon the essays, I think these philosophical reflections enrich and deepen them. There is in fact nothing contradictory about liking both football and philosophy, or in writing about the former through the lens of the latter. It is a lot easier though to say when one has won (and lost) in football than in philosophy!

Acknowledgements

No one can undertake a sustained period of academic research half a world away from their home without a great deal of assistance, financial and otherwise. I have already mentioned the crucial role played in this project's beginning by the year-long sabbatical leave granted to me by the University of New South Wales in 2009. Since that time, I have also enjoyed regular financial support from the Emeriti Research Fund of UNSW's Faculty of Arts and Social Sciences. While in the North-East of England I benefitted enormously from the unfailingly courteous assistance of staff in the Local Studies sections of the Newcastle and Sunderland Central Libraries; the archive staff of the Discovery Museum, Newcastle; and staff at the Northumberland and Durham County Record Offices. This book's first chapter, on the Alnwick Shrovetide football match, is especially indebted to Christopher Hunwick, the archivist of the Alnwick

Castle archive, as well as to staff at the Bailiffgate Museum in the town. Christopher saved me from making at least two embarrassing errors about the mid-Victorian Dukes of Northumberland, while the Bailiffgate staff gave me access to their invaluable 'Minute Book' of the match and a number of other important documents. Alex Jackson of the National Football Museum in Manchester was good enough to provide me with photocopies of some crucial FA documents related to 'the Crook Affair' when I was unable to consult them myself, and Dick Longstaff and his friends and colleagues at the Durham Amateur Football Trust also provided invaluable comments and feedback on the same chapter.

I would also like to thank Steve Tate for his kindness in helping a complete stranger find some crucial extra details on the Victorian sports journalist 'Mercutio' (see Chapter 3) and my son's partner, Louise Chesters, for using her Excel skills to help me produce the collated match attendance graphs for the same chapter. I also needed a place to live while in the North-East, and Pat Foreman, her husband Ian, and their delightful Border Collie Ben provided a most convenient, comfortable and friendly summer 'home-from-home' in Jesmond, Newcastle.

However, there are three individuals above all without whom this project would either never have begun or have shuddered to a halt well before its completion, and who are therefore deserving of special acknowledgement. The first of these is John Allan – 'football John' – who knows the old newspaper holdings of the Newcastle Central Library far better even than the library staff. He frequently – and absolutely invaluably for a researcher whose most limited resource was time – pointed me in fruitful directions and/or short-circuited time-wasting digressions. If I add that John is a Newcastle United fanatic, and provided me with this almost-daily friendship, assistance and stimulation despite knowing me to be a lifetime Sunderland fan, perhaps only north-easterners will fully appreciate his generosity of spirit.

The second person deserving special acknowledgement is my dear friend and colleague, Richard Holt. As well as originally suggesting the project to me, he gave me the consistent benefit, not only of his own academic expertise as one of Britain's leading sports historians, but also access to his equally helpful colleagues at the Centre for International Sports

History and Culture at De Montfort University, Leicester. Even more importantly, he provided me with an ever-welcoming and comfortable place to stay while in Leicester. And since his home was usually my first port of call after disembarking the exhausting flight from Australia, he also played a crucial role in safeguarding the health of an old friend.

Finally, I must thank my loving partner, Pamela Cawthorne, for once again bearing the significant personal costs involved in living with the very peculiar creature that is a 'research-active academic'. Those thanks are especially due when that academic is retired, and research has become a form of self-indulgence rather than a professional requirement. For while I was sitting alone in libraries and archives and allowing a mass of old newsprint to imperil my eyesight, I was aware that there were other things Pamela would infinitely have preferred me to be doing – the kind of things that 'normal' retiree couples do together. I hope we will be able to do at least some of them now.

GNK,
Sydney,
July 2020

'From Time Immemorial': The Alnwick Shrovetide Football Match and the Continual Remaking of Tradition 1828–1890[1]

Introduction

In the Bailiffgate Museum in Alnwick there is a large volume rather mis-leadingly entitled *Alnwick Shrove Tuesday Football Match Minute Book 1871–1953*.[2] The title is misleading in two respects. Firstly, the earliest entries date from 1869, not 1871, and secondly the book is not really a 'minute book' at all. It is a leather-bound scrapbook of over 200 unnumbered pages, proceeding in strict annual order from 1869, with two or three pages devoted to each year. But each annual entry consists of a miscellany of items. There are indeed individual pages of minutes stuck into the book which record, very briefly and schematically, the proceedings of the annual meeting of the match organising committee, usually held a week or so before the match. These hand-written entries appear to have been taken from an original minute book (or books) dismembered for the scrapbook. In each yearly entry the small, lined, exercise-book sheets of minutes are interleaved with press cuttings and (in later years) with press and other photographs of the match. Altogether the press cuttings

---

1   A version of this chapter was originally published as Gavin Kitching, ' "From Time Immemorial": The Alnwick Shrovetide Football Match and the Continuous Remaking of Tradition 1828–1890', *The International Journal of the History of Sport*, 28 (6), 831–52, reprinted by permission of the publisher (Taylor & Francis, <http://www.tandfonline.com>).

2   Referred to hereafter simply as 'Minute Book'.

and the photos take up far more pages in the scrapbook than the minutes themselves.

Nonetheless, whether strictly a 'minute book' or not, this document is an invaluable source for the history of Shrovetide football in the Northumberland county town of Alnwick, and I duly spent a number of days studying it in its museum home.

I was surprised, therefore, to find a second copy of the 'Minute Book' in the Northumberland County Records Office, and even more surprised that this second copy contained, at its beginning, some items not found in the Alnwick version. These included some press clippings reporting Shrovetide football matches in other Northumberland towns and in the border towns of southern Scotland, and, at the front of the book, a single typewritten page, unattributed, but dated '19.2.85'. This page, which is clearly meant as a kind of foreword, states *inter alia* that:

1. 'In Alnwick, we look upon this ancient Shrovetide game of football as dating from time immemorial.
2. Football Association rules have no bearing on the game.
3. The goals, or hales as we call them, are 400 yards apart.
4. The match is made up of three periods. The first two of half an hour each, and the last of 45 minutes.'[3]

In the chapter which follows I demonstrate that, whoever made these assertions in 1985, all of them are highly dubious. Specifically, assertions three and four are true now but were not true in the past, and assertion two was true in the past but is not true now. And this implies that the Alnwick Shrovetide football match has changed in many ways over the last 180 years. It changed particularly dramatically in 1828 (when it was converted from a 'street and field' game to a purely field game) and again in the early twentieth century (when it became a kind of large-scale soccer match in which, if 'Football Association rules' were not formally predominant, soccer forms of playing the game certainly were.) This chapter

---

3   Northumberland Records Office, Woodhorn (NRO 3851). This single sheet of typescript is inserted at the front of the scrapbook.

concentrates particularly on the Victorian period of the game's history (1828–90), which also saw major changes in both the organisation of the game and in play.

So while people in Alnwick may 'look upon' the Alnwick Shrovetide game of football as 'ancient', and 'as dating from time immemorial', whether anyone else should depends upon what they take the phrase 'the Alnwick Shrovetide game of football' in that first assertion to mean. If all it means is that a game called 'football' has been played, regularly but not continuously, on Shrove Tuesday at Alnwick, for some 250 years, then the assertion is true. But if it means that the same game, or even a broadly similar game, called 'football' has been played regularly, but not continuously, on Shrove Tuesday at Alnwick for centuries, then it is false, and can readily be shown to be so. The Shrove Tuesday football game being played today at Alnwick has almost nothing in common with the game as it was played there prior to 1828, and little in common even with the game as it was played there in the 1850s, 1860s and 1880s.

But if the Alnwick Shrove Tuesday football match, *as it is played now*, does not date from 'time immemorial' and is most certainly not 'ancient', why do people in Alnwick think it is? I will argue that, at least up to the end of the nineteenth century, there were reasons why they might reasonably have thought that it was. Because, at the end of the nineteenth century, the spirit, and – to a degree – the manner, in which the Alnwick match was played retained some genuinely old features. Today however, the game as such has nothing ancient about it. It has become little more than a mass, or larger-scale, soccer match, although still played on its Victorian venue, and surrounded by some 'traditional' ceremony – ceremony which, as we shall see, was also a Victorian invention.

However, even if they are aware of these facts, they simply do not matter to the vast majority of people who live in Alnwick. And they matter even less to the tourists or other visitors who come to the town every year on Shrove Tuesday to watch the match. Considering how and why this is – why the facts related in this article do not matter to anyone but a handful of historians – will lead me to some concluding reflections on popular attitudes to history in our postmodern world.

From Festival to Sports Event: The Alnwick Match 1828–1890

I first became interested in the Alnwick Shrove Tuesday match as part of a larger research project on the origins of association football in the north-east of England. I was attempting to discover why soccer became the majority participant and spectator sport in the North-East when rugby union had been well established there for some five or six years before soccer even arrived. I hypothesised that the forms of traditional or folk football being played in the region prior to the arrival of both modern football codes might have had more in common with soccer than rugby, and that this had facilitated the region's adoption of the former.

However, in common with many other researchers on the history of traditional football in Britain, I soon found myself mired in frustration. Because, though regional newspaper sources for the period 1840–1870 certainly showed that traditional or folk football was being played in the region in the decades prior to the arrival of rugby and soccer, they were far too brief and vestigial to tell me anything about the games involved and far too occasional and 'spotty' to provide any reliable guide to how frequently such games were played or how commonplace they were.[4] These sources

---

4   The general difficulty of finding detailed accounts of pre-modern football matches is one problem besetting academic research on the so-called origins of football, and one source of the many conceptual confusions marking a recent debate about it. For a survey of the debate and its confusions, as it was in 2015, see my 'The Origins of Football: History, Ideology and the Making of the People's Game', *History Workshop Journal*, 79 (1), 2015, 127–53. For some further contributions since that time, see especially Peter Swain 'The Origins of Football Debate: The Evidence Mounts 1841–51' and 'The Origins of Football Debate: Football and Cultural Continuity 1957–1859' (*IJHS*, 32 (2), 2015, 219–317 and 32 (5), 2015, 631–49). See also Graham Curry and Eric Dunning, 'The Power Game: Continued Reflections on the Early Development of Modern Football', *IJHS*, 33 (3), 2015, 239–50 and 'The Origins of Football Debate and the Early Development of the Game in Nottinghamshire', *Soccer and Society*, 18 (7), 2017, 866–79. However, in his journal article 'Early Football and the Emergence of Modern Soccer 1840–1880' (*IJHS*, 32 (9), 2015, 1127–42), his 2017 review of Curry and Dunning's 2015 book *Association Football: A Study in Figurational*

certainly suggested that traditional or folk football was not restricted to the large 'melee' matches played on Shrove Tuesday, but also included smaller-scale games played between groups of men and boys on fields and open spaces on many high days and holidays. But they did not tell me whether a contemporary observer, if time-transported to the 'sidelines' of such games, would be put in mind of contemporary rugby, contemporary soccer or of something else entirely.

In this factual famine, the more abundant newspaper sources for the Alnwick Shrove Tuesday match came as precious drops of water in a desert. They were all the more interesting because they concerned a traditional form of football that was played in a field, unlike the other major Shrovetide matches in Northumberland and Durham – at Chester-le-Street and Sedgefield – which, (like most Shrovetide matches in England and Scotland), were played in town streets. It was true that 'originally' – before 1828 – the Alnwick game too had been played, at least partially, in the streets of the town. But in that year, at the request of the town burghers, Hugh Percy, third Duke of Northumberland, had agreed to its transfer to an area of pasture adjacent to his seat, Alnwick Castle. He also made continuance of play in the streets illegal under the terms of the Alnwick Improvement Act, 1827.[5]

Sociology (*Sport in History*, 37 (4), 529–66) and in chapters 3–6 of his recent book *How Football Began: A Global History of How the World's Football Codes Were Born* (London: Routledge, 2019), Tony Collins has, in my view, essentially disposed of the debate. He shows, convincingly, that both its conventional sides underestimate the sheer variety of the games being called 'football', 'association football' and 'rugby football' in Britain between the 1860s and the 1880s. He also shows that the brief and ambiguous newspaper accounts which Swain collates for the period prior to 1860 are, at best, evidence of a variety of traditional football games in Britain before that date. Certainly, they provide no evidence of a vibrant pre-1863 *soccer* culture.

5   The Alnwick Castle Archive has recently had an important accession of material relating to these events. They include letters from the third duke and his agent to the town overseers agreeing to change the location of the match, and copies of handbills which announce the change and specify the penalties for continuing the street game. Alnwick Castle: ACC 107. I am very grateful to the archivist, Christopher Hunwick, for making this material, and some other vital papers,

But the Victorian Shrovetide match at Alnwick was not just a field game. I also discovered, that, in the mid-Victorian period, it was an 'all-kicking' game, with handling of the ball explicitly disallowed. It was also played on a clearly demarcated or roped-off area of grass of determinate length and width, with half-way markers, and with goals erected at either end of the playing area. These goals were arched in shape, and originally about 3 feet wide and 12 feet high. In short, it seemed that the Alnwick match *was* an example of 'soccer-like' traditional football in the North-East – a confirming instance of my initial hypothesis.

Subsequent research soon showed, however, that these promising appearances were deceptive. It soon turned out that that the match's 'kicking only' rule only dated from the early 1860s. It also turned out that the 'spatially organised' form of the game described in the paragraph above – with goals and roped enclosure, etc. – only began in 1856. In that year the game had been 'revived' by the fourth duke, Algernon Percy, following a nine-year hiatus after the death of Hugh, his elder brother. This 'revived' game featured not only the demarcated playing area with goals, etc., but the appointment of two umpires and the introduction of a set of match 'by-laws' read out to the players before the match commenced.

All these discoveries then raised a further question. What was the relationship, if any, between the 'revived' Alnwick match of 1856 and that played on the demesne between 1828 and Hugh Percy's death in 1847? How was this earlier game organised? And was it a kicking only game or did it feature more handling of the ball?

Appendix 1 of this chapter provides a chronological listing of all the newspaper accounts of the Alnwick match between 1828 (the year of its conversion to a field game) and 1847 (the year of the third duke's death) that I have been able to locate. They are placed in an appendix because, as will be seen, they are far too repetitive and formulaic to merit inclusion in the chapter body. They are as notable in fact for what they do not say, for what they do not tell us, as for any positive content.

---

available to me. I also took advantage of his expertise through a number of subsequent emails.

The Alnwick Match as Festival, 1828–1847

Even a cursory reading of Appendix 1 will readily reveal some clear patterns – patterns manifested in every single report with the only partial exception of the first. These are:

- Almost nothing is reported of the match itself, save that it took place, the winning side and (sometimes) its duration. Not even the number of participants is reported.
- The formal march of the participants from the Town Hall to the field, and the 'dance' or 'ball' afterwards, receive as much attention as the match itself.
- The Duke of Northumberland's 'donation' of (variously) five or ten pounds is always prominently featured, and it is made clear that this money is used primarily for the post-match festivities, not for the match itself.
- From the early 1830s all the reports have a strongly formulaic and 'pro forma' air. The same words and phrases recur – 'fierce contest', 'arduous contest', 'arduous struggle', 'numerously attended' – suggesting that they are being written from an annually recycled template. The few variations in description are entirely due to unusual events or occurrences – poor attendance, especially bad weather, a change in composition of the march or of the venue for the dance, etc.

So what may we conclude from all this? It seems fairly clear (as much from the omissions in the reports as anything else) that:

1. Having been transferred to the pasture, the match did not change much, if at all, between 1828 and 1847.
2. The match varies greatly in duration from year to year, depending mainly on the numerical strength of the two sides. When very closely contested it probably ended when darkness fell, and since this is Shrovetide – that is, mid to late February – this would be sometime between 4 and 5 p.m. (having begun, variously, between 1 and 2 p.m.).
3. The report of the first 'field' match, in 1828, is the only one to contain any description of the play at all. It tells us that the match

was divided into three 'games', with the victorious side in that
year winning two of these three 'games'. It does not say how such
winning was achieved, although it does make clear that spectators
joined in the play, and this clearly helped the single freemen on
this occasion.

4. Phrases like 'fierce contest' and 'arduous struggle' suggest that
   the matches typically involved physical confrontations between
   the sides, each of which almost certainly contained hundreds of
   players when the game was well supported. But we are given no
   details about this.

Almost certainly the reason for all this silence is that readers of the
Newcastle Chronicle or *Newcastle Courant* in the 1830s and 1840s did not
need the play described, because its main features were familiar to them.
Indeed, the same general point applies to descriptions of the play as to all
other descriptions in these reports; explicit mention is only made of innovations or novelties. Silence therefore betokens continuity, although it
is impossible from these reports to know what was continuing – what the
game would have looked like had we been there to see it.

It is clear, though, that all these brief passages are conceived as reports
of a popular festival not of a sports event. What matters to the newspaper
correspondents, and probably to the players, about the Alnwick Shrove
Tuesday 'foot-ball' match is its aristocratic patronage and the ceremony and
'entertainment' that surrounds it (in which the consumption of alcohol was
prominent) rather than the match itself or its nominal outcome. It is likely
that the players and many of the spectators were far from sober during the
game, let alone during the dances or 'balls' which followed.

In order to appreciate the next sections of this chapter it is also important to note the following:

1. There is no mention of demarcated playing spaces, constructed
   goals, rules or 'by-laws', or any of the other paraphernalia of
   modern or modernising sports in any of these reports. It is possible, therefore, that the 'games' making up the match were won
   either by putting the ball in, or near to, some natural feature, or

features, on or around the pasture, or by having the ball close to that feature at the termination of play.[6]

2. Each of the three games, and the match itself, ended either when a goal was scored or when darkness fell. The matches were therefore of highly variable duration. If one side was strongly preponderant in numbers, they could overwhelm the opposition and score the two necessary goals with ease, thus ending proceedings very quickly.

3. There is no reference, either to the goals themselves, or to the three 'games' making up the match, as 'hales'. This may be significant (see below).

4. It is made clear that no part of the Duke of Northumberland's 'donation' (apart from the ball itself) is used for any purpose to do with the match. As we shall see this also changes from 1856 onwards.

The Quasi-Modernised Match, 1856–1880

On 8 February 1856, the *Newcastle Courant* carried the following report:

From time immemorial, on Shrove Tuesday in Alnwick, the young men assembled at the gates of Alnwick Castle attended by a band of music. The porter then threw out a football which was followed through the streets and outskirts of the town by a numerous company and became the prize of the person who could carry

---

6   I have no direct evidence for this assertion, but in the Alnwick Castle archive there is a scrapbook devoted to David Smith, Commissioner for Estates under the second and third dukes. This contains, among other things, some hand-written comments by Smith on the game as it was before 1828. These suggest that the street game itself may have terminated on the Duke's pasture, the ball having first been kicked around the town. *A propos* of this, he also says that before 1828 "they had this diversion in the Castle Close, North of the Castle, between the South side of the River, and frequently it got into a Hole in the River (*sic*), called by them Jordan's pools – but the site of it is scarcely known at present." Alnwick Castle: DNP MS 187A/118.

it off. Such, with some slight modifications, was the ancient custom. Under the distinguished patronage of the Dukes of Northumberland ... it was determined this year to have a revival of the ancient pastime. ... A few weeks ago a committee was to make arrangements *(sic)* for a match to be played between the married and the single men of the parish on Shrove Tuesday. Captains of the respective parties were elected, and umpires appointed to whom reference might be had in case of a dispute arising. In accordance with the arrangements, the rival parties assembled at one o'clock on that day, in front of the barbican of the castle, where they were met by Wm. Forster, Esq, steward of the games, and the committee, from whence ... they proceeded to the north demesne in front of the castle, where the playground was staked out. On arriving at the centre of the goals, which were distinguished by a flagstaff, surmounted by the Union Jack, the captains marshalled their respective parties, and found that they mustered somewhere around 300 competitors on each side... The goals were two archways, 3 feet wide and 12 feet high, placed at a distance apparently 1000 yards apart; the party obtaining two hales out of three to be declared victorious. The game lasted from 1.30 p.m. to 4.30 p.m. with a break at 3 p.m. signalled by a trumpet. No goal was scored from 1.30 to 3 p.m. After this break, when bread, cheese and ale were served, the married men passed the ball through the goal to win the first hale, and since no other goal was scored before 4.30, the married were declared the winners. Henry Hutchinson, the married man who succeeded in kicking the ball through the goal, received the award allotted to the victor of the day. [6,7]

A local paper, the *Alnwick Mercury*, contained an even more detailed report of the 1856 match under the heading 'FOOT BALL AT ALNWICK'. This report contained the following information additional to that in the *Courant*:

1. 'A committee of six gentlemen prepared a few general laws and minor regulations in order that the game may be conducted in a regular manner.'
2. Thomas Vernon and Thomas Foster were appointed 'captains of the day'.
3. Robert Etherington and Robert Rutherford 'officiated in the honourable office of umpires'.

7   *NC*, February 8, 1856.

4. 'The laws of the game' were 'read out' and then 'the steward tossed up the ball at the Union Jack'.
5. There were 'more than 500 players' on each side.[8]

Thus the year 1856 brought a rash of changes to the Alnwick Shrovetide football match – the creation of a management committee making 'general laws' and 'minor regulations', the nomination of a 'steward of the games' (who also probably chaired the management committee) and the creation of team 'captains' and match 'umpires'. It is not clear whether the traditional bannered 'march' to the demesne took place in 1856 (the report uses the more flaccid verb 'proceeded') but the players certainly did not rendezvous at the Alnwick town hall anymore. Moreover, when the players got to the demesne they encountered a scene they would not have encountered before 1847 – a staked-out 'playground', a flag pole with Union Jack marking the half-way point, and two sets of arch-shaped goals constructed about 1,000 yards apart (not 400!).[9] It is almost certain, too, judging from slightly later reports, that a coin was tossed for choice of ends.[10] Most notably of all perhaps, the players now played a match of a predetermined length, with refreshments provided after ninety minutes of play, and the match ending after three hours at 4.30 p.m.

Finally, the post-match 'dance' or 'ball' disappeared in 1856, never to return. Among the refreshments served to the players after an hour was 'ale' (along with' bread and cheese'), but there was no longer a donation of ducal monies for post-match 'entertainment'. Indeed, and significantly, the only money paid out in 1856 was to Henry Hutchinson, 'the married

---

8   *AM*, March 1, 1856.
9   An *NC* match report twenty years later states that the goals were placed 'due east and west at a distance of 734 yards' (*NC*, March 3, 1876). The goals were said to be about 'three feet wide' in 1856. Another report in 1884, however, says that 'the goals were placed at a distance of about half a mile from each other, each goal being about six feet between the posts (undated, unattributed clipping for 1884 in Minute Book). With the exception of the curiously precise '734 yards', we should probably treat all these numbers as observer impressions rather than exact measures. But it is clear that the size of the playing area has declined over time, probably with the fall in the number of participants.
10   See, for example, *AM*, March 1, 1858.

man who succeeded in kicking the ball through the goal', receiving 'the award allotted to the victor of the day'.

As if to allay anxieties and doubts arising from all this novelty, the *Courant* correspondent immediately followed the remark about Henry Hutchinson: 'But to keep up the ancient custom, a ball was afterwards thrown up, to be the property of the person who should succeed in carrying it off. This prize, after a sharp run, was carried off by William Scott, plasterer, single man.' And further:

> A large assemblage of the inhabitants of the town was present during the proceedings, and the whole affair was managed so successfully, and such an admirable spirit of cordiality and good fellowship was manifested throughout, that it is resolved that the ancient game should be revived, *(sic)* and the match continued annually, in accordance with the immemorial usages observed on Shrove Tuesday.[11]

It will also be seen that both the *Newcastle Courant* and *Alnwick Mercury* accounts of the 1856 revival use the term 'hale', the *Mercury's* correspondent using it to refer to the 'archway'-shaped goals themselves ('Henry Hutchinson cleverly kicked it through the "hale" or goal'), the *Courant's* report being more ambiguous, referring either to the goals themselves or possibly to the three periods of the match ('the party obtaining two hales out of three to be declared victorious').

The term 'hale' here (also sometimes spelled as 'hail') is probably that given in the *Shorter Oxford Dictionary* as a 'rare' or obsolete Middle English word for a hall, or 'covered market place' or more generally, 'a place roofed over, but usually open at the sides; a tent, a pavilion, a temporary shelter'. Other sources from elsewhere in Northumberland and the Scottish borders suggest that the word was used, certainly from the eighteenth century and probably earlier, for the buildings, or partially open structures or places, (such as church porches or church yards, or walls of mills, or covered wells) that were used as 'goals'[12] in town-based Shrovetide and other feast-day

---

11   *NC*, February 8, 1856.
12   This relates to something else. In many of the Alnwick match reports, and in reports of the Chester-le-Street and Sedgefield Shrovetide matches too, the phrase 'their goal' is always used of the goal *attacked*, not of the goal defended. The goal

football matches.[13] It is therefore highly probable that the term was also used in Alnwick as a synonym for 'goal' prior to 1828, when the Shrovetide match was still a street-based game. As we have seen though, the term does *not* appear in any of the press reports of the 'converted' field game between 1828 and 1847. While this absence is hardly conclusive (given how short and schematic they are and the minimal attention they give to the game generally), it is possible that this piece of antique terminology was re-introduced in 1856 as yet another way of stressing historical continuity amid manifest change and discontinuity. Certainly the 1856 reports have a rather anxious ideological air, passing over the many innovations in a matter-of-fact tone, but lingering over any activity or practice that can be deemed 'ancient'. The reintroduction and refurbishment of the old 'hale' terminology would certainly fit in well with this.

We do not know who was responsible for this 'revival' that was simultaneously a radical restructuring. Neal Garnham suggests that Algernon Percy, the fourth Duke of Northumberland, was the 'prime mover' in the game's renaissance and relates this to the duke's wider antiquarian interests, his conception of himself as a 'neo-feudal' clan leader of the Northumbrian people and his 'Eton and Cambridge' education which may have made him 'a supporter of sports and games'.[14] But Algernon, as a younger son in an English aristocratic family, did not attend university at all, entering

---

of a team or side, in fact, was to reach its goal, and thus their goal was always in front of them, not behind. As well as being more semantically consistent, this shows, I think, how entirely devoid of any developed sense of tactics or strategy such matches usually were.

13 For a press clipping referring to a 'hailing point at the bridge' in an account of a Shrove Tuesday match at Howick in the Scottish borders, see 'Handba'at Howick' in NRO 3851. For the use of the term 'hail' at Hexham, south-west Northumberland, both for the goals themselves and for periods of the match, in a manner identical to the Alnwick usage (but referring to a much smaller-scale football match held as part of the Hexham Easter Sports), see *HC*, April 19, 1865, April 28, 1875 and April 27, 1878.

14 Neal Garnham, 'Patronage, Politics and the Modernization of Leisure in Northern England: The Case of Alnwick's Shrove Tuesday Football Match', *English Historical Review*, 117 (474) 2002, 1228–46, especially 1240.

the navy as an officer cadet at the age of 12, and spending nearly all his adult life there until becoming duke on his elder brother's death.[15] He did attend Eton's preparatory school between the ages of eight and twelve[16] and may have seen Eton field football then, but his enthusiasm for games and sports – assuming it to have existed – may not have been due to this. It could just as easily have had naval roots.

It was Algernon's nephew, Algernon George Percy, who succeeded as sixth Duke of Northumberland in 1867, who attended Eton and St John's College, Cambridge (as had his uncle, Hugh, the third duke, before him) and it was he who was duke when the full-blown 'kicking-only' by-law was first printed as part of the match advertising poster in 1869. But while this might lead to further speculations about Eton or Cambridge football influences on the Alnwick match's restructuring, it is probable that the 'kicking-only' rule was actually in force from at least 1866 and probably earlier.

It is true that several journalistic accounts of the 1856 events give the fourth duke the credit for the revival and for the 'by-laws' which regulated it.[17] This may be mere deference, however, for there is nothing in the Alnwick Castle archives scrapbook on the duke (which includes a mass of press cuttings about his life and several lengthy obituaries) crediting him with the 1856 revival, or suggesting that he took any interest in the match at all.[18] There remains too the puzzling question of why, if Algernon Percy was so keen on the match as an 'antiquarian' pastime, he allowed nine years to elapse between his succession to the dukedom and its revival, and why he 'revived' it in such a non-antiquarian form. But silence is by no means

15   Uncatalogued scrapbook entitled 'Percy Duke of Northumberland, vol. X, Fourth Duke', Alnwick Castle.
16   Email to the author from Christopher Hunwick, Alnwick Castle archivist.
17   A report of the 1871 match in the *Alnwick Journal* states that the passing of the Alnwick Improvement Act in 1827 led to the moving of the match from the town streets to the duke's pasture, and that "It was revived in its present form at the suggestion of Algernon, Fourth Duke of Northumberland. A committee was appointed to carry it out with proper spirit, and to regulate the game by a few definite by-laws." See also Garnham, *op cit*, p. 1239.
18   Uncatalogued scrapbook, 'Percy Duke of Northumberland, vol. X, Fourth Duke', Alnwick Castle.

conclusive, and at the least the match could not have been revived without the duke's consent, whether or not he was its 'prime mover'.

Equally frustratingly, although we know that the first match by-laws were introduced in 1856, there is no surviving written version of them pre-dating 1869. There is clear evidence, however, that the original 1856 by-laws did not include the 'kicking-only' rule. In the 1862 match, for example, Robert Blackford, having been 'carried through the goal by the press of the players; with the ball in hand' was awarded a 'no-hale' by the umpires, 'the rule requiring that it should be *kicked or thrown through the goal*' (my emphasis).[19] But in 1866 Humphrey Morrison, although scoring a winning goal for St Michael's parish, should not, a match correspondent tells us, 'Be, according to the rules, entitled to any prize' because 'the ball was thrown from the hand and not kicked through the goal.'[20]

These examples tell us two things of interest. Firstly, at some time between 1862 and 1866 the kicking by-law was tightened with the aim of eliminating ball-handling altogether. Secondly, this reform was being re-sisted by some of the local players, some of whom would have played in the match, or at least witnessed it, prior to 1847. This is the strongest evidence we have that the pre-1847 game was *not* a 'kicking-only' game but also in-volved catching and throwing of the ball, if not outright running with it.

This conclusion is strengthened by the fact that the match ball, prior to 1847, and indeed right up to the 1890s, was oval not spherical.[21] No

---

19   *AJ* clipping, February 1862, in Bailiffgate Exhibition on 'Football'.

20   *AM*, February 18, 1866.

21   An 1886 *NDC* match report cutting, in Minute Book, explicitly refers to the ball as 'the oval'. But it is likely that the ball used in the Alnwick match changed at intervals through the nineteenth century. J. Wightman Douglas in 'Shrovetide Football at Alnwick' (Minute Book clipping, undated, but probably early twen-tieth century) quotes an *AM* article of 1858, stating that, at that time, the balls were of India rubber (an invention of the 1850s) but says that the earliest footballs "were merely cases of leather or other materials stuffed with shavings, but later they probably … consisted of a beast's bladder covered with black leather, blocked to a spherical shape, and completely sown up without caps or lace, the result being an extremely hard ball much smaller than the modern article". However, from the 1890s onwards, a soccer ball was introduced and was used throughout the twen-tieth century and up to the present time.

one who has played or watched rugby needs to be told that the bounce of an oval ball is more unpredictable than that of a sphere, so that an 'all-kicking' game played with an oval is likely to make ball control difficult, all the more so if it is played on an uneven surface (as the Alnwick Castle North Demesne was, and is). So it seems likely that the pre-1847 Alnwick football match was a 'mixed' form of football, in which the ball was moved by a combination of handling and kicking. In this respect it was probably very like the pre-1828 street game which it displaced. Hence the fourth duke's attempt (if that is what it was) to turn the post-1856 match into a 'mass' form of 'kicking-only' Eton field football met with some resistance from those who knew this earlier history. And this resistance occurred despite the attempt to dress the revived match in the legitimising mantle of antiquity, and despite the introduction, in the 1860s, of cash prizes for the best kicking and kickers in the match and for the kicking of goals.

Not only was the form of play radically changed in 1856, just two years later the adversaries changed too. Out went the 'traditional' 'married v. single freemen' structure (which dated from the match's pre-1828 street days), to be replaced by a parish structure – the parochial district of St Michael's versus that of St Paul's. The parish of St Paul's had been created by the splitting of St Michael's just a few years before this change.[22] Neal Garnham relates the change to the wider modernisation of Alnwick, and particularly to the reduced role of the freemen companies in its economic and political life.[23] He is perhaps right to do so, but his explanation rests purely on social history 'first principles' as it were, rather than any direct historical evidence. In the 1858 press reports the change is passed over as briskly as the playing innovations of two years earlier, and with an equal lack of explanation.[24]

From the mid-1860s to the early 1880s the press reports of the Alnwick match repeat the brief, formulaic tone that distinguished them in the

22   Email to the author from Christopher Hunwick.
23   Garnham, *op cit*, p. 1241.
24   The *AM* report of the 1858 match, for example, simply says, *en passant*, and entirely without further comment, "The contest was between the parochial districts of St Michael's and St Paul's."

1828–47 period, although with rather more attention given to the match itself. However, a press report for 1876 suggests that in that year another significant change occurred: the setting of time limits to each of the three 'hales', in addition to the fixed half-time and full-time established in 1856.[25] (Prior to this a hale appears to have ended with the scoring of a goal, or was deemed to have been won by the side nearest to its opponent's goal when half-time or full-time was called). This may seem a small matter. But it is likely that the practice of ending play when a goal was scored went back to the pre-1828 street game, as did the tradition that, if no goal was scored, the match was won by the side nearest to its opponent's goal at nightfall. We certainly know that this is how the result was determined in the Chester-le-Street and Sedgefield Shrovetide matches.[26] If the tripartite structure of the match came with its conversion to a field game in 1828, then turning these three periods into fixed periods of time, and ruling that a hale was tied or drawn if no goal was scored by its end, was all part of the slow conversion of the Alnwick match from a time-elastic festive recreation to a time-programmed sports 'event'.

The Alnwick Match as Inadequate Sports Event: The 1880s

The most notable features of the 1880s Alnwick Shrovetide match press reports are their greatly increased length and their use of most of it to describe actual play. There remains, it is true, an amount of 'historic' scene-setting. The reports generally open with a potted history of the match, stressing its antiquity, with a nod to the Dukes of Northumberland and to the organising committee (whose names now regularly appear). This is usually followed by a brief, standardised description of the 'procession' or 'walk' by the committee and the players from the barbican of

25 NC, March 3, 1876.
26 On this see, for example, the reports of the Chester-le-Street match in NC, March 3, 1876, and in DCA, March 13, 1880. For the Sedgefield match, DC, February 28, 1879.

the castle – where the duke's match ball is now received – to the North Demesne. (The term 'march' is noticeably absent). Nearly always it is observed that this procession is headed by the duke's piper. And at the end of the reports, regular mention is made of the 'slight repast of bread and cheese and ale' served to the committee members (not the players) in the guest hall of the castle at the close of the game, and of the ritual toasts and awarding of cash prizes to individual players (for the scoring of goals or other feats of skill) after the said 'repast'.[27]

But having begun and ended in these 'traditional' ways, the 1880s reports give over most of their length to describing the match. In fact, it is in the 1880s that the newspaper reports of the Alnwick Shrovetide match begin, for the first time, to *be* match reports, which means, to resemble the match reports of soccer or rugby fixtures now found elsewhere in the north-eastern press. But just because of this several of them have a slightly patronising tone, featuring unflattering comparisons – explicit or implicit – of play in the Alnwick match with play in the 'proper', 'codified' football (both rugby and soccer) now abroad in Northumberland and Durham.

For example, a report of the 1884 match in the *Newcastle Daily Chronicle* has this:

> When the ball dropped both sides rushed upon it and the force of their meeting was such as to cause the leaders to fall over each other in confusion. After some scrambling the ball was sent freely away towards St Paul's goal; and being skilfully manoeuvred by a few of the St Michael's players, was quickly within easy possibility of a 'hale'. But here the unscientific formation of the sides showed to disadvantage. Each side was playing all in a lump, without either quarter backs, half backs or backs; and the two sides in consequence mingled in confusion. During a scrimmage at the goal – which was like a dozen orthodox scrimmages rolled into one – one of the St Paul's team kicked the ball through the goal of his own party; and the sounding of the trumpet announced that the ball was 'dead' and that 'no goal' had been scored. Thereupon the ball was carried back to the original spot, and again kicked out, the goals being placed the same as before. This time, the St Paul's runners carried the ball along in front of them; but unfortunately, missed the goal and shot behind the posts. Before they had time to dribble it back, the forces

---

27   Unattributed and undated press clipping – but probably *NDC* – of the 1885 match in Minute Book.

of St Michael's were upon them; and by a series of terrific scrimmages, effectually prevented them from scoring.[28]

In a report of the 1886 match in the same newspaper, the game's shortcomings were explicitly related to its rules, or lack of them. For in those rules 'which were of the old Northumbrian type, the Rugby or Association restrictions could not be recognized, the principal things stipulated being that the ball should be kicked only, not carried, thrown or jerked, and that the game should be carried on within certain boundaries'.[29]

Nor were such invidious comparisons restricted to journalists. In the 1881 meeting of the match organising committee 'A conversation ensued as to the desirability of asking the Association Football Club to play a match after the usual game is concluded; *in order to make the proper method of play known*' (my emphasis).[30] This 'conversation' came too late (February 14, 1881) to have any effect on that year's match, but in 1882 the Alnwick Association Football Club (which was formed in 1880) did play an exhibition soccer match, against Rothbury FC, after the Shrovetide game. So, interestingly enough, did the even more recently formed Alnwick Rugby Club (Alnwick Hotspur). This experiment was repeated in 1883, with both association and rugby clubs again playing exhibition matches,[31] but it disappears thereafter. Here it is curious both that the Shrovetide players were thought able to learn 'the proper method of play' from watching either soccer or rugby, and that it should then have been decided, after a fairly brief period, either that no such learning was going on, or that such learning was no longer desirable or relevant.

There is some evidence, though, that as the 1880s wore on, soccer forms of play may have become more common in the Alnwick match. A *Northumberland Gazette* report of the 1888 match has this for example:

28   Unattributed and undated press clipping – but probably *NDC* – of the 1884 match in Minute Book.

29   Undated clipping, annotated as 'Newcastle Chronicle' in the 1886 pages of Minute Book.

30   Minute Book, entries for 1881.

31   Minute Book, match advertising posters 1882 and 1883.

> Brannigan took possession and carried it to the hill above Clennel's Burn, where he delivered it to T. Roper, and the latter passed it on to J. Knox, and Roper and Knox, carried it along the flat almost to the goal, when it was passed through, after being kicked about a little by Bartholomew Thompson for St Paul's.

And later:

> Several players took it rapidly up the field towards the goal, from whom it was very easily taken by W. Pyle, who, after carrying it for some considerable distance up the field, passed it on to Joe Brown, who in turn passed it to Fred Bamborough, who delivered it with a kick to J. Brewis; M. Mavin intercepted it, and kicked it against the post, and on the ball rebounding, Brewis kicked through.[32]

If, as one can only assume, all this 'carrying' and 'passing' occurred with the feet, this certainly sounds very soccer-like.

But whether or not soccer was influencing actual play in the Alnwick match, from the 1880s onwards it, and rugby, were certainly influencing *descriptions* of that play. In the latter part of that decade in particular local press reports begin to include the Alnwick 'football' match in the same intellectual universe as the rugby and soccer codes of football. But it is included there only to be found wanting – an 'improper' kind of football match – one that should become more like the 'proper', 'codified' forms of 'the game'. But in saying that, or implying it in their descriptions, the journalists writing these reports were simultaneously changing the meaning of the word 'football'. They were saying, in effect, that only the modern codified games *are* 'football' – 'real football' – and that the Alnwick match is *not* 'real football'. Indeed, that is why the Alnwick players can learn what football 'is' – 'really is' (*and* what the word 'football' means – 'really means') by watching soccer or rugby, but rugby or soccer players can learn nothing from them.

In essence then, to classify the Alnwick match as not 'real football' (and its players as not 'real footballers') was to require the match to be played differently. In these 1880s reports the meaning of the word 'football' is being implicitly changed as part of an explicit attempt to change football play, or, more exactly, to change the type of play that is to be called 'football'.

32   *NG* clipping, 1888, in Minute Book.

Harbinger of the Future: 'Elfin' and the Alnwick Match as Bucolic Romance, 1890

But such changes are only necessary or desirable *if* the Alnwick match is treated as an inadequate sports event in need of yet further 'improvement'; and not everyone thought this even in the late nineteenth century. We have already seen how one correspondent explained the inadequacies of the match by reference to the rules – 'of the old Northumbrian type' – by which it was played.[33] But of the phrase 'old Northumbrian rules', we can be as sceptical as was Voltaire of 'Holy Roman Empire'.[34] The 'rules' that the 1886 match correspondent is referring to were certainly not old (at least not unless 30 years is 'old'), were dubiously 'Northumbrian' in origin and are very debatably classified as 'rules' of, or for, the game at all.

In 1890, however, another local journalist, 'Elfin',[35] produced the first full-blown account of the Alnwick match in which it is compared with the new 'codified' forms of football *not* in order to criticise it or to find it inadequate, but to place it in a separate and entirely superior category of its own. So remarkable is this account, and so redolent of later perceptions of the match (including those still dominant today) that it is worth quoting in full. It is headed, significantly enough, 'FOOTBALL AS IT USED TO BE', and reads as follows:

> I must confess that at a time when rules and restrictions largely circumscribe the game of football it is refreshing to see the game played in the old style, as it was

---

33 One could say much the same thing about reports in the *NC* and *HC* for April 1878 claiming that a traditional football match played in Hexham, as part of an Easter Sports day there, was played according to 'the old Hexham rules'. But this is a separate – though related – story: *NC*, April 25, 1878 and *HC*, April 28, 1878.

34 Voltaire, 'Essai sur l'histoire generale at sur les Moeurs et l'espirit des nations', ch. 70, 1756.

35 Elfin's column, 'Local Gossip', appeared in the *NDC* on the Monday or Tuesday of each week between the 1870s and 1890s. It provides a flow of intelligent, informed comment on many aspects of north-eastern life, including politics, economic and social conditions and cultural events. Very occasionally it also includes observations and comments on sports and recreations.

on the pasture at Alnwick on Tuesday afternoon. The sight was one of a kind that painters have loved to depict on canvas and that poets have immortalised in verse. A struggling mass of sturdy fellows, pushing, crushing and jostling each other, an unknown number of feet actively moving in quest of the ball, cheering youngsters, demure young ladies gazing amusedly on, with here and there old men seated on forms, gesticulating and living their youth over again – such has generally been the idea that the artist has conveyed to our minds. And such was the scene witnessed in front of the noble castle at Alnwick.

When football was played in the streets rowdyism sometimes prevailed, windows were smashed, and the horse-play was a trifle too strong for most tastes. On the pasture there is horse-play enough, and perhaps to spare, but there are no windows to break, and no one is much the worse. All the fun is spent over the game and over the pursuit of the daring mortal who collars the ball at its close, dashes off with it in hot haste, and maybe has to wade or swim the Aln in order to make the trophy his own.

Conventionality was unknown in the game at Alnwick on Tuesday. As usual, anybody played that liked, and from one end of the open space to the other there was fun and nimbleness of limb and hearty laughter. The weather was cold, but border blood heeded it not, while Northern limbs raced, struggled and kicked all over the field, and Northern cheers resounded as each goal was scored. It was worth a day's march to see it.[36]

Surely 'Elfin' only needed L. S. Lowry at work beside him to render the romantic, even bucolic, effect complete. Here, right at the end of the period of the Alnwick match's history with which I am concerned in this chapter, is the perfect literary evocation of it as ancient rustic festival – 'football as it used to be' 'from time immemorial'.

That evocation depends heavily, of course, on Elfin's assumption that he is watching something ancient, something descended directly from an old street game. In reality, he was watching a game that, since its 'reform' in 1856, had been increasingly rule-constrained and that some people at least had wanted to see even more constrained. But despite its distinctly underinformed antiquarianism, his description does capture some things that, in 1890, still set the Alnwick match apart from rugby and soccer, and things that probably *were* very old. These were: some surviving aspects of play on the one hand and the spirit in which the game was played on the other.

36   Unannotated, undated clipping in Minute Book entries for 1890. My own research confirms that the clipping's source is the *NDC*.

A Naive Game Played Festively

To understand these genuinely ancient aspects of the late Victorian game, its famous 'by-laws' (as they were in 1890, and as they had been, with some slight variations, since 1856) need first to be set out in full. There were seven of them:

1. The ball shall be procured by the Committee and kicked off in the North Demesne in the Centre between the Goals.
2. The goals shall be as near as convenient to the extreme end of the North Demesne; and when the ball has been haled, the same shall be announced by Trumpet.
3. The Ball shall be received at the Barbican of the Castle by the Committee at 1.30 pm, who shall then convey it to the North Demesne, preceded by His Grace's Piper, and shall be given to the victor of the former year, who shall have the honour of kicking it up in the centre of the Goals.
4. The Committee shall appoint two Umpires, who shall be Judges of fair play in the Game; and whenever they shall cause the Trumpet to be sounded, the Ball shall be considered 'DEAD', and in the event of the Umpires not agreeing on any appeal, the decision of the Committee shall be final.
5. Should the Ball at any time be declared 'DEAD' at or near the goal, the Umpires shall cause it to be taken a sufficient distance, in a straight line from the Goal, before coming again into play.
6. The Ball shall be KICKED ONLY, and shall not be carried, thrown, or jerked from the hand at ANY TIME during the Game.
7. After the final hale, the Ball shall be retaken to the centre of the Goals, and there thrown up, and it shall then become the property of the person who shall carry it off.[37]

---

37   1882 match poster in Minute Book.

It will be obvious why these are called 'by-laws' and not 'rules'. By-law 3, for example, is not the kind of thing that would be found in any rule book of modern sports, nor is the first half of by-law 1. Moreover, at various times between 1869 and 1890 there were other by-laws that were not rules in any sense. (One, for example, stated that, after the Shrovetide match, another game was to be held featuring the boys of the Duke of Northumberland's school.)

In fact, there is effectively only one rule of play in these seven – the sixth rule forbidding handling the ball. The rule forbids handling the ball,[38] but it says nothing about the handling of an opponent. It would therefore be perfectly possible, under by-law six, to play a game in which the ball was kicked up and down the field, but the people kicking it could in their turn be kicked, tripped, grabbed or tackled rugby-style and hauled to the ground, and in which defending looked a lot more like rugby than soccer. This is probably what was happening in 1890, what had been happening on the demesne since 1828 and was almost certainly a feature of the street game for a long time before that.

In the following chapter, we shall also see that the Alnwick football match, like the other pre-modern football matches in the North-East, was a very 'straight ahead' game, in which the aim was to score goals by forcing the ball through a mass of opponents rather than by attempting to go around them through lateral movement.[39] Mass rushes were met by massed defences, and a great deal of the play was scrimmage play. It was a game in which, to quote the 1884 report again, 'Every inch of the ground was gamely contested; and as the players massed together in one gigantic scrimmage, many hard knocks must have been experienced.'[40] Since phrases

---

38   Even in the 1880s though, this rule was still being resisted, or at least infringed. A report for 1888 has this: "Bob Keen, coming forward, took the leather right down to St Paul's goal. Near the goal Jimmy Kelly manipulated it, and carried it a short distance hugged to his breast, to the centre of the goal, where it was dislodged from his arms by W. Wakinshaw, and kicked through. The Committee, however, decided to disallow the 'hale', but agreed to allow Wakinshaw five shillings for his performance." Undated *NG* clipping, 1888, in Minute Book.

39   See Chapter 2.

40   Undated 1884 clipping, annotated as 'Newcastle Chronicle' in Minute Book.

about 'every inch of ground being contested' are the standard fare of reports on the Chester-le-Street and Sedgefield Shovetide matches too, it
seems very likely that this 'mass scrimmage' characteristic of the Alnwick
game also went back to its street days.

So much for the *way* the game was still being played in 1890. As for
the *spirit* in which it was being played, we have already seen that in 1828
the single freemen won because large numbers of the spectators joined in
on their side. It seems that in 1842 (see Appendix 1) the match was undecided because somebody, or bodies, absconded with the ball. In a report
for 1862, a full six years after the supposed reform of the game, we find this:

> After an interval of a quarter of an hour, which was merrily spent – in snow-balling
> and tripping each other on the snow – the ball was again thrown up; and after an-
> other 'no hale', by Robert Blacklock, who was literally carried through the goal
> by the press of players with the ball in hand – the rule requiring that it should be
> 'kicked or thrown' through the goal – it was won by Joseph Brewis, of St Paul's,
> who kicked it cleanly through after several alternations of success on both sides.[41]

In other words, 'Elfin' has the spirit of what he is observing right. People
had fun, festive fun, at the Alnwick Shrovetide match. That fun was certainly rough, and, despite the cessation of the duke's 'donation' after 1847,
may well have continued to be fuelled by alcohol ('the spirit of the game'
indeed!) It is also probable that the result of the match was less important
to its participants than the playing of it, in sharp contrast to what was
already the case in at least major soccer and rugby matches in the region
in 1890, and certainly in contrast to the 'results-based industry' which is
professional soccer today. In short, in 1890 the Alnwick match still retained much of the flavour of a festival, despite the fact that its players
had been forced, or cajoled, into taking on some of the constraints of a
modern sport.

One final example may serve to emphasise this. As we see in by-laws
4 and 5 above, participants in the late Victorian match had to abide not
only by the 'kicking-only' rule but also by the 'dead ball' rule. They had

---

41   Clipping from *AJ*, February 1862, in exhibit on 'Football', Bailiffgate Museum,
     Alnwick.

to accept that, when the ball went beyond the roped confines of the 'play-ground', the game stopped and had to be restarted. But given how much emphasis is put on this point in the by-laws (two of the seven are taken up with elaborating it) and how many capitals are expended on emphasising both it and the kicking-only rule, I suspect that, like the fulminations of the medieval Catholic church against sin, the intensity of both prohib-itions is a good index of the frequency of their flouting, at least in the first decade or so after 1856.

It is a moot point how much of a festive flavour the Alnwick match retains today, after another century or more of the impact of modern foot-ball, but it is only in so far as it does – in so far as it is played in fun – that it has any genuine claim to antiquity.

Conclusions: Who Cares? Bring on the Tourists

Were this chapter to be headlined on north-eastern regional TV, pub-lished in every newspaper in Alnwick and around, and read out daily by the current duke from the castle battlements, I am sure that Alnwick's certainty about the antiquity of its Shrovetide football match would barely be dented. And as for visitors to the town, consistency alone rules out all doubt. Alnwick has a genuine castle, it has a genuine duke, it has a genuine ancient arch giving access to genuinely ancient cobbled streets, so it must have a genuinely ancient Shrovetide football match.

In this minor respect, as in other more important and more damaging respects, I am struck by how little most people really care about history. Or at least, how little they care about it as a detailed, nuanced narrative of the messy outcomes of the complex actions and interactions of masses of people. History is altogether easier, and certainly more fun, as a few quickly grasped stereotypes and fantasies, especially if they can be stimulated by, and attached to, some 'historic' structures or other – castles, dukes, stone circles, ruined temples or churches, etc.

But I am not just struck by the indifference to history among most of my contemporaries, I am often equally struck by it in the case of many

historical actors themselves. Take those 'old men seated on forms, gesticulating and living their youth over again' whom 'Elfin' saw watching
from the sidelines in 1890. What were they gesticulating about? Were
they deeply engrossed in the match, or were they, perhaps, muttering to
each other that Duke Algernon had ruined the game back in 1856 – the
game they had played – and how the bloody thing had never been the
same since? There is no way of knowing, but I rather doubt it. Make the
changes quickly, keep, or say you're keeping, some genuinely old stuff,
and it is amazing how quickly people forget. Thirty years is an eternity
in the lives of most people. In fact, moderately healthy, moderately
happy societies seem to specialise in historical amnesia. It is only in
very unhappy and (often) very violent places where historical memory
is virulent. Think of Northern Ireland for a long time, or certain parts
of the Balkans now.

And yet, even in not unhappy societies, people can lose a sense of historical achievement through their indifference to history and the substi-
tution of easy pastiche for genuine knowledge. For example, the Alnwick
Shrovetide match is one of only two such matches in the whole North-East
still being held. As a result, it has become a tourist attraction, a source of
not inconsiderable attention and revenue for the town. But why is it still
being held? Because it changed and changed and changed. Had the third
duke not moved it out of the streets and into the demesne, it would have
gone the way of nearly all other Shrovetide matches once modern street
frontages and tarmacked roads made their playing far too costly for local
merchants and far too dangerous for the players. And having moved to a
field setting, the Alnwick match kept on changing, taking in aspects of an
emerging modern sporting culture and blending it with some traditional
elements and spirit. And in the twentieth century it went on changing. If
it hadn't, it would have come to seem far too strange, and far too boring,
for further generations of young people to have taken any interest in it.

We are all familiar with George Santayana's famous remark about
history – that those who cannot remember the past are condemned to
repeat it. That is true of many important aspects of history – of wars, dip-
lomacy, national chauvinism and our treatment of nature. But even in less
important, less 'life-and-death' ways, the costs of historical ignorance can

be significant. For those who know nothing about history – even minor history, the history of 'ordinary' 'everyday' things – both fail to pay adequate respect to their ancestors and have no idea what they are saying, in the present, about the past. Or rather, they have no idea what they are saying *means*.

Appendix 1: Alnwick Football Match Press Reports, 1828–1847

1828: 'The freemen having, previously, held a meeting for the purpose of making the necessary arrangements … assembled in the Town-hall, at half-past 1 o'clock on Tuesday afternoon, and, having arranged themselves in order, they marched in procession, preceded by a large flag, and a circular wreath of laurel, circumscribing a golden ball, surmounted with the Percy crest.' There were 'about 5,000 spectators'. The game was played as married v single, and 'the first game' lasted about an hour and was won by the married men. However, the singles 'gained … the two succeeding games … in consequence of numbers of the spectators, who could not be restrained, and, in the concluding game they formed the majority of those engaged in the sport.' The whole event went on 'for nearly three hours' (Unattributed press clipping, February 23, 1828, in Alnwick Castle: DNP MS 187A/118).

1829: 'From time immemorial, the Earls and Dukes of Northumberland have provided a football which was thrown from the castle for the amusement of the town's people, annually on that day, and generally kicked through the streets: of late years this has been complained of as inconvenient and dangerous, and, in consequence, his Grace … has presented a prize of five sovereigns to be played for by the freemen of the borough in a regular match, the married against the single, in the pasture opposite the Castle; and also another ball for the non-freemen. The freemen marched from the Townhall, preceded by the band of the Northumberland Militia, and the flags of the Skinners' and Shoemakers' companies (the latter borne by 'Lord Wellington') to the pasture, where the match, after being well contested, was won by the married party. The day's amusements was concluded by a ball in the evening, for which his grace provided another five sovereigns to furnish music and lights' (*NC*, March 7, 1829).

1831: 'On Shrove Tuesday, the annual foot-ball match, between the married and unmarried freemen of the borough of Alnwick, took place; his Grace the Duke of Northumberland presented the parties with 10l. [i.e., ten 'livres' – ten pounds] which he has also done for the last four years.

The burgesses marched to the scene of the action, preceded by the banners, music and other appendages; and, after a short contest, the married men were proclaimed victors' (*NCh*, February 18, 1831).

1832: 'The annual football match at Alnwick for five pounds given by his Grace the Duke of Northumberland, was played on Shrove Tuesday as usual; the procession went from the Town-hall at two o'clock, preceded by part of the band of the Northumberland regiment, and the flags of the Shoemakers and Skinners' Companies. After a short contest, victory was declared in favour of the married party. The weather was rather unpropitious' (*NC*, February? 1832).

'The sum of ten pounds annually given by his Grace the Duke of Northumberland, for a foot-ball match between the married and unmarried freemen of the borough, was contended for on Shrove Tuesday. The match was won easily by the married party. The dance in the evening was numerously attended, and was conducted with the true spirit of rustic revelry displayed on such occasions' (*NCh*, March 10, 1832).

1833: 'On Shrove Tuesday, the annual foot-ball match between the married and unmarried freemen of the borough of Alnwick, was played in the pasture opposite Alnwick Castle. The game was won by the married party. His Grace made a donation of 10ls with which refreshments were provided, and a dance held in the evening' (*NCh*, February 23, 1833).

1837: 'The annual premium of 10ls given by his Grace the Duke of Northumberland, for a foot-ball match between the married and unmarried freemen of Alnwick, was contested on Shrove Tuesday and won in the course of a few minutes by the unmarried party. The competitors were but few in number, and marched in procession with two flags of the free companies, preceded by the Alnwick Amateur Band. The premium was applied in the purchase of two barrels of ale, and in paying the expenses of a dance in the Town-hall in the evening, which was numerously attended' (*NCh*, February 11, 1837).

'The annual football match between the married and unmarried freemen of Alnwick for a prize of £5, given by His Grace the Duke of Northumberland, was played in the Pasture, in front of the Castle, on Shrove Tuesday as usual. The procession was this year attended with more than usual pomp and circumstance, in consequence of the voluntary and efficient services of an excellent amateur band, which has been lately formed at Alnwick.' (*NC*, Feb ? 1837)

1839: 'His Grace the Duke of Northumberland's annual prize of ten sovereigns for a foot-ball match between the married and unmarried freemen of Alnwick was contested on Tuesday last. The company assembled in the Townhall, and walked in procession to the field, accompanied with the trades' flags and preceded by the Alnwick band. After a keen contest of about two hours continuance, the bachelors were defeated, the game being won by the married freemen. The customary dance took place in the Townhall, in the evening, and was numerously attended' (*NCh*, February 16, 1839).

1842: [a section torn] 'The Duke of Northumberland presented the sum of ten pounds toward the annual foot-ball match between the married and unmarried freemen of Alnwick, on Shrove Tuesday, on which day the party marched in procession to the field, accompanied with banners, music &c. The game was undecided [...]ruders. The compete-[...]usual entertainment took place in the High Brewery, in consequence of the illness of a family residing beneath the Townhall' [If 'ruders' is the last bit of 'intruders', it may be that the ball got pinched!] (*NCh*, February 12, 1842).

1843: 'The Duke of Northumberland gave a donation of ten pounds to the borough of Alnwick, on Tuesday last, being his graces's [*sic*] annual prize to the ancient foot-ball match between the married and unmarried freemen, on Shrove Tuesday. The competitors proceeded in procession to the field, accompanied by the Alnwick Amateur Band, and the banners of some of the free companies. After a contest of nearly two hours the game was proceeding in favour of the married side, when it was prematurely terminated by the ball being struck into the river Aln. A dance was held in the Townhall, in the evening, which was numerously attended; and the usual refreshments were supplied by his graces's gift' (*NCh*, March 4, 1843).

1844: 'FOOT-BALL – The Annual foot-ball match between the married and unmarried freemen of Alnwick, to which his Grace the Duke of Northumberland makes an annual donation of ten pounds, was contested in the pasture ground to the north of the Castle, on Shrove Tuesday, and after an arduous struggle, was won by the superior numbers of the married party. His Grace's donation was expended in refreshments, and a ball in the Town Hall, which was numerously attended' (*NJ*, February 24, 1844, p. 2).

[Identically worded report in *NCh*, February 24, 1844, save for the omission of the opening 'FOOT-BALL', the spelling of 'Townhall' as one word and the phrase 'in the evening' after 'Townhall'].

1845: 'The Duke of Northumberland's annual donation of 10l. to the freemen of Alnwick for a foot-ball match, on Shrove Tuesday, between the married and unmarried freemen, was played for on that day; and, after an arduous contest, the game was won by the superior numbers and experience of the married party. His Grace's donation was appropriated to refreshments, and a dance in the Town-hall in the evening, which was numerously attended' (*NCh*, February 8, 1845).

'SHROVE TUESDAY. – At Alnwick, on Shrove Tuesday, the annual great foot-ball match between the bachelors and married men, in aid of which, his Grace the Duke of Northumberland, gives ten pounds, was played at the usual place. The game, as is generally the case, was carried by the superior energy and perseverance of the married men. The day was concluded with a dance in the town-hall, which passed off with uninterrupted hilarity and pleasure' (*Tyne Mercury* [or *Northumberland, Durham and Cumberland Gazette*], February 12, 1845).

1846: 'SHROVETIDE SPORTS AT ALNWICK – The annual donation of ten pounds by his Grace the Duke of Northumberland, for a football match between the married and the single freemen of the borough of Alnwick, was played for on Shrove Tuesday, the 24th inst. The parties met in the Townhall, and marched in procession with music and banners to the castle grounds on the north side of the Aln, when the ball was kicked off by Mr Matthew Gibson, the father of the borough, who has been for fifty-seven years a free member of the Cordwainer's Company. After a close contest of nearly two hours duration, the game was won by the party of the single freemen, who carried off the ball in triumph. His Grace's donation was expended in refreshments, and in defraying the expenses of the public dance in the Townhall in the evening, which was numerously attended' (*NCh*, February 27, 1846).

1847: Match cancelled because of death of third duke. Not resumed until 1856.

What's in a Name? Playing 'Football' in the Mid-Victorian North-East[1]

Introduction

This chapter is about a familiar topic in sports history, the transition from traditional forms of recreation (in this case a form of traditional or folk football) to modern organised forms of sport (in this case rugby union and association football). Like many such discussions it is set in the mid-late Victorian period (the 1870s and 1880s) but it deals with a particular region of England – the North-East – where soccer subsequently became a mass participation and spectator sport and an icon of regional cultural identity.

However, unlike many of the more conventional discussions of this transition, I shall not be concerned in this chapter with the way in which traditional recreations and modern organised sport mirrored or reflected the broader societies of which they were a part. I do not ignore this familiar story because I think it unimportant or false in some way. Rather I want to concentrate in this chapter on the empirical detail of *how* this transition occurred, rather than on the interpretive question of *why* (in a broader sense) it occurred. I am concerned with the transition from traditional recreations to modern sport as a lived experience of a particular group of historical actors at a particular – and brief – historical moment. I am therefore also concerned with it as a set of actions and activities of

1   A version of this chapter was originally published as 'What's in a Name? Playing 'Football' in the mid-Victorian North-East' (*Ethnologie Française*, XLI (4), 2011, pp. 601–14), reprinted with the permission of the publisher (Presses Universitaires de France).

particular people, rather than with the broader, longer-term consequences of those activities.

Given this focus, one preliminary point has to be made. In the 1860s, physically active young men in Northumberland and Durham were engaged in a range of pre-modern recreations, one of which was 'folk' or 'traditional' football. In 1914, another generation of young men were engaged in 'modern' sports, two of which were rugby and (much more commonly) soccer. But this transition did not occur instantaneously. Traditional football was not being played one day and modern rugby or soccer the next. This transition was indeed a transition, a process, which though occurring over a relatively short historical period (thirty or forty years) yet occurred slowly enough to encompass several generations of young men between the ages of eighteen and thirty-five, and to allow those men both to make changes in their recreational activities and to adjust to them.

Perhaps these are obvious remarks. But they have less obvious implications, one of which concerns the potentially obscuring role of names. As we saw in the previous chapter, in the 1840s, in Alnwick, Northumberland, large numbers of men were playing 'traditional' Shrovetide football. In the 1890s they were still playing 'Shrovetide football' in Alnwick, but the game they were playing under this name was different in important respects from that played fifty years earlier. Similarly, in the late 1870s a small number of young men on Tyneside were playing association football. In the late 1890s masses of young men on Tyneside, Wearside, and many other places in Northumberland and Durham were playing association football, a few of them professionally. But the game they were playing under that name was different in many ways from that which was being played under it twenty years earlier. And these remarks apply equally to rugby.

All this carries a lesson for the historian of sport which is easy enough to grasp in principle but is often missed in practice – that a game may have the same name at two different moments in time yet not be the same game. Moreover, if one of those times is the present, it is only too easy for the historian to assume that because s/he knows what (e.g.) the word 'football' means now, s/he knows what it meant in (say) 1880. But, as we will see, that can be a very unsafe assumption. An essential point of this chapter, in fact, is that soccer in the North-East of England evolved rapidly between the 1870s and 1890s, in part as a result of rule changes, but mainly as a result of players exploring and developing the game in playing it. Most importantly, it evolved more quickly in the crucial years 1880–5 than did its rugby rival. As a result, by the mid-1880s, soccer had become a more attractive and exciting game to play and watch than rugby. In fact this was the major reason *why* soccer became the mass football code of north-east England, despite the fact that rugby union had arrived in the region a full five or six years ahead of it and that a dozen or so rugby clubs were well established there before soccer even began.[2]

One final introductory point. When I began the research on which this chapter is based, I was concerned to answer the question 'why soccer?' Why did the 'association' or 'soccer' code of football become the mass sport of north-east England, rather than rugby, or indeed some other form of sport? In doing the research I have become convinced that any satisfactory answer to this question must focus on the nature and attributes of the games themselves, and on the precise way in which they are introduced to a region or population, and *not* simply on their wider economic, social or cultural significance. Comparative study shows conclusively that there are no economic, social or cultural functions fulfillable by one, and only one, sport. So the adoption of any specific sport by any group of human beings can never be adequately explained by broad functional generalities, but only in specific contextual ways. And that means it can only be explained in ways that are deeply contingent. Soccer did not have to become the dominant sport of north-eastern England. As we shall see, rugby could easily have done so, but did not. This chapter explains why.

2   In 1880, for example, there were 36 rugby clubs reported in Newcastle, Sunderland and Middlesbrough, but only 18 soccer clubs (nine of them in Middlesbrough). Middlesbrough was in fact the North-East's first urban soccer centre. As early as 1880 its reported soccer clubs exceeded its rugby clubs, but this only happened in Newcastle and Sunderland in 1884. See Table 1, p. 300 of Michael Huggins, 'The Spread of Association Football in North-East England, 1876–90: The Pattern of Diffusion', *IJHS*, 6 (3) 1989, 299–318.

Three Victorian Football Match Reports

There follow three lengthy quotations from newspaper reports of Victorian football matches. All three matches took place in the North-East (by which I mean the 'old' counties of Northumberland and Durham[3]) in the late 1870s and 1880s.

• *Quotation 1*

On the ball being kicked off, the Northumberland men, who were the heaviest team, made the most of their weight and bore down on their opponents' goal. The ball, however, was well returned by Cumberlege, whose play throughout was excellent. The Northumberland men again brought the ball back, and had several shots at the Tyne goal, Milvain being especially active. Bruce now made several fine efforts to get the ball through his adversaries, but his career was generally cut short by being charged over. Just before changing ends a scrimmage took place near the Northumberland goal, but by a united rush their forwards carried the ball away. After the change the Tyne goal was again in danger, and both Logan and Eicholtz had good shots at it. The Tyne men now began to play much better together, and for some time pressed the opposite side; Logan however carried the ball away and was only stopped close to the Tyne goal. The ball was then passed to Bruce and Cumberlege, who ran it down the field very smartly, and Blackburn secured the first goal for the Tyne. Time was now nearly up, and both sides redoubled their exertions, and just before time the Tyne forwards, playing together in excellent form, made a final effort and secured a second goal. In this affair Bruce and Cumberlege were especially conspicuous, and Blackburn was again lucky enough to get the final kick.[4]

• *Quotation 2*

A little after Milvain kicked off for the Tyne, but the ball going over the goal line was brought to the Tynemouth 25 yards flag and kicked off from there, and Milvain getting hold of it made a short run, and on being collared tried to pass it to Reid, but failing the first scrimmage was formed near the centre of the ground and the Tyne forwards worked the ball through, and their opponents had to touch down. The ball being again kicked from the 25 yards flag, Milvain returned it with a good

---

3   In the long period prior to the creation of the 'Tyne and Wear' metropolitan authority (and its associated boroughs of North and South Tyneside), the River Tyne marked the boundary between the counties of Northumberland and Durham.

4   *NDC*, November 5, 1877, p. 4.

drop, and Oliver made a good run only to be collared by C. Challoner and Benson, and a maul in goal ensued in which Oliver worked well, but was outmatched, and Challoner secured a try, which however gave no result. On the ball being again started, it was soon at the Tyne end, but their forwards carried it through. Logan now made a good try to get in but was securely held by Scott. The ball coming out of the scrimmage that followed was secured by Oliver, who was unable to get the ball past the backs; and Burridge getting hold of the ball, made a short run and a good drop sent the ball toward the Tynemouth goal line, but Logan and Cummins each made a run, and the ball was again at the Tyne end, soon to be sent flying back, and Tynemouth had to touch down twice. As if, however, to make up, they were soon within six yards of the Tyne goal line. Milvain, unfortunately for them, made a free catch, and with a good place kick relieved his goal … Tynemouth now got a touch in goal, and change was called. At first the Tyne men had to defend their goal; but at last they broke away and Tynemouth had to touch down. On the ball being brought out, Logan and Fenwick, by some good play, worked the ball away from their goal; but Milvain again ran it back, and scrimmage after scrimmage took place near the Tynemouth goal. Logan at last got away, and with two good runs took the ball nearly across the ground. The Tyne forwards once more took the ball away from their goal, but again Logan made a rush, only to be collared just as time was called.[5]

• *Quotation 3*

When the ball dropped both sides rushed upon it and the force of their meeting was such as to cause the leaders to fall over each other in confusion. After some scrambling the ball was sent freely away towards St Paul's goal; and being skilfully manoeuvred by a few of the St Michael's players, was quickly within easy possibility of a 'hale'. But here the unscientific formation of the sides showed to disadvantage. Each side was playing all in a lump, without either quarter backs, half backs or backs; and the two sides in consequence mingled in confusion. During a scrimmage at the goal – which was like a dozen orthodox scrimmages rolled into one – one of the St Paul's team kicked the ball through the goal of his own party; and the sounding of the trumpet announced that the ball was 'dead' and that 'no goal' had been scored. Thereupon the ball was carried back to the original spot, and again kicked out, the goals being placed the same as before. This time, the St Paul's runners carried the ball along in front of them; but unfortunately, missed the goal and shot behind the posts. Before they had time to dribble it back, the forces of St Michael's were upon them; and by a series of terrific scrimmages, effectually prevented them from scoring. The St Michael's men managed very cleverly to manœuvre the ball for half an hour, when the trumpet again announced the ball 'dead', and the first 'hale' was awarded to St Paul's by virtue of their

5   *NDC*, March 4, 1878, p. 4.

proximity to their opponent's posts. After an interval of a quarter of an hour, the ball was again thrown out, this time higher up the hill, where some excellent and determined fight on both sides was made for it. For a time it seemed as if the St Michael's men were about to carry the opposing ranks before them; but by skilful dribbling and steady pushing, the St Paul's gradually broke through the ranks of their opponents. Then their runners, keeping the ball well in front, made straight for the territory of the St Michael's party, where they came almost unopposed. Again however their haste prevented them from putting the ball through the posts; and their opponents managed to hold them in check until the half hour was over. Thus the second 'hale' was given to the St Paul's party, although in reality none had been scored. The third 'hale' was by far the most exciting of the three. On the ball being kicked out from the centre, it was at once carried by the St Paul's men (who excelled their opponents in running) down to the east goal ... Here the ball remained for nearly twenty minutes, neither side being able to effect any advantage over the other. Every inch of the ground was gamely contested; and as the players massed together in one gigantic scrimmage, many hard knocks must have been experienced. At last, however, the ball broke through; and just when it seemed likely that the St Paul's men would 'hale' it, it was cleverly dribbled by three or four of the St Michael's crew, who brought it swiftly to the west end of the field. Then, three men, Davison, Packard, and Graham, got it among them, and none of their opponents being able to overtake them, carried it right way to the St Paul's goal, where Davison kicked a clever 'hale', making the first score, and winning the only ten shillings prize given during the day. The play was then finished ...[6]

Quotation 1 is from a *Newcastle Daily Chronicle* report of an association football match between a soccer club, the Tyne Association Football Club (hereafter 'TAFC') and the Northumberland Football Club (a rugby club). The match was played at the Northumberland Cricket Ground in Bath Road, Newcastle on Saturday November 3, 1877. Quotation 2 is from a report of a rugby union match played almost exactly four months later, on the same ground, between TAFC and the Tynemouth Football Club (also a rugby club). And Quotation 3 is from an account of the Alnwick Shrovetide football match of February 1884, played on a field, called the 'North Demesne', immediately adjoining Alnwick Castle, the seat then as now, of the Dukes of Northumberland.

6   *NDC*, February 1884, in Minute Book.

Three 'Straight-Ahead' Games

Note how difficult it is, from a rapid reading of these reports, to clearly distinguish what game – what 'code' or 'sort' of football – is being described. For a start, their terminology is systematically ambiguous about one matter that any modern student of football would find vital – whether the ball is being moved around the field by being carried in arms or kicked. In all these reports balls are 'carried' or 'carried away', they are 'got hold of' or 'secured' in unspecified ways and then 'run' or 'brought back' or 'passed' or 'rushed through', but the writers seem almost indifferent as to whether this is all being done by hands, or feet, or both.

But this is not the most important reason why it is so difficult to decide what game is being played in the three cases. The difficulty derives largely from the fact that in all three accounts, a rather 'straight-ahead' game is described, in which packs or groups of forwards move the back and forth along the playing field while maintaining a tight group or 'clump' formation.

In both early soccer and early rugby in the North-East there is very little lateral ball movement. The aim is to move the ball straight down the middle of the field, 'through' (rather than around) the opposition, and to do so largely through sheer physical force. Thus, if an individual forward is stopped by an opponent (and whether running with the ball in hand or at feet) another member of the onrushing group 'follows up' to force the ball on. In rugby a fellow forward can 'follow up' by picking the ball up and running with it as well as by dribbling it. In association football he *must* kick it or 'dribble' it on. But in both cases his compatriots will be close by. Moreover, while passing of the ball occurs in early north-eastern soccer, it generally takes only two forms – very short passes exchanged by forwards running together in pairs or small groups, and long forward 'punts' by backs for those forwards to chase collectively. The sweeping lateral pass to the wing, or longer lateral or backward passes designed to set up subsequent forward movement, are effectively unknown in this early period. This is because the bulk of early soccer players were not spread across and along the pitch in clearly demarcated individual 'positions', as in the modern game. On the contrary, early soccer teams lined up and played with a goalkeeper, two or three backs and half backs, and the rest of the team (six or seven men) as a tightly packed 'swarm' of forwards.

Much the same pattern distinguishes early rugby teams. Here too the role of backs is simply to provide a last line of defence against an opposition forward break away, and to punt the ball straight forward (though this time from the hands) for their forward pack to chase. In the early years of rugby union, long and short lateral passing and free running and jinking with the ball in hand by backs and three quarters is effectively unknown, and in the North-East in particular, is *very* slow to develop. This is an important point to which I will return.

The same general point applies to the Alnwick game. It too is a 'straight ahead' game played in a group or pack fashion. The only difference is that since there are no goalkeepers or backs of any kind, the whole team effectively constitutes a forward pack, and the game occurs almost entirely in mass rushes, met by massed defences. As a result, a great deal of the play is scrimmage play. Indeed, writers use the term 'scrimmage' often in these years, whether they are describing traditional football, or what we would now call 'rugby' or 'soccer'.

So, while these three newspaper accounts *do* throw some light on the relationship between traditional or folk football and the modern codes, they do not do so in any direct 'predecessor/progenitor' way. Rather it is the 'straight ahead', swarm-and-scrimmage characteristics of *all* these games, which is important. Although it is extraordinary hard to find detailed action accounts of traditional or folk football for any period predating the 1860s (and not just for the North-East, but for the country as a whole),[7] we can glean something of the essential characteristics of those

---

7   Francis Magoun's 1938 book (*A History of Football from the Beginnings to 1871*. Cologne: Bochum-Langendreer) is the most exhaustive account to date of the *longue durée* history of football. It is the original source of many subsequent accounts – either directly or indirectly – and demonstrates conclusively the acute limitations of the available historical sources as accounts of play. Percy Young, *A History of British Football* (London: Arrow Books, 1973, 32–81) also has a good synthetic account, and Montague Shearman, *Athletics and Football* (London: Longmans, Green & Co, 1887, 245–78) is the earliest attempt at a history known to me. Adrian Harvey's *Football: The First Hundred Years. The Untold*

folk games, through the impress which they leave on the first playing of both rugby union and soccer.

When rugby and soccer were first codified, both codes left large amounts of room for interpretation. Both specified the objectives of their game, and forbad certain kinds of actions, but they did not tell anyone how to play either game. They did not, that is to say, tell anyone how to play as a forward, or a back, or a three quarter, or a goalkeeper. And in this vacuum it was only logical that the first players used whatever informal knowledge they had, either from their school days, or from forms of traditional football they had played and which continued all around them. And this is shown, I think, in the marked swarm-and-scrimmage characteristics of early rugby and soccer and (thus) in the almost total lack of lateral play, passing and 'open field' play generally in the first forms of both codes.

That it was these characteristics above all which both the modern codes initially inherited from folk football, is also suggested by what happened when a 'kicking only' by-law was introduced to the Alnwick Shrovetide match in the early 1860s. As we saw in the previous chapter, the by-law seems to have gradually eliminated the previous 'mixed' methods of ball movement (through kicking, throwing and running with it in hand.)[8] But it did *not* succeed in altering the 'swarm' and 'scrimmage' characteristics of the game, either in the 1880s or for many years afterwards. Indeed, when, from the 1880s onwards, both the new football codes gradually developed more open styles of play (much more gradually in rugby than soccer, as we shall see) it was the *maintaining* of these 'swarm' characteristics that increasingly distinguished the Alnwick match *as* 'traditional'.

Story (London: Routledge, 2005) has added considerably to our knowledge of pre-modern football in England in the 1830s and 1840s, and especially the Sheffield variant of 'association football' played in the late 1850s and 1860s, but his account is still short of detailed descriptions of play. For a longer discussion of the importance of forms of play, see my "The Origins of Football ..." *op cit*.

8   For a detailed account of the by-laws, their origins, and the way in which they were used to modernise a supposedly 'traditional' form of football, see Chapter 1.

There is also a suggestive typographical characteristic of football match reports appearing in north-eastern newspapers in the 1870s and 1880s. Such reports always appear in columns, or column sections, headed 'FOOTBALL', but, until the mid-1880s at least, no attempt is made to distinguish the matches reported by code. Instead a miscellany of short reports appear below the generic heading, distinguished only by the introductory capitals in which the names of the competing teams are set. In fact, it is only by paying close attention to the number of players in the team lists, or to the forms of scoring, that one can tell whether a soccer or a rugby match is being reported. It is clear, in fact, that for the newspaper editors of this period, what is being reported under the heading of 'football' are *two variants of one game*, not two different games. In 1870s and 1880s Northumberland and Durham, rugby and soccer are seen as two different variants of an older pastime. In that pastime two groups of people try to score 'goals' by forcing or bashing a ball through an opposing group. Whether the ball is forced through by kicking it, or by running with it, is seen as an entirely secondary matter differentiating two variants of one game, and not (as we now see it) as a primary criterion distinguishing two different games.[9]

---

9   "Notwithstanding the hard winter the popular game of foot-ball has been very greatly extended in our district. It is a grand exercise for our youth; if there is not too much rough tumbling about it. *But there seems to be a better set of rules for conducting the game than the Rugby rules*, which seem to be a little too "school-boyish" for men, many of them weighing eleven or twelve stone." (*NDC*, March 22, 1875, p. 3, italics added). This quotation is from a long-running weekly column in the *Newcastle Daily Chronicle* – 'Local Gossip', by the writer 'Elfin' (See chapter 1, note 35). Note that "the popular game of foot-ball" which was being "greatly extended" in the district around Newcastle in 1875 was rugby, not soccer. But no sooner has he said this than Elfin suggests that rugby is not 'foot-ball' as such, but just one set of foot-ball *rules*. In other words, Elfin is here operating two concepts of 'foot-ball' simultaneously, one of which is clearly much older than rugby. It is unsurprising to discover then, that he was a regular watcher of the Alnwick and other Shrovetide games, and indeed wrote a detailed account of the Alnwick game in 1890 [See Chapter 1].

Geordie Soccer Pioneers: The Tyne Association Football Club

The Tyne Association Football Club, which figures in the first two match reports above, consisted initially of about sixty[10] young Tyneside men from very elite backgrounds[11] playing their matches at the Northumberland Cricket Ground. The NCG was located in Bath Road, Newcastle on land very near the city centre and now mainly occupied by the University of Northumbria.[12] TAFC was not only the first association football club in Northumberland and Durham, for the two years 1877–9 it was the only active association football club in the two counties.[13]

Its initial problem, therefore, was to find opponents to play. In fact all its earliest matches were 'scratch' games of various sorts, either intra-club matches featuring shifting combinations of its members and their friends under various titles ('Tyne v Bankers', 'Tyne v Engineers', 'Tyne v Public School Team' were some of 1877–8 season fixtures, and speak volumes about the social composition of the club) or matches against well-disposed local rugby clubs willing to 'give it a go' under association rules.

The Northumberland (Rugby) Football Club – also based at the Northumberland Cricket Ground[14] – proved particularly congenial in this

10   This figure is based on my survey of the TAFC team lists published as part of *NDC* match reports for the 1877–8 and 1878–9 seasons. The 'about' covers a small amount of uncertainty deriving from the fluctuating spelling of names.

11   Paul Jouannou and Alan Candlish, *Pioneers of the North: The Origins and Development of Football in North-East England and Tyneside, 1870–93* (Derby: Breedon Books, 2009), 40–2.

12   *ibid*, p. 30.

13   The Newcastle Rangers club was formed in 1878 but did not play a match until the 1879–80 season.

14   *NDC*, December 11, 1877, p. 4. A collection of type-written documents in the Tyne and Wear Archives, appearing to be original research material for a history of rugby union in Northumberland, states that the Northumberland Football Club was the first rugby union club in the county, formed in 1872 "by premium apprentices at Armstrong's Works, Elswick and were (*sic*) permitted to play on the Northumberland Cricket Ground." *Tyne and Wear Archive, Discovery Museum, Newcastle*, documents S/RFC4/14/29-35. The quotation is from S/RFC4/14/35. Institutionally, it seems that the TAFC, like the Northumberland (Rugby)

regard. It played the TAFC at association football no less than four times, first in March 1877, then a further three times in the 1877–8 season. The March 1877 game ended in a 1–1 draw, but Northumberland won two of the three seasonal games. As this suggests, at first rugby players experienced no real difficulty in competing effectively under association rules. Indeed, in December 1877 TAFC suffered what the match report described as its 'first reverse … since its formation' losing 2–1 at home to a scratch team put together by G. D. Fawcus, a Tynemouth rugby player. In summing up the action the match correspondent noted that:

> The victory was well earned by the visitors, who, in spite of their being accustomed only to the Rugby Union rules dribbled remarkably well; the majority of them being Tynemouth players, and in the habit of playing a loose forward game.[15]

By the beginning of TAFC's second season however, things begin to change, and in November 1878 the Northumberland Rugby Club suffers its first heavy defeat – 5–0 – at the hands of the soccer players. The match correspondent is clear why. 'The forwards of Northumberland', he says, 'made several valiant efforts to turn the tide of the game, but the quick and clever passing of the Tyne seemed to baulk them.'[16]

Football Club, was an offshoot of the Northumberland Cricket Club. Joannou and Candlish claim that the TAFC was an offshoot of the 'Elswick Rugby Club' and played their very first match, on March 3, 1877 at the 'Elswick Football Club'. But it is fairly certain that the 'Elswick Football Club' and the 'Northumberland Football Club' were one and the same organisation, and that, like TAFC, it played its matches at the Northumberland Cricket Ground. What we are dealing with here, in the case of early rugby and soccer on Tyneside and in the North-East generally, is young men who were originally cricketers looking for a winter game to play. Indeed Joannou and Candlish's own profiles of the TAFC players suggest just that.

15   *NDC*, December 11, 1877, p. 4. Tony Collins has repeatedly emphasised that early rugby (i.e. rugby as it was played in the 1860s and 1870s) was much less of a handling game than it is now. See, for example, his *How Football Began …, op cit*, p. 21 "Forwards, who would usually comprise fifteen of what were twenty-a-side adult teams until 1877, aimed to break through their opponents by dribbling the ball with their feet through the scrum."

16   *NDC*, November 11, 1878, p. 4. Note the clear implication of this – the *forwards* must "turn the tide of the game", because if they do not no one else can.

TAFC still had some way to go, however, in fully exploiting the possibilities inherent in substituting a more dispersed passing game for the tight, 'pack' dribbling game in which rugby players could compete. On November 23, 1878, just a fortnight after their heavy defeat of Northumberland, TAFC met their most formidable foes – the Middlesbrough Association Football Club – formed a year earlier than TAFC. TAFC lose by a goal to nil and are fortunate not to suffer a heavier defeat. The correspondent is clear why:

> The play of the Middlesbrough men was marked by the unselfish passing and the way in which each man kept his place. Had the Tyne men done the same the result might have been different.[17]

Thereafter TAFC appear to learn their lesson, for their match reports for the 1879–80 season feature many more mentions of passing, both long and short, of wing play, and of 'dodging', that is, dribbling as a means of avoiding an opponent by left and right manipulation of the ball in space, not as the 'straight ahead' kicking of the ball by a pack leader 'backed up' by his fellow forwards.

These are fascinating glimpses of the way in which one early football team learned to 'de-clutch' 'de-cluster' its way of playing, to make forward play looser and more positional, and spread its play generally, so that collective effort could allow greater room (both literal and figurative) for individual action and initiative. But they are just one microcosm of a 'learning through playing' that was going on widely in the game at this time. In fact, the North-East of England, as a relatively late starter in adopting soccer, was able to short circuit its own learning by copying teams from Teesside and Cleveland, and (even more importantly) from Scotland,[18] who had made these developments earlier.

17   *NDC*, November 25, 1878, p. 4.
18   In January 1880 several of the leading TAFC players played for a 'Tyne and District' eleven against a touring team of Scottish internationals, and in February 1880, TAFC itself played against an Edinburgh University team, the latter also containing two internationals.

Soccer and Rugby

However, rugby union clubs in the North-East were much slower to make equivalent changes in the playing of their code. Until at least the mid-1880s north-eastern rugby clubs seem to have been dominated by big forwards, both in their membership and on the pitch, with backs and wing three quarters treated as strictly ancillary second-class citizens, doing little or no running or jinking with the ball, or even much passing. For at least the first decade or so of play, rugby union backs and three quarters in the North-East seem to have been restricted to 'last ditch' tackling of breakaway forwards and to punting the ball ahead for their pack to chase. Certainly, the detailed accounts of the development of rugby union in the North-East in the 1883 and 1884 season found in the short-lived *Northern Athlete* magazine[19] (hereafter *NA*) broadly confirm this thesis.

At the beginning of the 1883 season an *NA* editorial on 'Scientific Football' felt the need to defend rugby union from the charge (made by its 'ignorant opponents') that it was just 'a confused medley of pushing, struggling beings without any theory or skill in their frantic struggles'. In defending the game from this charge, the editorial pointed to the highly 'scientific' form of rugby developed by the Oxford University side of 1882–3, 'perhaps the most perfectly drilled and scientific team ever seen in the field'.

> Every man had his special work and duty, and although individually better players could very easily be selected from the London and country clubs, the dark blue fifteen … was invincible and vanquished in turn every club it opposed. Furthermore, the 'passing' game, as practised by the Universities, has now been generally recognised as the chief secret of their success, and all the leading clubs are, this season, gradually adopting the tactics which proved so irresistible in the previous winter.[20]

However, a close survey of local rugby match reports and 'football gossip' columns of this same paper for the 1883–4 season suggests that, if this

---

19   This version of the *Northern Athlete* lasted only two years. But a magazine under the same title was refounded in Newcastle in the Edwardian period.
20   *NA*, November 28, 1883, p. 471.

adoption was occurring in the North-East at all, it was 'gradual' indeed. Reviewing a Christmas holiday match between the Northern Rugby Club (by common consent the best north-eastern club at this time) and Wakefield Trinity, the *NA*'s correspondent found that:

> our players have a very great deal to learn before they can cope successfully with the crack teams from Yorkshire, Lancashire and other centres of the game. The forward play of the locals is good […] and when it has been a matter of footwork, they have proved themselves quite capable of holding their own, but they still need great coaching in the all-important department of passing. The game has, during the past few seasons, undergone great changes, the old-shoving style of play has given place to a prettier and more effective one, in which dribbling and passing play the most important part. The key note of success is unselfishness […] The forwards should learn to pass amongst themselves, and to cross (this word is one largely used in the Association game, but recently it has been applied to the Rugby, and is the best one to express our present meaning) the ball from one to another. They should also be ever ready to give their half-backs chances, whilst the latter should be constantly feeding the three-quarters. The Wakefield Trinity men gave a good exhibition of the long passing game, and must have proved, to all who witnessed it, that it is the paying game.[21]

If allegiance to an older-style 'shoving' forward game was this strong in what was regarded as the best and most progressive rugby club in the region, it is hardly surprising if many of the *NA*'s other rugby match reports show that, despite the journal's constant admonitions, the 'new', 'prettier', 'scientific' style of the game was still more notable by its absence than its presence throughout Northumberland and Durham. So there are repeated complaints that local backs 'did not pass nearly enough, and showed very badly when compared with the Yorkshiremen' while forwards 'were weak in the tight scrimmages, and […] when near the other goal line, appeared to lose their heads by kicking instead of dribbling'.[22] Or again, north-eastern forwards might have benefitted 'if they had availed themselves of the heeling out system' but 'this they did not once do, but simply endeavoured to play the honest forward game […] of working the

21   *NA*, January 9, 1884, p. 566.
22   *NA*, November 14, 1883, p. 442. See also *NA* November 7, 1883, p. 424 and March 19, 1884, p. 728 for almost identical comments repeated.

ball through the scrimmages, and even when any individual succeeded in doing this he was alone and unsupported'.[23]

Under such circumstances it is unsurprising that, at the end of the season, in March 1884, an *NA* editorial called for a change of the 'Mauls in Goal' rule. By doing so, long passages of scrimmage play (following from the inability of one side to touch the ball down in goal, and the inability of the other to wrest possession), could be eliminated, and the amount of play consisting 'almost entirely of tight scrimmages' which 'from an onlooker's point of view [was] by no means interesting' reduced.[24] Because, whatever may have been the case elsewhere, the 'prettier style of play [...] in which dribbling and passing form no unimportant features' seems to have found only slow acceptance in the North-East.

There are three possible explanations of this. It may have reflected a uniquely 'forward-dominated' culture and conception of the game in north-eastern rugby clubs. It may have been the result of rule constraints deriving from the original forms of the game. Or it may reflect the greater technical difficulty posed by lateral passing from the hands, in comparison with the feet.

On the first hypothesis I can find no direct evidence one way or the other.[25] On the second (rule constraints), Montague Shearman, discussing early rugby union in his *Athletics and Football*, says, *inter alia*:

23   *NA*, December 5, 1883, p. 448.
24   *NA*, March 19, 1884, pp. 728–9.
25   Although there is one observation that may be tangentially relevant. Shearman re-
     marks: "To our mind the delight of the Rugby Union game – a delight which was
     not given to the same extent to the Association play – came from its resemblance to
     mimic warfare. Not only was the game 'not destitute in some sort of the policies of
     war' as Carew said of it, but there was something of the stern joy of warfare in the
     rushing attack, the stubborn defence, the grapple breast to breast, the overthrow,
     and the rise again to face the foe." (Shearman, *op cit*, pp. 308–9.) This is a Victorian
     example of a much longer running phenomenon, viz. the claim, made by many
     of its followers and enthusiasts, that rugby union is the true lineal descendent of
     'manly' folk football in Britain. ('Carew' was the author of a well-known seven-
     teenth century account of one variety of that football – Cornish hurling). I have
     found similar claims in centenary histories of the Durham City Rugby Club and
     Durham County Rugby Union, and in an official history of the Gosforth Rugby
     Club. Interestingly, they are based as much on the fact – or alleged fact – that folk

The Union code very properly abolished hacking, tripping and scragging, the last named of which […] consists in the twisting of an opponent's neck round, with the gripe of the arm to make him cry 'down', if he had any available voice; but the abolition of all these practices, and especially of the hacking, tended to make the game 'tight' and to render of little value the best and most skilful forward play, which can only be exhibited in 'loose' scrimmages.[26]

On the third hypothesis, Shearman dates the full development of the 'second phase' aspect of rugby football (in which lateral passing allowed backs and wings, as well as free running centres, to come into their own) only to the period 1882–4 for the country as a whole[27] and it certainly came later to the North-East. Moreover, a number of *NA* match reports for the 1883–4 season do suggest that initial experiments with passing led to frequent loss of possession.[28] This may have reinforced old preferences for shoving, dribbling and for individual running with the ball (with 'back-up').

But *whatever* may have been the reasons, by the time a more open style of play (featuring longer passing amongst forwards and between forwards and backs, and having lateral ball movement at its core), came to north-eastern rugby, it was already too late. From 1883–4 onwards the number of working-class soccer clubs in Northumberland and Durham begins to multiply rapidly as workers (coal miners, iron-and-steel workers, shipyard and engineering workers) take up the game in increasing numbers. If I am right, this is because the earliest soccer clubs (which were just as 'middle class' or 'white collar' in their composition as any of the early rugby clubs), in loosening, spreading and individualising their play, made their game – for this crucial early adoption-determining period – a

---

football involved a head-to-head clash of forwards as on its being a handling game. Equally interestingly, no such claim is found in official histories of north-eastern soccer clubs and associations. This may be one source of early rugby's resistance to any changes in its pattern of play – the belief that such changes were 'unmanly'. Or at any rate, it may have provided an historical/ ideological rationalisation for that resistance, and for maintaining the centrality of forward play.

26 Shearman, *op cit*, p. 297.
27 *ibid*, p. 308.
28 *NA*, September 26, 1883, p. 335 and October 31, 1883, p. 410.

more exciting and varied spectator and participant sport than the rugby then being played.

Spectators

Contemporary spectators of soccer and rugby union are generally informed spectators (in the sense that many of them have at least attempted to play the game they are watching). But by definition this could not have been true for the first generations of spectators of either code. Being 'naïve', such spectators were bound to be attracted by aspects of play which were spectacularly eye catching or visually exciting. And there is little doubt that individual players passing the ball quickly and running freely in the open field while 'dodging' opponents, or being bravely and spectacularly arrested by an open-field tackle while trying to dodge, *were* visually attractive and compelling features of the soccer code as it developed in the North-East. And they seem to have been features which it acquired before regional rugby did.[29]

On Saturday, November 12, 1881, at the Blue House Field in Hendon, Sunderland, there was a trial match – 'Probables v Improbables' – to select a Northumberland and Durham Association side to play Cleveland

---

29   The reluctance to reform rugby play to make it more attractive to spectators, was not restricted to the North-East. It also reflected a growing hostility, among the national leadership of the Rugby Football Union, to working-class involvement in the sport, whether as players or spectators. At the root of this hostility was a deep opposition to professionalism. Having in the 1870s and early 1880s been keen to expand their code to the working classes, the RFU leadership had, by the mid-1880s, come to believe that, if rugby became widely popular, it would face demands for professionalisation, just as soccer was doing. Hence, the RFU repeatedly denied requests from local associations (including those in the North-East and South Wales) for rule changes which would make the game more attractive to watch. For more on all this, see Tony Collins "Early Football and the Emergence of Modern Soccer" *op cit*, and his *How Football Began …*, *op cit*, chapter 10, pp. 75–81.

Association a week later. A correspondent for the *Sunderland Daily Post* was present and noted that:

> The players selected from the different clubs of Northumberland and Durham were undoubtedly men of fine physique and promise fair to make popular the Association game in the North of England. Three years ago there were only six clubs in the Northumberland and Durham Association, now they number between twenty and thirty, with about 1,500 playing members. The public who were able to witness the match on Saturday had a real football treat. Smart passing, fine dribbling, good tackling, and above all the amusing dodging kept the onlookers delighted. There is no doubt that the Association game only requires to be known to be generally adopted by football players.[30]

This report, and especially its last sentence, enraged one reader, 'a rugby player', who immediately fired off an angry letter to the *Post*. In it he took to task, not only the match report, but an editorial in the same edition of the paper, in which the editor, 'Ariel', had remarked of the same match that: 'For the first time in my life I saw a game of football played on Saturday afternoon last under what are called the association rules. The association game differs from that of the Rugby system in some important particulars. No hugging or lifting of the ball with the hands is allowed. There is an absence of what is known as collaring or scrimmaging. I should fancy, from a scientific point of view, the association game ranks highest, but to the onlooker is not nearly so exciting.'[31]

Notwithstanding Ariel's 'last instance' commendation of his game, 'a rugby player' was not mollified. He commented: 'Is the Association game more scientific? I am inclined to think not. It is true by our rules we *handle* the ball, and this appears to be the enormity of our offence. But why? Good dribbling may be witnessed at any of our good Rugby football matches, as also loose scrimmages, a plenitude of tackling and amusing dodging, a pretty passing game, some excellent running, and, with due deference to our Association friends, some fine drop, punt and play kicking.'[32]

---

30   *SDP*, November 14, 1881, p. 4.
31   *SDP*, November 14, 1881, p. 2.
32   *SDP*, November 16, 1881, p. 3.

But whatever might have been the case for 'good' games, a 'plenitude' of such things could *not* be witnessed at the average rugby union game in the North-East of England, or certainly not before the mid-1880s. It need not have been so. The more rapid development of the second phase and back play elements of the rugby game could have made it just as compelling a visual spectacle as soccer and may have been doing so in other parts of England and Wales at this time. But until the mid or even late 1880s, rugby in the North-East remained predominantly a tight, breast-to-breast 'slog' between packs of forwards, with such demanding, not unskilful, but visually rather dull close 'warfare' being relieved only by long and high punting of the ball by backs and forwards. And by the time this changed it was already too late. The proletarian young men of the region had by then already voted, with their eyes, as well as with their feet.

Conclusions: Substantive and Methodological

The primary aim of the first stage of my research was to answer the question 'Why soccer?' Why did soccer become the predominant participant and spectator sport of the North-East of England? Before I had done any research, when I was totally naive about the matter, I rather suspected that the obvious answer would turn out to be the right one – that is, 'because young men in the region liked it more than any alternative they were offered'. However, when I proffered this explanation to my sports historian colleagues I was met mainly with scepticism and amusement. This explanation was, I was told, naive in the extreme. How, to take only the most obvious objection, could it possibly account for the fact that coal miners and other workers in West Yorkshire took up rugby league, or that Welsh miners played and loved rugby union as much as any north-eastern miner loved soccer?

But such objections are logically compelling only if assertions about 'liking' or 'preferring' a game are treated as timeless, de-contextualised, 'essentialist' assertions about the intrinsic attractiveness of a game. If so meant, they are indeed completely question-begging. Tell any elderly Welsh miner that rugby union is somehow unable to allow exciting open-field running and evasion, or enormously skilful long and short passing, and he will – quite rightly – laugh one out of court, beginning with a litany of the great Welsh, and other, exponents of such skills.

However, assertions about the comparative attractiveness of a game do not have to be essentialist. They can be deeply contextual, historically situated assertions, and then they can be true, and be demonstrated to be true, but only for a particular time and place. Rapidly developing early soccer in the North-East of England 140 years ago *was* a more attractive game to watch, and to play, than less rapidly evolving rugby union was at that place and time. It could easily have been otherwise if the early rugby clubs had also maximised the excitement strengths of their 'brand' (to use current marketing speak.) But they did not, chose not to, or at least not quickly enough.[33]

Another way of understanding this is even more interesting. If we treat both early soccer and rugby, as their first Victorian spectators did, as semi- or quasi-modernised variants of the ancient game of 'football' or 'foot-ball', then we see that early soccer clubs in the North-East developed and further modernised their variant more quickly than did the exponents of the rugby variant. And putting matters thus helps us to see something even broader and more important – that turning the traditional, popular pastime or recreation that was 'football' into a modern sport involved *more* than formulating written rules, *more* than bureaucratically organising associations and leagues, *more* than producing coaching manuals, *more* than developing enclosed stadia, or taking advantage of modern forms of transport like railways and trams (the kind of factors on which many standard accounts focus). It also involved developments on the pitch.[34] It

33   This is important, not only because exciting passages of play attracted more spec-
       tators, but because, in this very early period, spectating was as much a prelude to
       playing as *vice versa*. Soccer *playing*, as well as spectating, was increased by making
       the code pleasing or exciting to watch.

34   I use this phrase for its familiarity, but strictly it is anachronistic. Victorian soccer
       players did not play on 'pitches', they played on fields, and that was a very different
       matter. Playing on very uneven surfaces, and on grass which rapidly metamorph-
       osed into mud and then into hard-compacted earth under heavy winter wear,
       posed problems for the Victorian soccer pioneers unknown even to the modern

involved new ways of *playing* the game that were learned by doing, and by emulating, ways that were learned – or certainly were learned at first – in physical practice, rather than from rule books or coaching manuals.

And this reflection brings us directly to questions of historical methodology. If we are to write good sports history, we must, I believe, pay at least as much attention to the sport (any sport) as a physical activity as we pay to its forms of organisation or social setting.

It was only after I had been working on the history of football in the North-East for several months that I began to appreciate the importance of match reports – and in particular the 'action' sections of the reports – for my research. At first, I treated them only as sources to be quarried for the names of early players, for first mentions of clubs or their grounds, or for spectator tallies. Only slowly did I understand that the more detailed reports (of which there were a surprisingly large number, even for the very earliest years) were telling me a story about how the playing of one form of football was changing – was actively being changed – by the young men involved, while the other was remaining largely static. I was also slow to grasp that the *language* in which soccer and rugby match reports were expressed was important, that I could learn a lot about the assumptions and expectations of the men doing the describing through their choice of terminology. In particular, I could learn something, at least by implication, about what the old 'foot-ball' had involved, through the way such men first described its two 'new' variants.[35]

---

amateur player. It was also an important factor in the instability and ephemeral character of many early clubs. Fields were usually rented by the year from landowners or farmers, and renewal of the leases could be difficult once the owners grasped what a season of football could do to valued pasture. Many early soccer clubs went in and out of existence as they 'lost their field' but obtained another one after a passage of years. In this respect TAFC, and indeed the first 25–30 soccer clubs in the North-East, were relatively privileged because, unlike the large number of proletarian clubs that succeeded them, they were allowed to play on the only areas of grass then existing which were specifically designed for human sporting use – cricket fields.

35 For the use of match reports to shed light on the early development of association football in England and Scotland more generally, see my "The Origins of Football" *op cit*.

But why was I slow to recognise these things? Because I had been influenced by a tradition of sports history that generally marginalises sport as an activity in pursuit of its deeper social or cultural significance. That sport does have such significance no one can doubt. That one can learn a great deal about class relations, about community and other identities, about dominant conceptions of masculinity and femininity, as well as about structural economic and social change, by studying the history of sport, is indubitable. Sports history is as significant, as important, a form of social, economic and cultural history as any other. But it is equally true that no one plays or spectates sport *in order* to relate classes, *in order* to express community or ethnic identity, *in order* to express masculinity, *in order* to bring about structural social change. To be naive once again, people play and watch sport *because they enjoy it*. And generally speaking, even people who play sport professionally also enjoy it.

To put that methodologically, it is important not to confuse a description and/or explanation that an observer can properly give of the concomitants, consequences, implications of someone else – some other individual or group of people – playing or watching sport, with an account of the motivations that person, or group of people, may have for playing or watching sport. It may be perfectly right for someone else to say that, when I attend a football match and cheer for my team, I am, among other things, and objectively speaking, 'expressing my sense of community identity'. But it does not follow from this that the reason – the subjective reason – that I went to see Newcastle play Everton last night was to express my sense of community identity.[36]

36 It is clear that the explanations historians give of human actions and motivations *must not be inconsistent* with the explanations that historical actors themselves give of them (if we are lucky enough to find such). But this is not nearly as restrictive a requirement as is commonly supposed. The accounts that people give of their motivations are often – indeed usually – logically and factually consistent with a wide variety of broader explanations of their actions. Indeed it is this problem – of under determination by 'subjective' evidence – that makes debates over competing explanations in history and social science so intractable. Cases in which explanations are point blank contradicted by actors' own assertions are both much less common and much easier to deal with. (Despite some significant literature in the philosophy of social science suggesting otherwise.)

What we must understand though, if assertions about enjoyment are not to be philosophically naive, is that the category of 'enjoyment' is itself enormously complex and multi-layered, embracing everything from physiology (e.g. the production of testosterone and adrenalin) to aesthetics, to the pursuit of social prestige and approval. But though that is true, it is also true that one will never grasp the complexity which is the enjoyment of sport, unless one pays due attention to the actual play itself. The game may not quite be *the* thing, but it is at least *a* thing – a real and important phenomenon. Moreover, it is a phenomenon which (in the case of soccer and rugby certainly) has given millions of people enjoyment, formed an important part of their lives, whether as players or spectators. It is therefore fully as worthy of serious intellectual attention as any other aspect of human life. We must therefore grasp in detail what happened – what they did – 140 years ago, when those young men of the Tyne Association Football Club first ventured out to play soccer. Because that detail shows us that they were venturing out, not just to play soccer, but to make it, mould it, develop it, modernise it, on the cricket grounds of the Victorian North-East. In short, through their playing, they helped, in however small a way, to change the very meaning of the words 'soccer', 'association football' and indeed 'football', forever. (But that is what we understand now. It is not what they would – or could – have understood then).

Mercutio and Friends: The Press and the Commercialisation of North-Eastern Football 1885–1892

Introduction

On January 29, 1892, the Middlesbrough-based *North-Eastern Daily Gazette* reported that:

> Sportsmen generally throughout the North of England will learn with mingled regret and pleasure that one of the ablest and most impartial of Northern sporting journalists is about to leave the district for a higher appointment. Mr T.W. Gale ... well-known in the football world under his *nom-de-plume* of 'Mercutio', has been appointed to an important position on the staff of the *Sporting Chronicle*, and his friends and admirers on Tyneside intend to embrace the opportunity to mark in some lasting fashion their appreciation of the man and the journalist ...[1]

Three weeks later, on February 22, the *Northern Echo* told its readers in what this 'marking' had consisted. There had been a banquet in Mr Gale's honour at 'the Crown Hotel, Clayton Street, Newcastle'. It had been attended by a large number of local worthies from the city, but also from Sunderland, South Shields, Hartlepool and Middlesbrough, and Mr Gale had received a 'substantial cheque' and his wife a 'valuable ring'.[2] Later the same evening, according to the *Shields Daily Gazette*, a large number of friends had congregated in Newcastle Central Station (hot foot from

---

1   *DG*, January 29, 1892, p. 3.
2   *NE*, February 22, 1892, p. 3.

the banquet presumably) 'to bid "Mercutio" God-speed' on his journey to Manchester and the *Sporting Chronicle*.[3]

As all this indicates, the departure of 'Mr T. W. Gale' from the North-East was an event of note. But, though his banquet and impending departure were reported in the *Newcastle Daily Chronicle* and *Evening Chronicle*,[4] neither informed their readers that T. W. Gale was none other than the *Newcastle Daily Leader's* famous 'Mercutio'. Perhaps even more remarkably, not a word of Gale's departure was breathed in the columns of the *Leader* itself.

There was a good reason for the latter omission though. 'Mercutio' had been the sports editor of the *Leader* from its very first edition in late September 1885. In fact, he was the first full-time sports editor ever employed by a Newcastle newspaper, and he had been an outstanding success. So popular had his reports and reflections on local sports – especially his

3   *SDG*, February 22, 1892, p. 3. The *Sporting Chronicle*, founded in 1871, was part of the Edward Hulton-owned group of newspapers in Manchester which included the *Athletic News* (1875) the *Sunday Chronicle* and later (1897) the *Manchester Evening Chronicle*. Interestingly, James Catton ('Tityrus'), probably the most prominent sports journalist of the late Victorian and Edwardian periods, was appointed as a 'news editor' of the *Sunday Chronicle* in November 1891 and wrote regularly thereafter for the *Sporting Chronicle* and the *Athletic News* (which he edited from 1900 onwards) as well as the *Sunday Chronicle*. (The three papers were produced out of the same offices in Withy Grove, Manchester.) The near perfect coincidence of Catton's arrival in Manchester with Gale's appointment to the *Sporting Chronicle*, together with the fact that Catton had spent some time in Nottingham (as a reporter on the *Nottingham Daily Guardian*, 1883–91), strongly suggests that Catton played some part in Gale's appointment. Certainly we know that Gale had worked for the *Nottingham Express* newspaper, probably in the early 1880s (see note 7 below). After the second world war until its demise in 1983, the *Sporting Chronicle* was exclusively a 'racing' paper, concentrating entirely on "the turf and the dogs" in Tony Mason's words. But for the first seventy-five or so years of its existence it covered a much broader range of popular sports. For all this see Steve Tate, 'James Catton, "Tityrus" of the Athletic News (1860 to 1936): A Biographical Study', *Sport in History*, 25 (1), 98–115, and especially pp. 102–4, and Tony Mason "Sporting News 1860–1914" *op cit*, especially pp. 171–3 and 185.

4   *NDC*, February 20, 1892, p. 7, *EC*, February 20, 1892, p. 2.

weekly 'Sports and Pastimes' column – become, and so vital to the paper's commercial viability, that its editor resolved to retain the by-line and its columns even after their original creator had departed. In fact, the *Leader* continued to use the by-line 'Mercutio' for eight years after 1892, leading its football coverage with it until 1899, relegating it to occasional 'Golf Notes' in 1900 and dropping it entirely only in 1901.

The need to retain a popular by-line explains why the departure of its 'first Mercutio' went unmentioned in the *Newcastle Daily Leader*. It does not so obviously explain why none of the *Leader's* Newcastle competitors saw fit to inform their readers that Gale and 'Mercutio' were one and the same person. But there was a reason for that too. Virtually all Victorian press reportage occurred under pennames, and before the legal creation of 'intellectual property' those names were regarded as the property of the newspaper in which they appeared, not of the journalists using them. Thus, the *Leader* was entitled to change the writer behind its 'Mercutio' by-line as many times as it liked. But it could only do that without its competitors revealing the changes by joining them in a kind of mutual self-denying ordinance. In return for their remaining silent about T. W. Gale's journalistic identity, the *Leader* would in turn remain silent when the *Newcastle Daily Journal* changed the human being behind its 'Custos' sports by-line, or the *Newcastle Daily Chronicle* changed the author of its 'Notes by Offside' football reports. But this convention only operated within a shared local market, in which all the newspapers involved risked losing readers if these changes became known. Papers more distant from that market (in this case, from Newcastle) were not constrained by it.

The *Newcastle Daily Leader* ceased independent publication in 1903, being merged with the *North Mail*.[5] And with the disappearance of the latter newspaper – by then the *North Mail and Newcastle Daily Chronicle* – from the Newcastle market in 1939, all its records and those of its component

---

5   The *Newcastle Daily Leader* was founded in 1885 by James Joicey, a prominent north-eastern coal owner and Liberal politician. He bought it as a weekly paper (*The Northern Weekly Leader*) based in South Shields and edited by James Annand, "the foremost Liberal journalist on Tyneside". Annand continued to edit the *Leader* as a daily and as a "consistently radical Gladstonian newspaper" until 1895 (i.e. throughout Gale's time there). He resigned in 1895, having quarrelled

titles were lost.[6] So we will never know how many more 'Mercutios' there were between 1892 and 1900, or their real names. Indeed, we only know that T. W. Gale was the first because the popularity of his pioneering efforts gave him a region-wide reputation and provided a reason for newspapers in Middlesbrough, Darlington and South Shields to reveal his penname.

Beyond these accounts of his departure from Newcastle we know very little personally about Thomas William Gale – just enough to discover his Christian names, that he was born in London in 1855 and died there fifty years later, that he was married to Elizabeth Ellen Gale, and that he had been working as a journalist in Nottingham immediately before his arrival in Newcastle.[7] But what he wrote while in Newcastle survives in the battered copies of the *Leader* held in the city's Central Library. And in reading his prose, over 130 years later, one can still enjoy the charm, humour and

---

with Joicey over Irish Home Rule, and was succeeded by Aaron Watson, who edited the paper until 1901. In 1903 Joicey sold the *Leader* to the Conservative Charles Pearson, then owner of the *Daily Express* and of a stable of Conservative/ Unionist papers in the midlands and north, including the *North Mail*, which he had founded in Newcastle in 1901. Pearson then merged the *Leader* into the *North Mail*. For some details, including the disagreement with Joicey over the Boer War which led Aaron Watson to resign as editor of the *Leader*, see Maurice Milne, *Newspapers of Northumberland and Durham: A Study of their Progress During the 'Golden Age' of the Provincial Press* (Newcastle: Frank Graham, 1971), 128–30 and 215, and Laurel Brake and Marysa Demoor (eds), *Dictionary of Nineteenth Century Journalism in Britain and Ireland* (Gent: Academia Press, 2009), 460–1. The story of the *Leader*, and in particular of its relationship with the Joseph-Cowen-founded *Newcastle Daily Chronicle*, is part of a much larger national story of the rise and decline of the Liberal press in Victorian England. For the important role played in that decline by Liberal splits over Irish Home Rule, the Boer War and imperial preference, see Alan J. Lee, *op cit* especially pp. 135–6, 174–7 and 218–19. The characterisation of Annand above is from Milne, p. 128. The characterisation of the *Daily Leader* as a "radical Gladstonian paper" is from Lee, p. 136.

6   At least that is what one is told when one enquires at the offices of the *Newcastle Journal* (into which the *North Mail and Newcastle Daily Chronicle* was incorporated at the onset of the war.)

7   'Mercutio' says very little about himself in any of his *Leader* writings. However, census and some other press sources tell us that Thomas William Gale was born in Battersea in 1855 and died in Nunhead, now a suburb of Peckham, in 1905. He was living in Croydon in 1881, in St Thomas Street, Newcastle (very near the city

general *bonhomie* which made its writer so popular. More importantly, through Mercutio's astute observations and reflections on early north-eastern football, a contemporary reader can learn a great deal about a short but crucial period (1885–92) when the sport that was to become a regional obsession underwent rapid expansion and significant structural change.

When T. W. Gale arrived in Newcastle in the autumn of 1885, its foot-ball teams were entirely amateur, and its main 'city' clubs (Newcastle West End and East End) were just two of a clutch of small Northumberland football clubs of broadly similar status and levels of support. When he left, in early 1892, both East End and West End had professionalised, were the dominant clubs in both city and county, and the former's transformation into 'Newcastle United' was only months away. When 'Mercutio' arrived in the North-East, Middlesbrough FC was still the region's outstanding football club. By the time he left that mantle had passed to Sunderland.[8] In those vital three or four years of the late 1880s Sunderland too emerged from a clutch of small amateur football clubs (this time in County Durham), rapidly expanded its support, and professionalised.[9] By the time Mercutio boarded his train for Manchester in February 1892 it had become the region's first Football League club. He himself acknowledged, even celebrated,

---

centre, and just south of the current Newcastle University campus) in 1891 and ap-pears to have been staying in a hotel in Nottingham at the time of the 1901 census. A brief obituary in the *Nottingham Daily Express* confirms that Gale had worked as a journalist for that newspaper immediately before coming to Newcastle. (*NDE*, July 21, 1905, p. 5). To date however I have not been able to learn anything of his time at the *Sporting Chronicle*. I am enormously grateful to Steve Tate for first tracking down most of these details.

8   In the same story in which it reported the plans of his friends to mark T. W. Gale's departure, the *DG* said that "Mr Gale ... delights to tell how, when he first came to the North seven years ago, he had invariably to journey to Middlesbrough to see a first-class football match." *DG*, January 29, 1892, p. 3.

9   It is worth listing the football clubs in Northumberland and Durham with which Sunderland and Newcastle West End and East End were broadly on a par in 1885. They included: Shankhouse, Morpeth Harriers, Sleekburn, Bedlington Burdon, Elswick Rangers, Elswick Leather Works and Rendel in Newcastle and Northumberland; and Whitburn, Southwick, Birtley, Gateshead NER, Durham University, Darlington, Darlington St Augustine's, Stockton and Bishop Auckland Church Institute in Sunderland and Durham County. At this period

Sunderland's achievements, but he also challenged the major Newcastle clubs to match them. And for that to happen – for Newcastle to 'catch up' with Sunderland in football – he thought that the East End/West End split would have to end. In this, as in much else, he was to be proved right.

However, Mercutio did not confine his activities to Newcastle, or even to the Tyne-Wear conurbation. He perambulated widely and incessantly, no doubt at his paper's expense, through the entire North-East – from the northern edges of the Northumberland coalfield to Tyneside, through the length of County Durham to Middlesbrough and Teeside – reporting and reflecting on football as he went. He watched matches in Newcastle and Sunderland, but also in Ashington, Morpeth, Shankhouse, Gateshead, Darlington, Bishop Auckland, Stockton, Middlesbrough and Redcar. Indeed just before his departure from the *Leader*, at the beginning of the 1891–2 season, T. W. Gale initiated a series of lengthy reports under the title 'Around the Grounds'. In these he described not only the football action at 'Park Lane, Gateshead', or at 'Linthorpe Road, Middlesbrough', but the appearance of the grounds concerned, the size and composition of the crowds they held, and the views and attitudes of various club 'committeemen' or 'directors' whom he met while there. (See Appendix 2 of this chapter for a typical example.) 'Around the Grounds' was continued by his successor (or successors) for another season after he left, and, along with the original Mercutio's fair-minded and non-partisan approach to football reporting, further reinforced the by-line's regional reputation and popularity.

In short then, in the writings of Mercutio we can find invaluable descriptions of a period in the history of north-eastern football for which we have no film or broadcast media, very few photographs and just a couple of paintings. In fact, the only football illustrations from this period found in any quantity are stylised newspaper engravings, and even these are only abundant from the late 1890s onwards.

In the rest of this chapter, therefore, I shall use the writings of this 'first Mercutio' to discuss: the football grounds of the late Victorian north-east; the size and behaviour of the crowds which frequented them; the

_____

the Northumberland/Durham county boundary was of no significance in football competition, *all* these teams playing each other regularly in friendly matches.

excursion and other trains on which some of the people in those crowds travelled to matches; football rivalries within and between Newcastle and Sunderland in these early years; and the relationship between the major north-eastern football clubs and the local press. But before doing all that I must introduce readers to T. W. Gale's endearing prose.

A Charming Bonhomie

1. … last Saturday week I was foolish enough to entrust myself to the tender mercies of the excursion train which the West End people considered would be of value to those of their admirers who wanted to follow them to the great town of iron, [i.e. Middlesbrough – GK] although they themselves, the West End executive and the eleven, travelled by the 10.40 ordinary from the Central …

… it was a very popular excursion and well filled before we left Newcastle. Then, although the train could not have held a dozen more, to all appearances, we seemed to wait a long time after the appointed hour of departure to see if any more passengers came. Then we crawled to Gateshead, where there were enough people waiting to fill another train … Staying elsewhere we picked up a lot of other passengers, and I fancy that by the time we reached Sunderland we must have had a lot of people on the roof.

How late we were after we had crossed the Wear I don't know. I only know that at Sunderland were assembled enough people to fill two more trains such as we had. I was by this time in despair and precipitately fled. How the adventures of the excursion train were concluded I have not heard. Whether a further train was made up, or whether the officials piled passengers on the carriage roofs, slung them in hammocks underneath, and gave the driver and stoker some companions on the tender – the guards had company already I fancy – I have never sought to discover, nor have I asked how the hundreds that must have been waiting at other roadside stations got on. One thing that looked certain was that I should see nothing of the game at Middlesbrough, and so, sadder and wiser, I walked away to Roker.

I had been footballing every Saturday of the season so far and thought that a little rest would do me no harm. But down by the sad sea waves at Roker … a melancholy mist hanging over them – I could not get away from the great winter game. Two or three teams were playing about me, and I saw a ground very neatly marked out and a side in practice which seemed to boast a pretty smart goalkeeper and one or two rather good shots at goal. These youngsters, I reflected, will grow up to take places in good teams, and with so many juveniles fired with enthusiasm in the districts round our big towns there may be a time when importation of players is unknown …

2. West End, like most popular clubs, are never short of shouters on the skirts of their field, nor do they go begging for captains in the same position. On Saturday, however, they developed a champion so far as shouters go. Doubtless the gentleman in question has been to many matches before; but it was never my fortune to get so close to him as on this occasion. I hereby congratulate this son of the sunny south on his lung power and his energy. Throughout the game he kept up a running fire of cheering words, and his 'At 'em West End', 'Go on West End', 'Now then West End', 'Now pass it', 'Go on', 'Played West End' and so on, could be heard a long way off. He had, though, one merit as a personage in the front row of the shouters, and that was that he did not give vent to a howl of derision or pass a vote of censure when a player did not do as he thought he should when he got on the ball.

3. One had only to pay a visit to Sunderland last Saturday to realise the rapidity with which Association football in the North has advanced … during the past two years. The crowds now number thousands where hundreds used to assemble, there is a businesslike spirit among those who manage our grounds, and our players – aided a little by some few from over the Border – show a better appreciation of the science and attributes of the game … The Sunderland and West End clubs have decidedly done a great deal of what has been done to advance the best interests of the sport and it is rather lucky for all concerned that such a keen rivalry has grown up between them. The public get the benefit of good games, and the clubs are able to fight their way better with the sinews of war which the public provides. The paying people feel meanwhile that the clubs are under no obligation to them, seeing what good value they receive for money. Moreover something has been done to help their club and, therefore, to forward the game; and thus Mr Tom Watson and others associated with West End must have carried with them a nice little salve for their wounded feelings when they commenced the journey home from Sunderland.

4. It is as dangerous to go out poaching for football players as for salmon or rabbits just now. Kelso is game on which more than one club have their eye, and numerous are the offers he has had to leave West End. The other day two gentlemen came over from a town not a hundred miles away to open negotiations with the celebrated half-back, but they were discovered in the act of turning from his door by a party of West End players and partisans, some of whom had been called away from practice at St James Park. Fortunately one

of the visitors – a well-known player – could run, and he took to his heels and caught a train home to Gateshead. The other was not so fleet and he was severely handled and had to seek shelter. This new method of preventing annexation is certainly effectual when your poacher is caught, but its legality is, I think, questionable.[10]

These four passages will, I hope, give the reader a sense of Mercutio's genial personality, lively sense of humour and capacity for astute observation. And we will see more of all of these attributes as we explore this chapter's main themes.

There is one last introductory point before that. The *Newcastle Daily Leader's* weekly 'Sports and Pastimes' column made 'the first Mercutio's' reputation, but it was not a product of his pen alone. It also featured contributions from a small stable of associates calling themselves – variously – 'Sunderland Correspondent' (or 'Wearside Critic'), 'Darlington Correspondent' and 'Stockton Correspondent'. Again we know nothing about the human beings behind these pennames (although the 'Sunderland Correspondent' position stood vacant for short periods in 1886 and 1889 and had to be re-filled). What we do know is that Mercutio took pains to hire people in these roles who could also write well, even if not (usually) quite as well as he. We will hear from some of these 'friends' of Mercutio too as the chapter progresses.

The Grounds

In January 1889 a football match between Sunderland and Sunderland Albion ended in a riot, at least in part because, the goals not being netted, there was widespread confusion about whether a very late Sunderland winner had gone over or under the bar. But this was just one respect in which early north-eastern football grounds would have appeared odd to

10   Mercutio, 'Sports and Pastimes', *NDL* November 16, 1891, p. 6, February 27, 1889, p. 7, November 9, 1887, p. 7, November 21, 1888, p. 7.

a contemporary fan. For in 1889, and indeed in the entire period between 1885 and 1892, they lacked rather more than goal nets.[11]

On Monday, January 4, 1886, Mercutio attended a match between Corinthians and a 'Newcastle and District' eleven, held on the then ground of the Tyne Football Club in Brandling Place, Jesmond. This was a much-anticipated 'association' fixture, and the most significant that Mercutio had attended since his appointment to the *Leader*. There were nearly 3,000 people present when the match kicked off and though Corinthians went on to win 8–2, Mercutio was glowing about the entire proceedings. The size of the crowd was unprecedented ('the gate was the largest ever taken at a dribbling code match in Newcastle'); the spectators 'enthusiastically followed the various phases of the game and took up the points (*sic*)'; and the 'arrangements' for the game, were 'excellent'. He had only one reservation:

> I should like to suggest to the Northumberland Association that on future occa-sions it would add to the interest of the encounter if the ground were marked out with the orthodox white lines and the usual small flags were flying at the corners.[12]

White lines were to become something of an obsession with Mercutio in these early years. Just a few months later he visited Sunderland Football Club's then newly occupied 'Newcastle Road' ground at the north end of the town. On the whole he was impressed, but again:

> I should recommend … the committee to have the touch-lines marked with white on match days. Not only does it look better but it enables umpires and referees to judge better. Many other local clubs are guilty of omission in this respect, although the operation of marking out the lines is simple and inexpensive.[13]

A week later he attended a Northumberland County Trial Match ('Probables v Possibles') at the 'Bedlington Burdon' football ground near Ashington. Once more he observed that:

11   Goal nets were first trialled by the FA in 1891 and made compulsory for football league matches in the 1891–2 season.
12   *NDL* January 6, 1886, p. 7.
13   *ibid*, September 22, 1886, p. 7. "It was not until 1883 that lines were placed at the borders of the pitch, with the first internal markings, indicating a centre line and

… it would have cost very little to mark out the touch and goal lines in white, albeit I was told by the Bedlington Burdon secretary, Mr Metcalf, that this would have been done only time did not permit the carrying out of the intention of the local club on Saturday morning. It may not be out of place to remind those interested that a little machine for the work of running a white line over the lines of play can be procured at small cost.

Whether it would have made any difference to the play had Mercutio's 'little machine' been procured and the boundary lines better marked is not clear. But it might have, because the Probables' left-wing had its problems. In fact their left-winger, Aitken of West End:

… would not go to work with the bad support accorded him … and left the field in disgust, although it would have been a more dignified thing to have seen the game out. Still I can vouch for the provocation being great, for Muir, his colleague on the left-wing, hardly ever came near him, and never attempted to join him in a passing run.

Mercutio however did *not* think this was due to poor delineation of the sidelines. Rather it was 'probably … because the East End man [i.e. Muir] did not understand the needs of his playfellow'.[14]

In the same week in which he visited Sunderland's new Newcastle Road ground, Mercutio also made a visit to Newcastle West End's newly acquired 'Leazes Ground', already better known as 'St James' Park'. The ground had stood unused for several months, having previously been the home of Newcastle Rangers, one of the city's pioneering clubs. Having acquired its lease, West End had spent around £200 in the 1886 close season on improvements, levelling some 'undulations' in the pitch and enclosing

---

12-yard lines and 6-yard semi-circles from either goal, arriving in 1892." Taylor, *op cit*, p. 87. In 1886 then Mercutio's white lines would have been restricted to the pitch boundaries only.

14 *ibid*, September 29, 1886, p. 7. Mercutio also complained that: "The players, although announced to appear in distinctive jerseys, were after all very much mixed as to colours, several of them sporting those of their club instead of those the county had been expected to provide."

it with 8 feet high palings (a standard method for forcing would-be spectators to pay an entrance charge).[15]

Having been improved in these ways, the ground was 're-opened' in early October 1886 with a match against East End. On seeing St James' Park in its new form Mercutio found no shortage of white lines, and:

> the only defect appears to be the incline ... towards the goal at the town end of the field ... If the West End can see their way to raising the level at the lower end ... the enclosure will be almost perfect.[16]

However, although the West End executive said it would level the incline 'when funds permitted', the work involved was expensive, only began in the 1890 close season, and even then the slope was only 're-duced'.[17] As the years passed Mercutio expressed ever-increasing exasperation with the quality of the St James' Park pitch and the ground's general lack of facilities for public and press. His complaints became particularly insistent from the summer of 1888 onwards, when Sunderland, (involved in a life-and-death struggle with Sunderland Albion for the loyalty of the town's football public), made extensive improvements to their Newcastle Road ground, erecting first 'a new dressing pavilion ... and ... press box', and then, in the 1889 close season, an actual covered stand.

But even before this Mercutio had compared St James' Park unfavourably, not only with Newcastle Road, but also with the 'new' ground in Heaton (it opened almost coterminously with the renovated St James' Park) of Newcastle West End's intra-city rivals, Newcastle East End. Although, as everyone now knows, St James' Park was to become the undisputed heart and home of Newcastle football, Mercutio was just one of a number

---

15   *ibid*, October 4, 1886, p. 6.

16   *ibid*, September 22, 1886, p. 7.

17   Just a month after its grand 're-opening', in November 1886, the 'Athletics' correspondent of the *SDE* claimed that at "the West End ground ... the crossbar of the bottom goal is on a lower level than the centre of the field, also ... the ground slopes into one corner." *SDE* November 14, 1886, p. 4. Certainly until 1893 teams kicking towards what is now called the Gallowgate End of St James' Park enjoyed a distinct advantage.

of visitors to East End in the late 1880s and early 1890s who contrasted the Heaton ground favourably with its western competitor – at least as a spacious and *level* playing surface. At various point he called it 'a splendid playground', 'the very finest ground in the county' and even 'undoubtedly the best [ground] in or near the city'. Despite this, East End's new Heaton 'headquarters' suffered both from its distance from the then city centre and from problems of access. The latter were cruelly exposed in March 1887 when it hosted a Northumberland Cup Final between West End and Shankhouse. Totally unexpectedly, a crowd of over 5,000 turned up, or more than four times the number at the previous season's final. The result was chaos, and according to Mercutio:

> When our reporter arrived at Heaton there could not have been less than 300 people surging around the entrances and spectators were arriving in scores. They entered so slowly however ... that a considerable sum of money was lost to the authorities by hundreds climbing the fencing. Had the Association [the Northumberland Football Association – GK] made more complete arrangements for the ingress of visitors they would have been more than recouped in preventing the illegitimate and undignified entrance of those who 'got over' – in fact I may say they would not have been got over by those who got over.[18]

However, despite Mercutio's conviction that the East End authorities should have 'anticipated' a large crowd and altered the ground's entry arrangements accordingly ('... the second entrance was within three yards of the first, thereby drawing the entire crowd to the centre ... The second gate ought to have been at the other end of the field which would have divided the crowd') this was just one case of many in these years in which north-eastern clubs and grounds were caught totally unprepared for the speed at which the sport was gathering devotees.

For example, 7,000 people (including several hundred 'excursionists' from Sunderland) turned up at St James' Park on Saturday December 17, 1887 to see Shankhouse play Aston Villa in a fourth Round FA Cup tie (the Northumberland colliery village team's most famous fixture, remembered to this day). As a result the entrance gates were unable to cope with

---

18   *NDL*, March 23, 1887, p. 7.

the press of people, and as kick-off approached 'many people' (according to Mercutio) climbed over the palings and got in without paying.[19]

Not only were there problems in giving large crowds speedy access to grounds in these years, there could also be severe problems controlling them once they were inside. For spectators simply stood around the pitch, sometimes behind a low picket fence, but very often, and particularly on minor grounds, behind a rope, or with no barrier at all between themselves and the play. As there was often no police presence and ground stewards were unknown pitch invasions were a doddle.

On Saturday, October 20, 1888, a match between Sunderland and Middlesbrough, at Middlesbrough's Linthorpe Road ground, ended prematurely when a 'packed' crowd invaded the pitch. The author of 'Sunderland Notes' described a sequence of events familiar to any contemporary football fan. The invasion, he says:

> … would never have taken place if proper arrangements had been made to keep the crowd from getting inside the ropes almost to the touch line. They crowded in in a most excited manner and there was no one to keep them back. When W. Peacock fell with the ball between his legs he was … kicked rather badly by Walsh, one of the Middlesbrough halves. Andrew Peacock ran up to Walsh under the impression that his brother had been kicked purposely and asked the reason for such action (*sic*). The Sunderland umpire then claimed a foul, the referee blew his whistle and the spectators, believing that the game was over, rushed on to the field, effectively preventing any further play.[20]

Pitch invasions – in response to playing incidents, controversial refereeing decisions or simply to stop a match being completed with an unpopular result – have since become a feature of football the world over, if a rather infrequent one. Direct interventions in the play by spectators have been much rarer. But in the early years of the game in the North-East they happened too.

In January 1886, Mercutio received a letter from someone calling himself 'An Eye Witness', concerning a second round Northumberland Cup tie

19   *NDL*, December 19, 1887, p. 6.
20   *NDL*, October 24, 1888, p. 7. See also *NDL* November 28, 1887, p. 7 for an earlier pitch invasion on the same ground.

between a colliery team, Rising Star of Ashington, and a Newcastle-based railway club, 'North-Eastern'. According to 'An Eye Witness' (who could clearly barely believe them):

> Later in the game the visitors got the ball between the Ashington goal-posts, and obtained what I considered a goal, but the goal-keeper seized and fell down with the ball in his hands, and after a severe struggle, with the help of his own team and about a score of onlookers behind the posts, got it clear of the goal. While this scrimmage was going on, one of the N.E. men was lifted bodily up from behind and thrown, and another was seized by the foot and tripped up by a supporter of the home team. I understand that a protest will be lodged by the captain of the N.E. team with the officers of the Association, by whom, no doubt, the matter will be thoroughly investigated. It is to be hoped that in future the Rising Star members will govern their tempers and request their followers to do likewise and not interfere with the play, or I anticipate that many of their dates on their fixture card will become vacant.[21]

Unsurprisingly, given that they only lost the tie 1–0, North-Eastern *did* protest on the grounds that 'a spectator sent the ball back into play after they had put it through their opponent's goal,'[22] but to no avail, Rising Star going through to the next round. Whether this was because the Northumberland Association disbelieved North-Eastern's account, (and 'Eye Witness's' letter), or because such events were too commonplace at the time to merit action, Mercutio does not, unfortunately, tell us.[23]

But whatever went on in them, what, when all is said and done, did north-eastern football grounds look like between 1885 and 1892? As we have seen, the most developed (which included St James' Park, East End's Heaton ground, and the grounds of both Sunderland and Sunderland Albion) were surrounded by high paling fences with a small number of

21   *NDL*, January 27, 1886, p. 7.
22   *NDL*, January 25, 1886, p. 7.
23   Quite possibly the latter. Certainly Tony Mason reports a rash of similar incidents at football matches around the country from the 1870s to the 1890s. See Tony Mason, *Association Football and English Society, 1863–1915* (Brighton: Harvester, 1980), chapter 5, pp. 158–66. For the entire period before 1914, "many grounds were simply too small to contain the increasing numbers of people clamouring to watch ... Clubs often did not know the capacity of their own grounds and the issue of whether the house was full or not was largely decided by trial and error ... facilities inside the grounds were often inadequate; mounds of earth might not be

gated entrances (without turnstiles) to allow access. Inside, the pitch itself was surrounded by a rope or wire or (later) by a low fence, behind which the spectators stood. It had wooden goal posts with no nets, and even if marked out with Mercutio's beloved white lines, did not feature a penalty area or spot, because these had not yet been introduced. High wooden palings were, however, only a feature of the grounds of the most successful urban clubs with larger crowds. Most other football grounds, in smaller towns or villages, were simply open fields which were roped off on match days. There was no entry control, and club volunteers simply circulated during the match collecting the 'gate' or 'entrance' money from those who had turned up. By today's standards all the football pitches of the time (or 'football fields' as they were properly and accurately called) were incredibly rough. They were often uneven or undulating even when not overtly sloping, and their surfaces were composed of natural grasses. Those grasses, even when cut, were far longer than present-day turf and greatly impeded the roll of the ball. Being grass fields without any form of artificial drainage, Victorian football grounds also quickly transformed into hard-compacted earth, or into deep cloying mud and standing pools of water, under the combined assault of heavy boots, rain and snow.

This was the situation up to the summer of 1887. Between 1887 and 1891, the first stands were erected on the grounds of Newcastle East and West End, Sunderland and Sunderland Albion. At first they were simply mounds of earth in the shape of a 'right-angled-triangle', with spectators standing on the shallow slope of the hypotenuse letting down to the pitch. At their higher levels wooden supports with adjoining beams were driven into these slopes so that spectators were supported against the gradient. Before the 1889–90 season *nobody* at any north-eastern football ground (including those in the 'Reserve stand' provided for club members) had

---

steep enough to afford everyone an uninterrupted view but they were usually steep enough to cause people to slip and sway about. The surprise is not that there were crowd invasions and occasional incidents, but that there were not many more of both." (p. 164). Moreover, these generalisations are distilled from press reports of crowd behaviour at major league and other urban grounds before the First World War. At lower league and minor grounds there were even fewer physical or human impediments to crowd misbehaviour.

any cover from the elements, and the only seated spectators were press reporters. In the earliest days, the latter sat at a table or tables just behind the touch line. Later they were provided with 'press boxes'. The first of these was erected by Sunderland FC in the autumn of 1887, but by the early 1890s all the major Newcastle and Sunderland clubs had installed them at their grounds (see below).

In 1888, as part of general improvements to Newcastle Road, Sunderland extended their stands around the entire ground (previously they had covered only two sides) and built 'a new dressing pavilion with separate accommodation for the home and visiting teams at the north-east corner of the field'. It was 'so arranged that the players will not have to leave the playing ground to reach it'. In the following close season (of 1889) Sunderland added to this unprecedented luxury by erecting the first ever covered football 'grandstand' in the North-East. It did *not* have seats however. As its name implied, it was simply the pre-existing earthen 'Reserve' stand covered with a roof. When West End became a limited liability company in 1890, and acquired a longer lease to St James' Park, it announced plans to build a covered stand 'something after the style of Sunderland's grandstand'.[24] But with the failure of the company, and then of the West End club as a whole, one was not built until after Mercutio left the area, and St James became the home, first of East End, then of Newcastle United.

Though the elite grounds of Newcastle, Sunderland or Middlesbrough, even when improved, were decidedly primitive by contemporary standards, things were a great deal tougher elsewhere. In early December 1887, for example, East End travelled to 'Low Flatts Farm' in Bishop Auckland to play Bishop Auckland Church Institute, a quite successful and well-supported team in central County Durham. According to Mercutio:

> getting out at Hunwick Station …[the team]… ran a couple of miles to the Low Flatts Farm, and then unrobed at a hostelry which did not offer great comforts. I believe also that the club will remember a *poor creature* – I beg pardon a *pork creature* – they encountered at Auckland for a long time to come.[25] [A bad-tempered pig on the pitch? – GK]

---

24   *NDL*, November 5, 1890, p. 7.
25   *NDL*, December 14, 1887, p. 6.

The Crowds

Until 'manned' gate entrances were constructed at north-eastern 'elite' football grounds (i.e. until 1887) all reported crowd figures were estimates, and even after that, and until Mercutio's departure, most remained so, as can readily be seen by the general penchant for round numbers – '500', '1,000', '5,000' – etc. Also, according to people who research these things, observer 'guesstimates' of crowd numbers almost always exaggerate, and the larger the crowd the greater the exaggeration.[26]

Having said that, all the *Leader's* football writers, and Mercutio in particular, were extremely interested in the size of match crowds, and their growth. It is therefore possible, from the paper's match reports, to derive rough aggregate and average figures for attendances at Sunderland, Newcastle East End and Newcastle West End home matches from the 1886–7 season on, and these are shown in the first appendix to this chapter (Figures 3.1 and 3.2). It should be emphasised that estimates tended to be given more frequently when crowds were perceived to be bigger than usual. They are therefore upward-biased for this reason, as well as for the 'psychological/perceptual' reasons mentioned above. One can hope however that the overestimations are roughly similar for all three clubs and thus that their comparative magnitudes are generally reliable.

As will be seen from Figure 3.1, the average attendance at West End matches rose from under 700 in 1885–6, to a peak of over 5,500 in 1890–1, before falling back to just over 2,000 in 1891–2, the club's last season before its collapse. Over the same period East End attendances rose steadily,

---

26   A *Leader* report from a couple of years after the first Mercutio's departure confirms this. When, in February 1894, Sunderland played Aston Villa in a Football League match at Newcastle Road, 'Sunderland Correspondent' estimated the crowd at 22,000, and he noted that other journalists had put it as high as 25,000. But by this time the club was able to supply reasonably exact admission figures. It turned out that the paying crowd ("up to a thousand" might have got in without paying) was just 15,956, that is, even the more conservative estimates were more than a quarter too large. *NDL*, February 14, 1894, p. 7.

averaging just 250 people in 1886–7, but peaking at nearly 7,000 in 1891–2.[27] Attendances at Sunderland over the same period however were of a completely different magnitude. Averaging around 2,250 in 1885–6, they rose sharply to over 8,000 in 1886–7 (when the club moved to its Newcastle Road ground) and peaked at over 20,000 in 1890–1 (the club's first season in the Football League). Indeed between 1888 and 1891 Sunderland attendances were consistently more than double those of West End and East End combined As shown in Figure 3.2, it was only from 1895–6 onwards that attendances at St James' Park (by then the home of Newcastle United) began to outstrip those at Newcastle Road.

It is easy enough to understand then why, by the time he left the region, Mercutio was enormously impressed by the explosion in football's popularity on Wearside and frustrated by the failure to match it in Newcastle. This frustration reached a peak in 1890 when Sunderland attained Football League status, but both major Newcastle clubs were still confined to the Northern League. In January of that year he wrote:

> … it has to be allowed that they [East End and West End] have so far done little this season in the way of pleasing the public. It is true that both … have been hampered by the Northern League, of which I hope we shall hear nothing next season,[28] and we must give them credit for the excellent clubs they have brought here for the

---

27   Sunderland Albion home attendances are not included in Figure 3.1 because the figures available are even more patchy than for the three other clubs. But for what they are worth, they show that Albion enjoyed their highest average home attendance in the 1889–90 season, at 5,800. This then dropped to 3,680 in 1890–1 and to 2,042 in 1891–2, Albion's last season. In other words, even at their peak Albion's home attendances were less than a third of SAFC's, and dropped dramatically – to a sixth, then to an eighth – once the latter became a Football League club. See Chapter 4 for more details.

28   One would never guess it from this remark, but in 1888 and 1889 Mercutio had been an excited *advocate* of the Northern League, which, at one point, he thought might be a kind of regional rival to the newly created Football League. See, for example, *NDL* April 25, 1888, p. 7, and especially March 20, 1889, p. 7 and April 3, 1889, p. 7. In fact, that Mercutio had a shrewd appreciation of football's potential popularity in the North-East does not mean that he always got the details right. As well as over-estimating the Northern League's capacity to challenge the Football League, he also over-rated (albeit briefly) the potential appeal of county

holidays *[the Xmas holiday period of 1889–90 – GK].* But their aim should be to do as the two Sunderland clubs have done and bring us a succession of first-rate clubs from a distance. However, there is hope of improvement, because, before long we shall have to hail a WEST END COMPANY *(sic)* on the limited liability principle which is being worked in connection with the Ironopolis club at Middlesbrough. If this works satisfactorily a number of new men will come in and combine a pecuniary and sentimental interest in the game, the playing ranks will be strengthened, the much-needed stands will be erected, and the enclosure otherwise improved. And better clubs … will be induced to visit us.[29]

Mercutio eagerly seized on any larger-than-usual attendances as the prime indicator of the game's growing popularity. Between 1885 and 1892 there were no less than ten occasions in which he hailed gates as, 'the largest ever taken', 'far and away the largest gate ever taken', a 'prodigious' crowd, 'a best on record', 'the biggest crowd I ever remember seeing at St James's Park', 'the largest at any match in Sunderland', etc. Unsurprisingly therefore, he treated the growing disparity of crowds between Sunderland and Newcastle as a significant problem for the game on Tyneside.

However, though Mercutio was intensely interested in crowd sizes, he was much less curious about their social composition or appearance. In fact, he showed no real interest in crowd *behaviour* at all, except when it was disruptively over-partisan or a fount of obscenities. After an afternoon spent at St James' Park in October 1887 watching a match between West End and Sunderland, he came away disgusted by the 'blasphemous and obscene language' used by the crowd, much of it by 'mere lads'. Something should be done about it by 'the West End committee and other authorities' – perhaps 'a few extra policemen' – because:

Few men of sense would … be inclined to take their wives, sisters and sweethearts to one of our leading Association matches on account of the vile language that rises up on every side of the field … The time has arrived when it is necessary to be outspoken on this subject.[30]

---

representative football in comparison with club football. See, for example, *NDL*, January 30, 1889, p. 7, and October 15, 1890, p. 7.

29   *NDL*, January 8, 1890, p. 7.

30   *NDL*, October 10, 1887, p. 10.

Fortunately, Mercutio's indifference to the sociology of crowds was not shared by other *Leader* football correspondents. In particular the writer – or writers – who served as his 'Sunderland Correspondent' often provided the newspaper's most striking descriptions of crowd behaviour.

On March 7, 1887, Sunderland played Shankhouse at Newcastle Road in front of a crowd estimated at 'nearly 3,000'. 'Sunderland Correspondent' reflected on the scene as follows:

> Week after week hundreds visit the Newcastle Road ground, and the utmost interest is manifested in the matches, not only by the old admirers of the game, but also by the juvenile portion of the community, who always form a large percentage of the attendance. For some time past the committee have allowed these youngsters admission on the payment of one penny … On Saturday a very young admirer of the game – he was hardly taller than the proverbial six penny worth of copper – entered the gate in front of me and tendered as his admission fee a halfpenny – probably the sum total of his week's pocket money. He was however refused admission without the additional halfpenny, and the disappointment shown on the little fellow's face was almost as great as if he had to go without a meal. The influence which the game has had upon these youngsters is shown at every street corner; where you come across half a dozen lads dribbling a ball made of paper and rags from one side of the road to the other … Strange to say both young and old prefer the Association game, and this, there is no doubt, is the reason for the very small 'gates' which are got at the grounds of the Rugby fifteen in Chester Road. If the Rugbeians desire to make their game popular they must play more for the people.

Eight months later, Sunderland hosted West End in a second round FA Cup tie, and:

> … the sight which met the eyes of the visitors to the ground will be long remembered by them. The stands which had been erected by the Sunderland committee all around the ground were crowded to the utmost extent by a black mass of people. Every point of vantage was occupied, not even excepting the top of the new press box on which some persons, whose ideas of cleanliness and decency were of a very small order indeed, had perched themselves, and budge they would not, notwithstanding the threats of committeemen and stalwart policemen.

Two years later the match was Sunderland v Blackburn Rovers, the Newcastle Road crowd had risen to 11,000, and:

Even the guinea and half-guinea stands were almost uncomfortably crowded, while the lesser priced stands presented a black mass of excited, enthusiastic beings, some of whom had marched off direct from the shipyard and engine works with grimy and greasy hands and faces.[31]

In the nature of things, many members of these early football crowds must have been quite uninformed about the game they were watching, and must have learned about it, in part, *by* watching. In March 1886, Sunderland played Darlington at Bishop Auckland in a Durham Cup Final. 'Sunderland Correspondent' was there, and noted that:

Novices at the game were present in strong force, and their remarks on the play caused no end of amusement among those who had been let into its mysteries.

And finally, in January 1890 'Sunderland Correspondent' provided an interesting description of shifting crowd psychology, a description which any contemporary fan will instantly recognise. The stimulus was another Sunderland v. Blackburn Rovers match, this time a second round FA Cup tie at Blackburn. Sunderland lost the match 4–2, but for some reason a 'bungled' telegram reached the town reporting the defeat as a victory:

31   This is however just one of a mass of 'impressionistic' press accounts of Victorian and Edwardian football crowds from which historians have struggled to distil a more accurate or precise understanding of the class (and gender) composition of such crowds. On class, the literature has not moved much beyond Tony Mason's general conclusions that "by 1915 the majority of the spectators who went to watch football matches were working class in origin, occupations and lifestyle.", that probably in the 1870s "the proportion of middle class people was greater than it was to be later" and that the working-class men who came to dominate crowds in the 1880s and 1890s were from the more skilled, higher-earning levels of the class. As a result, "it was probably only in the inter-war years that association football in England was watched by representatives of all sections of working men more or less in proportion." Mason, *Association Football, op cit*, 150 and 157. On gender, it is effectively impossible, from press sources, to provide even rough estimates of the number, or proportion, of women in Victorian and Edwardian football crowds, although probably "female attendance fell as the overall size of crowds increased and that … the practical and financial constraints on the leisure opportunities of working-class women militated against regular attendance." Taylor, *Association Game, op cit*, 99. See also Mason, *op cit*, 152–3.

'The streets were filled by excited crowds of people and the place generally reminded one of an excited political contest just ended by the return of the popular candidate.' [*But, when the truth came out*]...'they (the team) were looked upon as martyrs and the people cheered out of sympathy. There was an immense crowd outside the station when the train came in. Stern justice, in the shape of a dozen policemen or so, cruelly closed the doors shortly after eleven and shut all out, but those who could get to the front lined the windows with their faces and waited on patiently until the train came in ... over half an hour late. The people had by this time got somewhat reconciled to their fate – but only somewhat. The general cry now is – 'Lost, but not defeated.' Lingering hopes are built on the protest made by Sunderland. [*A protest over the state of the ground, which was rejected – GK*][32]

Going by Train

Excursion trains for association football matches appear from the 1886–7 season onwards, but they did not originate with football. There were excursion trains run to major north-eastern rugby matches from 1885 or earlier and there were 'special trains' to horse race meetings, flower shows and other major events from as early as the 1870s. Moreover, excursion trains did not become a regular accompaniment to major soccer matches until at least 1887. On November 5 of that year, for example, the *Sunderland Daily Echo* carried a long account of a first round FA Cup tie at Newcastle Road between Sunderland and West End. As part of his introduction the reporter commented:

That the North-Eastern Railway Company are gradually awakening to the fact that football has a strong hold in this district was proved by the running of an excursion train from Newcastle specially for this match, and that the Tynesiders were anticipating a hard match was evident from the large numbers who availed themselves of the opportunity afforded by the company. The train left Newcastle at 1.30 pm, and upon its arrival at Sunderland a large number of the passengers

---

32　Sources for crowd descriptions: *NDL*, March 9, 1887, p. 7, November 7, 1887, p. 6, September 5, 1889, p. 7 and January 20, 1890, p. 7.

went straight to the Newcastle-road ground, in order to secure a good 'stand' from which to witness the game.[33]

From the beginning fares varied by distance, but, judging by classified advertisements, were rarely less than 1s. even for short-distance trips around Northumberland and Durham. (Up to 1892 ordinary supporters rarely travelled outside the region and long-distance train travel to away matches was effectively monopolised by players, club executives and officials and press reporters.[34]) As the Mercutio account at the beginning of this chapter suggests, excursion trains were often very crowded, mainly because the North-Eastern Railway Company (NER) charged lower-then-standard fares to attract customers. And, in these early years they not infrequently ran late, leading supporters to miss significant amounts of the play, or – in a few instances – to kick-offs being delayed until a train arrived.[35] In a time when there were no floodlights, the latter practice could in turn lead to matches being finished in semi-darkness, or not being finished at all.

In October 1887, for example, 900 Sunderland supporters travelled on an excursion train to Morpeth, to see their team play the Morpeth Harriers in a replayed FA cup tie, but only got there twenty minutes after the match had begun. However, they did better than the 1,500 Middlesbrough fans who, three months later, came on an excursion train to Sunderland to

---

33   *SDE*, November 5, 1887, p. 4. Tony Mason cites an *Athletic News* story of August 1891 on the NER "agreeing" with SAFC "that cheap excursions should be run to Sunderland from many of the colliery settlements on match days.", but whatever the nature of this agreement, excursion trains to Sunderland home matches certainly predated 1891. Mason, *Association Football … op cit*, p. 146.

34   In January 1890 Mercutio reported there being "pretty nearly a thousand people" on an excursion train from Sunderland to Blackburn for a first round FA Cup tie, but his subsequent description of "two saloon parties" with a "number of ladies" taking "the long journey", does not suggest that most of these people were ordinary working-class supporters. *NDL*, January 20, 1890, p. 6. It *does* suggest however, that by the eve of Sunderland's promotion to the Football League, football supporting was colonising a part of the town's middle class as well.

35   See, for example, *NDL*, October 24, 1887, p. 7 and November 28, 1887, p. 7.

see another FA Cup tie. Their train arrived so late that they only saw the second half of the match.[36]

However, although brief references to excursion trains – the number of people they carried, their times of departure and arrival – are abundant from 1888, descriptions of the trains themselves, or of the experience of travelling in them, are much rarer, which makes Mercutio's 1891 account all the more interesting. One can certainly infer from that account that excursion trains were significantly less comfortable than regular services, not only because they were so crowded, but also because, in all probability, the NER allocated its older and less comfortable rolling stock to them.

Certainly we know, because he says so, that Mercutio only wound up on the excursion train because he *missed* 'the 10.40 ordinary from the Central' on which the West End executive and team had travelled to Middlesbrough.[37] His taking 'the Peoples' train' was not, therefore, any deliberate sociological experiment. And we have several accounts suggesting that going to Middlesbrough on the '10.40 ordinary' would indeed have been a more comfortable experience than taking the excursion. This would have been especially true if he had travelled in one of the more luxury 'saloon' carriages, which, by the early 1890s, were routinely provided for club officials, players and pressmen.

In September 1891, for example, Mercutio's Sunderland Correspondent (or 'Wearside Critic' as he was calling himself then) travelled to Birmingham for a match between Aston Villa and Sunderland in a saloon carriage attached to a North-Eastern Railway mail train. This carriage, which he joined at Newcastle:

> … was one of the most commodious saloons, and although one or two of the followers of the team had been provided with seats there was still plenty of room without overcrowding. Mr J Harley of the Three Crowns and Mr Jas McQueen of the Waverley at Sunderland had decided to make the journey. Consequently the journey was a merry one, and that seductive game 'nap' kept away any desire for the other kind until the New Street Station was reached about twenty minutes late. The Colonnade Hotel had been selected as headquarters, and after a light meal which

---

36   *NDL*, October 24, 1887, p. 7 and December 5, 1887, p. 6.
37   *NDL*, November 16, 1891, p. 6.

was in waiting for them, the whole of the eleven retired to seek that rest which by
this time they needed much.[38]

However, as this account also suggests, even travelling by luxurious
team saloons, did not guarantee punctuality. Indeed, just a few months
earlier, in March 1891, 'Wearside Critic' had adopted an altogether less
self-satisfied tone when describing the journey home from Sheffield,
where he had watched Sunderland lose an FA Cup semi-final replay to
Notts County. Apparently:

> Fate seemed against both team and committee, for the express from Sheffield by
> which they returned … was three minutes late at Leeds, and before the saloons
> could be detached from one train and put on the through express to Sunderland
> the latter had left … As a result all had to make the best of an hour and a quarter's
> stay on the platform and in the cold wintry night until the time arrived for the next
> train – a slow one to Thirsk – to leave. Instead of being home before eleven o'clock
> it was quarter past one the following morning before Sunderland was reached –
> and Sheffield was left at 6.35.

And he added sourly:

> It is a pity that the North-Eastern Railway Company are not always so anxious
> about punctuality in the starting of their trains as on this occasion.[39]

'Put Doon What's Reet': Local Rivalry and Press Impartiality

As we have seen, the *North-Eastern Daily Gazette* hailed Mercutio as
'one of the ablest and most impartial of Northern sporting journalists'
and he deserved the accolade. His impartiality however did not take the

---

38   *NDL*, September 29, 1891, p. 6.
39   *NDL*, March 19, 1891, p. 7. Despite his complaints, Wearside Critic did a great
      deal better than a Derby Junction team in December 1887. On that occasion their
      'carriage' arrived so late in Sunderland for a Saturday match that the game had to
      be postponed until the following day! *SDE* December 27, 1887, p. 4.

form of a bland neutrality, but of evaluating football matches and other sporting events as he saw fit *irrespective* of partisan opposition or where it came from.

For example, at the beginning of October 1890 (when Sunderland had begun their first Football League season) Mercutio received a letter of complaint about his 'Sports and Pastimes' column. His response was at once typical, and utterly unlike anything to be found in today's football press:

> This person says that the West End matches are hardly spoken of in these Wednesday morning notes and referring to the prominence given to the Sunderland club, says he considers it 'the duty of a Newcastle paper to report Newcastle clubs before going further afield'. The first statement is not true, and with regard to the latter the correspondent must allow me to know my own business best. When the Newcastle clubs attain the prominence to which Sunderland has risen then will be the time for complaint if the former is neglected.[40]

Mercutio's dismissal of this complaint, however, did not indicate any bias towards Sunderland. Four years earlier, in February 1886, when Sunderland played Newcastle East End at their (then) ground at Fulwell, Mercutio was appalled by the behaviour of the Sunderland fans. They had 'hissed' the East End team after their winning goal and also the referee as he left the pitch (for awarding it). He commented:

> the majority of the spectators seemed to have the impression that the goal was not a fair one …[despite the fact that]… the referee was a member of the Sunderland club and gave his decision in favour of the visitors.

Mercutio also felt that, given the behaviour of the Sunderland supporters:

> the East End eleven will probably hesitate before visiting Sunderland again.[41]

A week later, in a pattern that would become all too familiar in later years and decades, Mercutio was fielding further fallout from these comments. There was a letter from the Sunderland secretary, J. B. Wallace, claiming that his account was inaccurate because the crowd 'only' hissed the

40　*NDL*, October 1, 1890, p. 7.
41　*NDL*, February 24, 1886, p. 7.

referee and not the East End team, and therefore Mercutio's claim that East End would hesitate to play at Fulwell again was 'far-fetched'. There was another from someone called 'Alexander' claiming that East End had no right to complain about being hissed at Fulwell, given the way East End fans had treated the Sunderland team on their visit to Byker 'a few weeks ago'; and a third from someone called 'Mercurios' who claimed that Mercutio's condemnations of bad behaviour were never directed at Newcastle clubs.

In reply to Wallace Mercutio simply denied that his allegation was 'far-fetched', saying that he had by him 'a letter from a prominent member of the East End club in which such a feeling is given explicit expression'. But his real ire was reserved for 'Alexander' and 'Mercurios', to whom he replied:

> I never endeavour to hide unseemly proceedings at matches, because I think that by giving publicity to them, and showing their absurdity, they may be stamped out. When people are making a disturbance they lose half the pleasures of a match, and no real lover of sport will think of participating in the unseemly behaviour of the kind that appears to have gone on in Newcastle and Sunderland, where it is at least admitted that a referee belonging to the home club had been hissed.[42]

These sentiments tell us quite a lot about Mercutio the man, and in particular about the quintessentially Victorian middle-class values of 'fair play' and 'gentlemanly' behaviour that he espoused. They were of a piece with his strong distaste for 'vile language', especially in the presence of 'ladies', already noted. What is more unusual, however, was both his capacity to distinguish myopic and fact-denying partisanship from full-hearted support for one's team (hence his amused appreciation of the West End 'shouter') and his conviction that gentlemanly behaviour need not be the monopoly of any social class. Thus, after watching Shankhouse lose to Sunderland in October 1887, (in a kind of 'championship' match between the Northumberland and Durham Cup holders) he expressed his admiration for the way in which:

> ... the Shankhouse spectators and the club itself bore their defeat. The spectators, at the close of the match, freely admitted that the best club won, and referred to

several pieces of good play on the part of the victors in a manner which many a field of onlookers in Newcastle or Sunderland would do well to take as an example. It shows that the interest excited by the game itself overshadows more partisan feeling.[43]

However, even in these early days, myopic localism manifested itself much more frequently in the dealings between north-eastern football clubs and supporters than the generosity of spirit that Mercutio saw, or thought he saw, at Shankhouse. It certainly drove nearly all the allegations of partisanship which regularly punctuated his *Leader* career.

In November 1886, for example, he was defending East End from allegations of playing improperly registered players against Sunderland (he checked and found no evidence of impropriety). This did him little good though, for less than a month later he was having to deny allegations in a letter (probably from the East End secretary) that he was 'persistently biased' in favour of West End![44] And, as we have already seen, from 1890 onwards he aroused widespread Newcastle wrath when he regularly praised the Sunderland club's achievements and contrasted them with the general 'lack of advance' of football in Newcastle.[45] What these allegations missed however, was Mercutio's genuine frustration at Newcastle's major clubs falling behind Sunderland in football, and his oft-expressed wish that they 'get their act together' and do better. Their relative decline was particularly galling to him because, as he continually insisted, up to 1889 or so both Newcastle clubs had been on a par with Sunderland.[46]

More fundamentally, all these allegations missed the most essential point about Mercutio and his assistant 'correspondents' – viz. that they all saw themselves as partisans of football in the North-East as a whole, not of any particular club, town or city.[47] Thus, while Mercutio was clear that

43 *NDL*, October 5, 1887, p. 7.
44 *NDL*, November 3, 1886, p. 7 and December 8, 1886, p. 7.
45 *NDL*, January 8, 1890, p. 7.
46 *NDL*, December 4, 1890, p. 7.
47 In December 1890 Sunderland Correspondent attended a fourth qualifying round FA Cup match between East End and Sunderland Albion at Heaton. His report praised the East End team warmly, claimed that they had a "perfectly valid" third, (and winning) "point" disallowed, and concluded "it does seem strange … that the East End ground is not better patronised on ordinary occasions, for

in the years from 1886 onwards football in Newcastle and Sunderland had caught up with, and surpassed, football in Middlesbrough, he nonetheless retained an interest in the progress of the game in the North Yorkshire 'town of iron'. He became especially interested, and curious, when, in 1890, the Ironopolis club there became the first limited liability 'football company' in the region, and threatened (or promised, as Mercutio saw it) to raise football standards in Middlesbrough to their old prominence.[48]

The truth was that, whether visiting football grounds, teams and officials in Morpeth (where he was warned to 'put doon what's reet' by a Morpeth Harriers' enthusiast) Ashington, Shankhouse, Newcastle East End, Newcastle West End, Elswick, Gateshead, Sunderland, Sunderland Albion, Darlington, Bishop Auckland, Middlesbrough, Middlesbrough Ironopolis or Redcar, Mercutio *always* arrived as a well-wisher, keen to see good football and to write appreciatively about it and those who produced it. And some people in all these places clearly understood that and liked and admired him for it. Others, however, did not, and even in these early years there were at least as many of them as there were of his admirers.

To be an admirer – to appreciate Mercutio's impartiality and even-handedness – one required to be something of a regional football patriot oneself. And in these early years there *were* more such people to be found than there were to be even five years after he left. For between 1885 and 1892 club and area allegiances were still somewhat fluid, shifting and inchoate. And thus some actual 'north-eastern' football patriots were to be found – travelling from Newcastle to Sunderland to cheer them on against 'big-name' opposition from England or Scotland,[49] or taking an

---

undoubtedly the team is one which could play a good game with any club about here." *NDL*, December 8, 1890, p. 7.

48   *NDL*, December 16, 1889, p. 7.

49   A few months after the first Mercutio left the North-East, in December 1892, Sunderland played Preston North End in a top-of-the-table League clash at Newcastle Road. On this occasion the *Leader's* Sunderland Correspondent (now calling himself 'Ilex') actually thought to collect some statistics from the Sunderland station master on the numbers arriving by train from various localities. It turned out that, of a crowd estimated at 16–17,000, 1,800 (over 10%) had come from Newcastle, another 4,400 (26%) from various places in County Durham and 400 from Saltburn in North Yorkshire. (There were just 300 from Preston itself.)

excursion train from Sunderland to Newcastle in the hope of seeing the Northumbrian miners of Shankhouse knock over the great Aston Villa in a St James' Park FA Cup tie.[50]

Having said that, it was far easier to adopt an 'all-region' football patriotism if, like Mercutio, you were an informed, privileged outsider. As an informed outsider he could compare north-eastern football with the game elsewhere, understand the ground the region still had to make up, and be an 'even-handed' cheer leader for its advancement. As an outsider he could also adopt a regional football patriotism as an intellectual position rather than a visceral expression of identity. And as a privileged outsider he could travel the entire region as few local people could. As a result, the North-East was probably existentially real to him in a way that it was not – could not be – to an Ashington miner, or an Elswick shipyard worker, or a Middlesbrough steel worker.

Symbiosis and Competition: Football Clubs and the Press

At the end of 1887, as part of his reflections on that Shankhouse v Aston Villa cup tie, Mercutio wrote:

This implied of course that nearly two-thirds of the crowd had come from the town of Sunderland or its immediate environs. Somewhat surprisingly, rather more fans had arrived on scheduled services (3,800) than had come by excursion trains (3,100). *NDL*, December 19, 1892, p. 6.

50   *NDL*, December 19, 1887, p. 6. However, in the minds of north-easterners (as against Mercutio) a broader, milder 'regional' football patriotism may have coexisted with – rather than conflicted with – more emotionally intense localisms, even in these early years. In mid-November 1887, for example, the difference of crowd behaviour in a Sunderland v Blackburn Rovers 'friendly' game at Newcastle Road was contrasted with that in an FA Cup replay against Newcastle West End just a week earlier: "Then, it was war to the knife ... and in the tense state of excitement that prevailed it would have been more than human nature had local feeling kept itself within bounds ... To-day all that was changed. The game partook more of a friendly character, and the demeanour of spectators was more benevolent than hostile to the visitors." *SDE*, November 14, 1887, p. 4.

> When the *Leader* was first started I was laughed at by brother press men for putting
> in an appearance at football matches, but now so great is public interest in the game
> that there is quite a gathering of scribes at important encounters … and I believe
> that a certain old-fashioned organ which continually follows where we lead have
> discarded … their amateur cum-professional critic who used to blow hot and cold in
> one sentence and are leaving the work to men on the regular staff, so we may expect
> the conscientious work of men trained to serve the public in a journalistic sense.[51]

This was not the first time its sports editor had 'puffed' his newspaper in
this way. A year earlier, in some comments on an East End v Sunderland
match, he had said, just in passing, that '*The Leader* was the first paper in
Newcastle to devote a lot of space to the noble winter game.'[52]

Nor were these empty claims. Until the late 1880s the *Newcastle Daily
Chronicle* or *Newcastle Daily Journal* gave far less space than the *Leader* to
all sports coverage, tended to focus primarily on horse racing in the coverage
they did provide, and gave rather more space to rugby than association
football in their scanty coverage of both codes. This meant, for example,
that up to 1887, about the only football content in the *Newcastle Daily
Journal* was a Friday list of upcoming weekend fixtures (rugby and association) and a Monday column with a motley collection of very short match
reports. These too covered both codes (sometimes with scores, sometimes
without) under the omnibus heading 'FOOTBALL' and often featured
games from elsewhere in England and Scotland as prominently as local
fixtures. For its part the *Newcastle Daily Chronicle* and its sister papers
of the 1880s (see below) reported slightly more association football than
the *Journal*, and gave somewhat more space to local matches, but their
coverage was still largely restricted to fixture lists and very short match
reports. And as in the *Journal*, these reports were usually supplied, not by
their own reporters, but by club secretaries, and provided little detail and
no background analysis.

It is not clear whether the 'old-fashioned organ' to which Mercutio
referred was the *Chronicle* or the *Journal* (probably the former), but we
know, from an extraordinary little spat which occurred in February and

51 *NDL*, December 21, 1887, p. 7.
52 *NDL*, December 8, 1886, p. 7.

March 1887, that, up to that point anyway, neither of them had employed professional journalists in their football coverage.

On February 23, 1887, for reasons at first entirely opaque, Mercutio suddenly informed readers of 'Sports and Pastimes' that all the north-eastern 'football material' in the *Newcastle Daily Chronicle*, *Evening Chronicle* and *Weekly Chronicle* (as well as in the *Athletic News's* occasional 'Tyneside Talk' column) was supplied by just two men 'Mr George Hall and Mr James Phillips', respectively the Treasurer and Secretary of the Northumberland Football Association. Hence: 'I, and those associated with me in this office, are the only professional pressmen in Newcastle who supply comments on football.' And he added, *a propos* of apparently nothing, that George Hall, as well as being Treasurer of the NFA, was a 'gentleman engaged in commerce'.[53]

Two weeks later 'Sports and Pastimes' reported that James Phillips had resigned as the NFA's Secretary, and that Mercutio had 'been told' that 'a statement of fact in last week's Sports and Pastimes had led to this happening'. But Mercutio denied this, saying that Phillips had expressed his intention of resigning 'weeks ago', and that he (Mercutio) received 'a communication' from him confirming this 'the day before the publication of my notes last Wednesday'. But in any event, so Mercutio assured his readers, his motive 'in showing how press appointments were held by Association officials' had not been motivated by any wish to provoke resignations, whether of Phillips or anyone else, but 'to bring about an alteration of the manner in which official communications were sent to the *Leader* through the office of a contemporary at hours which were unsuitable to our time of publication'. And the matter was now resolved, because 'the Association officials have – as I have often asked them to do – procured the simple and inexpensive means of producing three copies of an official report at one writing, so that all three morning papers will now receive the Association information at the same time. I have, therefore, gained what I sought and am satisfied'.[54]

53　*NDL*, February 23, 1887, p. 7.
54　*NDL*, March 2, 1887, p. 7.

In other words, Mercutio had felt that Hall and Phillips were abusing their dual roles as NFA-officials-cum-part-time-journalists to give the *Daily Chronicle* and *Evening Chronicle* an 'inside straight' to NFA information (probably fixture lists and Northumberland Cup draws) and to freeze out the *Leader*. So he breeched the penname 'self-denying ordinance' to 'out' the real people behind 'Captain' in the *Daily Chronicle* and 'Ajax' in the *Weekly Chronicle*, and gesture at the conflicts of interest inherent in their dual roles.[55] And his action speedily did the trick in restoring competitive parity. But his intervention also prompted, or at least hastened, the *Daily Chronicle's* decision to replace 'amateur' part-timers with professional sports journalists of their own, a change which he approved and thought overdue.

In fact, one wonders what the editor of the *Leader* made of this little episode, because, just as in the case of football, Mercutio appears to have cared more about raising the general standard of sports reporting in the North-East than about the success of any particular paper, including his own. And since he had been appointed primarily with the intention of giving the *Leader* an advantage over 'old-fashioned' competitors (who marginalised sports reporting generally and football reporting in particular) his employer, just like many a North-East football fan, may have felt that Mercutio was a tad too impartial, or perhaps partial to the wrong things.

So the rapid growth of the popularity of football in these years, in combination with the astuteness of the *Leader's* owner and editor and Mercutio's energy, charm and (when necessary) combativeness, changed the balance of power in the Newcastle press, at least for a while. But if the growth of football helped change the press, the press also changed football, or rather, it changed football grounds in a quite specific way.

Not long before he left the North-East, in September 1891, Mercutio paid a visit to Newcastle Road to watch Sunderland play Newcastle East

---

55   A week later Mercutio reported that at an upcoming AGM of the Northumberland Association there could be "a movement afoot to make it conditional on gentlemen holding office not to undertake work for the public press beyond supplying duplicated reports of an official nature to the newspapers." There is no further mention of this 'movement' in the *Leader*, and (unsurprisingly) no mention of it at all in the *Daily Chronicle* or *Daily Journal*, so one must assume it came to nothing. *NDL*, March 9, 1887, p. 7.

End. This was the beginning of Sunderland's second, and championship-winning, season in the Football League. Mercutio took the opportunity to heap praise on the Sunderland executive – 'Mr Tyzack, Mr Thompson, Mr Marr and others' – for their achievements. But he also used his visit to reflect on the relationship between the press and Sunderland, saying: 'The press has admittedly done a great deal for the Sunderland Club, but in doing so the press has only done its duty to club and public. By way of compensation the Sunderland club has done much for the press. Since my last visit to the ground a new apartment has been raised on the south side solely for the use of the fourth estate.'[56]

The 'new apartment' was a press box and Mercutio's 'Sunderland Correspondent' had already lavished praise on it a year earlier:

> It is nearly nineteen feet long, very spacious and is raised ten feet from the ground. The windows, looking on to the field, are made on the railway carriage window principle, so that they are very easily pulled up and down. A capital view of the field is obtainable, much better than from the old box. The floor will be covered with linoleum and stools will be provided instead of the hard wooden benches. The entrance to the box is from the back [of Sunderland's South Stand – GK] up an easy staircase kept entirely separate from the crowd.[57]

This was not the first nor the last time that the subject of press boxes – their presence, absence and attributes – would figure in the reports of Mercutio and his *Leader* colleagues. In fact, it can sometimes seem that it was the Sunderland's committee's decision to provide an enclosed press box at the Newcastle Road ground in 1887[58] and to further improve it in the close season of 1888, that did more to commend the club to Mercutio than anything else – *including* its winning League status. Conversely it was the dilatoriness of both East End and West End – and especially of West End – in providing such boxes that perhaps irked him more than

---

56 *NDL*, September 28, 1891, p. 6.
57 *NDL*, December 4, 1890, p. 7.
58 The box appears to have been built, probably in October 1887, in preparation for a second round FA Cup tie between Sunderland and West End in November. See *SDE*, October 18, 1887, p. 4 and November 5, 1887, p. 4.

anything else, including their failure to match Sunderland's achievements on the pitch.

Thus it took until January 1889 for East End to 'erect a pavilion for the sole use of reporters' and even then, despite Mercutio's encouragement ('Now West End, will you follow suit?') they didn't.[59] Even when West End adopted limited company status (between May 1890 and July 1891) ground improvements were slow to come, mainly because the company spent most of the capital raised on players and on attracting 'big-name' opponent clubs to St James' Park. And even when, in the summer of 1891, significant improvements *were* made to the ground these still did not include a covered press box.[60]

But Sunderland's provision of a fully covered press box in 1888[61] was not simply, or even primarily, motivated by the desire to please Mercutio or his *Leader* colleagues. As will be seen in the next chapter, it was just one aspect of the Newcastle Road club's internecine battle with Sunderland Albion. Albion had also built a covered press box at their Hendon ground in the summer of 1888 (in preparation for their first playing season) and improved it further in the 1890 close season. 'Sunderland Correspondent' was one of the press men invited to view Albion's new box before its formal opening. He waxed both lyrical and ingratiating: 'It is certainly the best accommodation for reporters on any football field in the North. The box, which has been erected at the expense of Mr William Adamson, one of the club patrons, and built by Mr Mark Howarth, is placed above the grand

---

59   *NDL*, January 9, 1889, p. 7.

60   *NDL*, September 3, 1891, p. 7. The first reference to a press box at St James' Park in the *Leader* is in an edition for September 5, 1892 (p. 6), which may mean that it was built in the 1892 close season.

61   However, the precise extent to which either the 1887 or 1888 boxes were covered is unclear because, frustratingly, we have no clear descriptions of either of them, the nearest being some remarks made about the 1888 box by 'Sunderland Correspondent' some two months after its construction. "… the new box proved itself in every way suitable for seeing the game, but owing to the ends not being closed up the rain came in very freely … It only, however, took a word to the committee and last Saturday the box had been glazed and the front of the box had been sheltered." *NDL*, September 12, 1888, p. 7.

stand *(sic)*. Pressmen owe a debt of gratitude to Mr Adamson for his kindness and forethought.'[62]

It was Sunderland's desire to 'top' Albion in the 'press box battle' that led to the building of that '19 feet long, linoleum covered' box at the top of the Newcastle Road south stand, completed just three months after the Albion box. That, and the fact that the club's 1888 box was unintentionally compromised by the building of a grandstand in the summer of 1889.

'Sunderland Correspondent' allowed that the grandstand would be of great benefit in bad weather, but: '... it is not an improvement to the press box. This is in the same position as last year but ... rendered very much darker by the roof ... two small windows have been placed at the back, but these are not sufficient, and towards the finish of the match reporters were writing in darkness.'[63]

So lo and behold, an improved press box appeared at Newcastle Road about a year later, its announcement being greeted with the usual fanfare by Mercutio and his 'Sunderland Correspondent': 'It was very annoying to the ladies on the grand stand having the "copy" boys for the evening papers continually running backwards and forwards, and this is about to be remedied. The new box will be erected on the south side of the field, above the stand situated there ... The entrance will be only from the back, and is, therefore, separated from the stand. The box will be very lighted and warmed, as there is to be a stove put in.'[64]

Now all this may just seem the determined pursuit of self-interest, and of course it was. Sitting at a table in the open air in the middle of a northeastern winter and trying to produce hand-written copy with frozen fingers or rain-soaked paper, must have been a trial,[65] and Mercutio was perhaps the first north-eastern sports journalist to understand that he could trade

62   *NDL*, September 3, 1890, p. 7.
63   *NDL*, September 5, 1889, p. 7.
64   *NDL*, November 5, 1890, p. 7.
65   In March 1891 'Sunderland Correspondent' was at Bramall Lane, Sheffield to cover a Sunderland v Notts County FA Cup semi-final. The antiquity of the ground, and the prestige of the football club which was its home, was not reflected in the quality of its provision for the press: "To write sitting on your haunches like a pitman at a village street corner is neither easy nor comfortable, not to speak of

positive coverage for physical comfort. Accordingly, he and his *Leader* colleagues were implacable, incessantly 'puffing' the clubs and grounds that made them comfortable and using those puffs to try to chivvy other clubs into doing the same. Nor were their efforts restricted to Sunderland and Newcastle. When Mercutio visited any football ground in the North-East – be it Gateshead, Darlington, Stockton or Middlesbrough – he always made a point of commenting on the press box, or its absence, or its improvement.

But seen in a wider perspective the provision of press boxes in exchange for good publicity was just an early – and physical – expression of that broader symbiotic relationship between football clubs and the press which began with the commoditisation of the sport itself and has continued to this day. Commercialisation of football was first made possible by the money that came from 'gates' – from spectators paying an entrance fee to see a match. Therefore, and obviously, the more spectators the bigger the gates and the bigger the gates the bigger the revenue to be spent on players, ground improvements, etc. This was the financial relationship at the heart of football capitalism from the 1880s until the emergence of Pay TV a century later.

But people will not – indeed cannot – come to a game they do not know about, and so from the first (which means in the North-East, from about 1883 or 1884) football clubs were keen to see their matches advertised in the local press. They could take out classified advertisements of course, and clubs in Newcastle and Sunderland did that from the early 1880s. But 'press coverage' – whether in the form of match reports or (even better) in the form of match previews – performed the same function as an advertisement and cost a club nothing (or not in direct cash terms). And match reports, especially if they were colourful and exciting, provided a far more potent incentive to 'be there' at the next match, than a brief advertisement

---

the danger of contracting an illness. The policemen and understrappers on the ground should know that reporters are not exactly a gang of thieves to be hustled and jostled about at their sweet wills. If some of the constables had endeavoured to keep the people from crowding at the corner of that miserable table instead of interfering with the pressmen they would have been doing their duty much better."
(Apparently there were over thirty 'pressmen' at the match, although whether they were all working at the same 'miserable table' is not clear.) *NDL*, March 4, 1891, p. 7.

could ever do. So press coverage aided football clubs in furthering their commercialisation, and one of the first ways in which they were willing to reciprocate that aid was to make press reporters physically comfortable.

But, as the *Leader* was the first paper in the North-East to discover, press coverage of football could also aid the press, by selling more newspapers. And, as we have seen, where the *Leader* led its competitors were forced to follow. Following the *Leader's* example meant expanding the coverage of football beyond a single column list of three-or-four-line match reports in small type, and producing both proper fixture lists, and long, detailed match reports on a prominent 'football' page or pages. It also meant giving column inches to the sport *beyond* match reports, whether reflections on previous matches, thoughts on upcoming ones, or analyses of administrative or technical developments in the game. And at all of this Mercutio excelled.

All that is perhaps self-evident. What is rather *less* self-evident, but emerges from detailed local research, is that in order to transform their football coverage local papers had first to replace football officials 'moon lighting' as football journalists with professional sports reporters. And here too the *Leader* in general, and Mercutio in particular, were north-eastern pioneers.

Predicting the Future: Mercutio and Historical Winds and Tides

In February 1886 Mercutio wrote of north-eastern football:

> Comparatively speaking, the sport here is in its infancy, but, to my mind, the material for making players fit to meet the best sides England and Scotland can produce is with us in some quantity, and with the development of skill and the free use of the energies of the Northumberland Association, after the manner we are now experiencing, the time is not far distant when the game will have taken a great hold on the public, as well as its exponents, and a 6,000 or 10,000 gate will be little of novelty in the district. When that time comes, gentle reader, I prithee, embrace me as Mercutio the prophet.[66]

---

66   *NDL*, February 24, 1886, p. 7.

In claiming his prophetic status Mercutio was being a little disingenuous. His 'prediction' appears in the same edition of the *Leader* as a report on a Shankhouse v Morpeth Harriers Northumberland Cup semi-final which had attracted a crowd estimated at 4,000. And just seven months later, in November 1886, 'fully 6,000 people' turned up at Newcastle Road to witness a Sunderland v West End match.[67] So he was reporting and projecting an already-discernible trend, not imaginatively postulating some astonishing future.

But in addition Mercutio was, as already noted, an outsider. He had come to Newcastle from Nottingham and had clearly witnessed the rapid growth of football's popularity there and possibly elsewhere. Certainly, he was well-enough informed to know how popular football had become in western Scotland, Lancashire and the Midlands in the 1870s and early 1880s. So he may well have come to Newcastle hoping, or even expecting, that something similar would happen. In short, he thought he knew the way the wind was blowing or about to blow, perhaps he even took the job at the *Leader* on that basis. And having got the job he recruited helpers to monitor the wind direction and strength in other parts of the North-East.

I say this because in the endless debates among historians and philosophers about the existence or otherwise of 'direction' (let alone 'progress') in history, it has been too readily assumed that, even if there is such a thing, it can *only* be known in hindsight. Historians can (perhaps) chart directions of historical change in the case of – say – the reformation or the industrial revolution, but only decades or even centuries after the fact. There can be no question of identifying the direction of historical developments contemporaneously. But this conventional wisdom is false, or at least it is not invariantly true, and certainly not of the short term. Some people living through them *can* see or sense social or economic trends as they are emerging and act on that sense. (Economic entrepreneurs do it all the time. It is one of the things that makes them entrepreneurs). And like Mercutio, they are sometimes right. The wind is blowing in the direction they think it is, a tide in the affairs of 'men' *is* running and *can* be ridden on to fame and fortune.

---

67   *NDL*, November 29, 1886, p. 6.

Mercutio was right. Football in the North-East did take a 'great hold' on the public and the region did produce 'players fit to meet the best sides England and Scotland can produce', and lots of them. His being right was not some extraordinary feat of unaided intellect or imagination, but an extrapolation from what he knew from elsewhere and (probably) from what he had already lived through elsewhere – an extrapolation from the immediate past in one place or places to the immediate future in another. But it was a correct extrapolation nonetheless, and in 1886 a lot of people in the North-East (including the owners and editors of the *Newcastle Daily Chronicle* and *Daily Journal*) would not have endorsed it.[68]

There is another point about this, and one that also abuts on innumerable philosophy of history discussions. Mercutio was not simply an observer of the football explosion in the North-East. He did not simply sniff the wind or watch the tide. Like an economic entrepreneur (a genuine one) he played his part in *creating* what he was observing. He was not just a witness to this particular historical change, he was an advocate of it, an enthusiast for it. And insofar as his writing and his advocacy influenced people to attend football matches that they might not have attended, or influenced football clubs to build stands or press boxes (especially press boxes!) that they might not have built, his advocacy and his enthusiasm added to the tide, made the wind stronger.

But *how much* did Mercutio matter? How much did he influence what he observed? Had the *Leader* hired, not T. W. Gale, but somebody else as their sports editor, might they have done the job just as well? Or might 'the job' have been done by somebody else entirely at some other newspaper? Or perhaps none of these things mattered? Perhaps north-eastern football would have mushroomed in exactly the same way if neither Mercutio nor the *Leader* (nor any other Newcastle paper? nor any north-eastern paper?) had ever existed. None of these questions are answerable, none of these speculations can be proven or disproven. Even if we accept that Mercutio

---

68   By 1888 they would have been having severe doubts about their scepticism, and by January 1891 (when 20,000 people turned up at Newcastle Road to see Sunderland play Everton) they would have been forced to abandon it. Such was the speed at which this process unfolded.

did contribute to the creation of what he observed, it will never be possible to say by how much, let alone whether his doing so was in any way essential or irreplaceable.

But not merely can we not answer these questions about Mercutio, we cannot answer them about anybody. We cannot know, cannot ever know, how much anybody – any individual – has contributed to, or is contributing to, any social, cultural or economic phenomenon. We can know that we have played a role, and that some people have played more of a role than we, but we can never quantify these things, never know by how much we have influenced anything, or by how much others have exerted a greater or lesser influence than we. And we cannot do any of these things for a reason also endlessly commented upon philosophically – that history is not an 'experiment' one can re-run with changed variables, not a set of engineered 'events' that one can reproduce with different control groups. History is an unrepeatable 'one-off', which means that none of its postulated counter-factuals can ever be tested.

But that that is so doesn't mean that we – anybody – should stop trying to influence things now, and it certainly doesn't mean that we shouldn't enjoy what we are doing when we are trying. Mercutio enjoyed what he did and tried to make a difference. I think he did make a difference, but even if he didn't, he still enjoyed the attempt and over 130 years later we can still enjoy his enjoying it.[69]

---

69   When T. W. Gale died, in July 1905, his obituary in *The Sportsman* newspaper claimed that the journalist "universally known" to his 'host' of friends and 'numerous' acquaintances as 'Tommy' Gale, was "the best of good fellows", "a bighearted comrade", who did not have "an enemy in the world" and was "never out of temper". It also claimed that "few more able journalists have ever lived" and that he was "equally at home with racing, boxing and many other forms of sport." 'Vigilant's Note Book', *The Sportsman*, July 21, 1905, p. 2. Certainly, if to write well is to *express oneself* while hardly saying a word *about* oneself, then T. W. Gale was a fine writer.

Appendix 1

Home Attendances, Sunderland FC, Newcastle West End and East End and Newcastle United 1885–1900

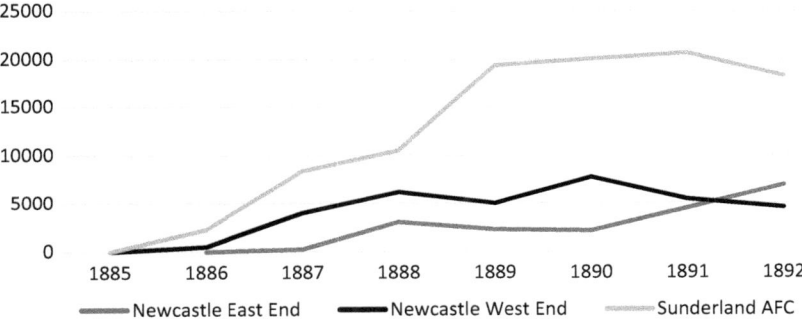

Figure 3.1: Home Attendances 1885–1892

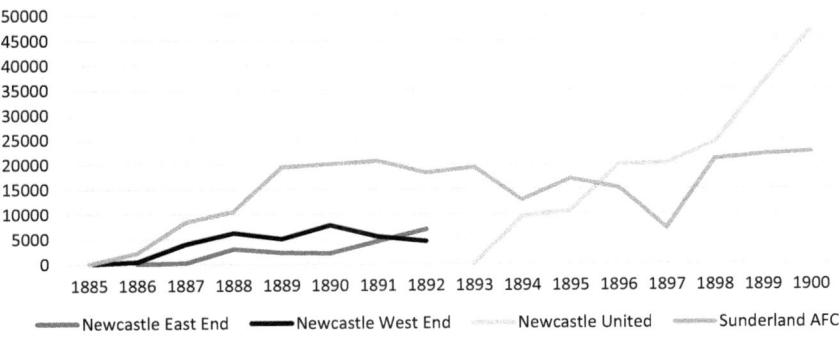

Figure 3.2: Home Attendances 1885–1900

Appendix 2

Excerpts from 'Round the Grounds No. 8'
(Middlesbrough v Stockton at Linthorpe Road, Middlesbrough)
'by Mercutio'
Newcastle Daily Leader, Monday, November 2, 1891

'Time was when I had to go to Middlesbrough if I wished to see any Association football. Now sport of this kind is plentiful in Newcastle and its immediate vicinity, and it is seldom that I can spare a Saturday in the enterprising town of iron. Therefore I have been eagerly looking forward to a trip in that direction in connection with this series of articles. Opportunity served me on Saturday, and not only did I enjoy a very interesting game in the Northern League between such keen but friendly rivals as Middlesbrough and Stockton, but had the pleasure of shaking by the hand many old friends. First and foremost there was Alderman Weighell, whom I was glad to see in better health than he has been for a long time. How proud the genial alderman should be – and doubtless is – of the fine set of plates which adorns his sideboard at the Cleveland Bay and bears testimony to his kindness to the poor during that terrible year of 1878!

Pleased was the genial alderman to tell me that his old mare Lady Middleton, the dam of Linthorpe, has at last her first filly foal by her side, so that her blood will be transmitted to other equine generations, although I hope that, before the time comes for her to assume matronly duties, Linthorpe's own sister – for such she is – will have won many races.

Then, too, there was that excellent fellow and sound journalist, my 'Middlesbrough Correspondent', to look up; Mr John Reed, the Cleveland Association honorary secretary, and many others, to meet, and the only regrets I came away with were that a genial old gentleman whom I encountered at the door of the press box on the ground should have expressed his affection for a rival journal in preference to this, and that I did not have time to visit that esteemed athlete David Bookless. But, no matter, I shall be able to see my friend David when I visit the Ironopolis ground shortly, and as to the champion of a contemporary – well, he is at liberty to choose for himself, of course, but I think he will find the *Leader* a pretty good pennyworth.

Mr Alfred Borrie, the hard-working secretary of the Middlesbrough club, I found after the match a veritable 'king in the counting house, counting out the money'. He was too busy to afford me much time for a talk about the club, but Mr John Reed, jun., was on hand, and ready to tell me all I wanted to know, so I left Mr Borrie to count up the $200 or so taken at the gates, not without remembering, however, that his place was once in the field, where he was probably the best centre forward the North of England ever produced.

Yes, Middlesbrough was a rare club in those amateur days. Of all the old band Tom Bach – now turned pro. – is the only playing member left, although I hear that grand back, George Millar, will don the old colours again. Borrie's rushes and Jackson Ewbank's shots will be seen no more, nor will O. H. Cochrane, in his day a brilliant forward, again wear football jersey. During my time in the North, Middlesbrough has been amongst the last eight in the English Cup, and they were six or seven years ago decidedly the best eleven between Sheffield and Edinburgh. Established as long ago as 1876 the club was the first ever formed in the district, and its earliest rival was the defunct Tyne – the first Association club formed in Newcastle. Professionalism was not adopted until it became absolutely necessary to go with the times, but once the new order of things was realised an energetic committee spared no pains to get the very best men available, and to-day Middlesbrough is in an excellent position. In Mr J. B. Cooper they have an enthusiastic honorary; in Mr F. Hardisty – like Mr Borrie, an old playing member – they have a practical working one, and they have besides hosts of followers, as my readers are well aware.

There were two features in Saturday's game. In the first place a new stand erected at the Linthorpe Road end of the ground was opened for the first time and McKnight, a new centre forward, made his first appearance with the club. Prices of admission were raised all round too – for the committee argue that if the public want talent they must pay for it. But nobody grumbled, and the patrons of the game are evidently in accord with the committee for between nine and ten thousand spectators assembled. By the erection of the new stand the authorities have now made stand accommodation all round the field, the building in which the press box is situated being nicely sheltered and having specially reserved places for subscribers, the committee, &c. The field of play is perfectly level and well-turfed, and altogether the enclosure is such a good one that it is to be hoped that it will be long spared from the devouring grasp of the builder, who has made much encroachment on the Linthorpe Road since I first remember it.

'Sweet are the uses of advertisement,' says the poet or some other fellow. So think the Middlesbrough tradesmen, for the stands are extensively used to set forth the value and virtues of their wares. Before I left the town I should add that I visited the Football Institute in the Marton Road, Mr Reed, who is one of the founders of it, showing me round. It is a capital place, and is open to all the members of all the clubs in the town and district. There are rooms for committee meetings, a large apartment in which smoking concerts and other entertainments can be held, recreation and bath rooms, supply of dumb bells, boxing gloves and other athletic appliances, and a carpenter's and joiner's workshop. All the best literature of the day is supplied, and there is a drawing class in connection with the Institute which is largely patronised. The charge for membership is very small, and altogether this establishment is a boon and a blessing to local football and footballers ...'

'It was a splendid autumnal afternoon and there was hardly any wind to interfere with play. The following list will show the names of the respective teams and their positions:-

MIDDLESBROUGH	POSITION	STOCKTON
Mackay	Goalkeeper	McLaughlin
Crone	Right Back	Shaw
McManus	Left Back	Lindsay
Waller	Right half-back	Monteith
Ball	Centre half-back	Chatt
Bach	Left half-back	Hutton
Wilson	Right forward (outside)	Strachan
Campbell	Right forward (inside)	Cooper

McKnight .... Centre forward .... Welford

Wood .... Left forward (inside)........................ Allan

Black .... Left forward (outside).................. Jones

Referee – Mr Stacey, Sheffield ...'

'... In a word the sides were remarkably well matched, and play was very fierce at either end. There was a time when the Middlesbrough side had the best of it, and it was astonishing how the Stockton position was kept. A corner kick as nearly as possible brought a goal, and the citadel was in jeopardy from a free kick for foul play by Chatt, but the backs and goalkeeper defended well and all was made safe so that the forwards of the visiting team got down and Jones caused Mackay to handle. McKnight just afterwards got rather into a muddle at the other end, but Campbell came to the rescue and shot past. It was a very near thing, and we all from the stand thought a goal had been registered, but it was "a bye", as they say in Middlesbrough, when the ball passes the uprights.'

[Middlesbrough won the match 2–1]

CHAPTER 4

Shamateurism, Corruption and Prejudice on the Eve of Professionalism: The Sunderland AFC/Sunderland Albion Split of 1888

Introduction

In 1888 there was an acrimonious split in the management committee of Sunderland Association Football Club (hereafter 'SAFC'). The split was so acrimonious that it resulted in the man who had created SAFC – the Scotsman James Allan – resigning his post as Treasurer and founding a rival club in the town, 'Sunderland Albion'. There then followed an often ill-tempered and nasty rivalry between SAFC and Albion lasting almost until the latter's demise in 1892.

That much is easy to recount, but to gain a clear understanding of *why* these events occurred is much more difficult. In fact it is impossible, even now, to know definitively what led Allan and his associates in the Sunderland club and committee to take the radical step of splitting the club, or why, after the split, there was such unremitting hostility between the two clubs, at least for as long (about three of the four years) as Allan remained closely associated with Sunderland Albion.

In this chapter I attempt – using the reports not only of Sunderland's major newspaper (the *Sunderland Daily Echo* – '*SDE*') but of a number of other north-eastern newspapers of the time – to provide some answers to these questions. But even at the end of a tortuous interrogation of a mass of old newsprint all I can offer are plausible hypotheses – informed guesses – about the motivations involved. The reason for this is that the *Sunderland Daily Echo* engaged in a systematic cover-up of the causes of the split, a cover-up acquiesced in by other north-eastern newspapers, and especially by the major Newcastle newspapers of the time – the *Newcastle Daily Chronicle* (*'NDC'*), *Evening Chronicle* (*'EC'*) and *Newcastle Daily Leader* (*'NDL'*).[1]

The reason for the original *SDE* cover-up was simple enough. The split involved an unsavoury combination of administrative incompetence, financial corruption and widespread ethnic prejudice. More importantly (for the *SDE*), it led to a division in the football community of late Victorian Sunderland that put some major local firms and their owners, and some other major municipal figures, on opposing sides. Hence the *Echo's* desire not to offend the locally powerful severely hamstrung its entire reporting. It made it impossible for the paper to offer any account of the causality of the split without offending somebody. Thus, in a classical case of media self-censorship, it offered none, simply reporting the fact of the split and its consequences but offering no explanation or evaluation of it.

The motives of the Newcastle newspapers in acquiescing in the cover-up are more complex. At this time the owners and editors of the *Newcastle Daily Chronicle* and *Evening Chronicle* in particular were distinctly unenthusiastic about association football. On the whole they disapproved both the sport's growing professionalism (overt and covert) and the behaviour of its rapidly growing body of fans. In this situation the football correspondents of these newspapers felt themselves to be minimally tolerated functionaries, accepted only because the sport they covered had become too popular, in Newcastle and throughout the North-East, to be totally ignored.[2] In fact they saw themselves as embattled advocates of the game as a whole in the region, rather than (as became the case later) partisans of any particular club or clubs.

The case of the *Newcastle Daily Leader* was somewhat different. The aim of its owner and editor was to build the readership of a relative newcomer to the crowded Newcastle newspaper market by offering more

---

1   However the Middlesbrough-based *North-Eastern Daily Gazette* (*'DG'*) having, for reasons which will become apparent, less interest in maintaining the cover-up, provides something of a corrective to the Sunderland and Newcastle papers.

2   This does not seem to have been untypical. Andrew Walker notes of the late-nineteenth-century Lincolnshire press that "those engaged in reporting sports

systematic coverage of sports generally, and football in particular, than their competitors. To that end the *Leader* was the first newspaper in the North-East to employ a full-time sports editor.[3] But that simply made the paper and that editor ('Mercutio') even less inclined than his compatriots on the *NDC* or *EC* to give undue attention to any doings of football clubs or their supporters that might call the respectability of the sport into question. The *Leader* had hitched its wagon to the football horse and was therefore inclined to ignore any of its unpleasant smells. And at this time SAFC was the premier football horse in the North-East, so noxious emanations from there were thought to be especially damaging to the regional image of the sport.

Thus the *SDE* covered up the reasons for the SAFC/Albion split because those reasons were highly unsavoury on both sides and because it did not wish to offend the locally powerful. The Newcastle papers acquiesced in the cover-up because of an ideological commitment shared by all their football correspondents. That commitment led those correspondents to protect the reputation of a sport which was still the object of considerable suspicion amongst the upper classes of the region – which meant amongst a great many newspaper readers as well as owners.

However, though the cover-up makes it very difficult for the contemporary historian to obtain a clear picture of the split and its causes[4] it is *not*, in the end, what makes its study historically significant. Rather the SAFC/Sunderland Albion split encapsulates, in one short period and a dramatic little story, virtually all the contradictions that arose from the extraordinarily rapid transformation of football at this time. Between 1886 and 1890 SAFC changed from a small, self-funding group of amateur enthusiasts to a quasi-professional, quasi-commercial organisation 'selling' football

---

stories often appear somewhat detached from the newspaper themselves" and that this could have been "a result of the low esteem in which sports reporting may have been held at this time." Walker, *op cit*, p. 461.

3   For some relevant history of the *NDL* in particular see Maurice Milne, *op cit*, pp. 128–30 and Alan J. Lee, *op cit*, pp. 135–6 and 218–19.

4   There is a fan history of the split, Paul Days, *The Battle for a Town*, which makes extensive use of the *SDE* reportage and which contains much useful information, but it makes no attempt to get beyond the paper's own account of events.

as a mass spectacle and having an income and turnover measured in the thousands of pounds. And all this occurred even *before* SAFC became a professional club, let alone a Football League club. In fact the essential transformation happened in just two years, between 1886 and 1888, and it provided the financial background to, and a major cause of, the 1888 split.

My main aim in this chapter therefore is not to 'solve the mystery' of the causes of the SAFC/Sunderland Albion split (although I make a plausible attempt). Rather I use the split to explore the process of the commoditisation of association football in a booming shipbuilding town on the north-eastern coast of England in the late 1880s and early 1890s. I show in detail *how* that process unfolded within SAFC and how it brought out the worst in some of the people affected by it and benefitting from it. I suggest, in fact, that some of the suspicion with which the educated upper-middle classes of the North-East regarded football may have been justified. But I also show that, given the social backgrounds, attitudes and values of the people caught up in that bewildering and exhilarating process (both north-easterners and others), it could hardly have been otherwise.

The Background

On Saturday, November 26, 1887, at its Newcastle Road home ground, SAFC defeated Middlesbrough FC 4–2 in a fourth qualifying round FA Cup replay. Shortly afterwards Middlesbrough protested their defeat to the Football Association (hereafter 'FA') on the ground that Sunderland had played 'unregistered' professional players and had employed a 'professional trainer' for the tie. The FA Council then appointed a Commission of Inquiry to examine Middlesbrough's allegations which met at Darlington on the evening of Tuesday, December 27, 1887.[5]

---

5   *DG*, December 28, 1887, p. 4. At this time the qualifying rounds of the cup had been regionalised, and a club had to win all the qualifying rounds in its region to enter the national competition proper. Then it could meet the 'big-name' national clubs and play really lucrative matches. The Sunderland v Middlesbrough tie was

By the end of December it was clear that the Commission had upheld Middlesbrough's appeal and recommended SAFC's expulsion from the FA Cup. However, the Commission not having formally reported to the FA there was considerable uncertainty about the precise grounds of the expulsion. In particular it was unclear whether the Commission of Inquiry had endorsed Middlesbrough's complaint of 'professionalism', or whether it had 'only' found SAFC guilty of not properly enrolling newly acquired players as club members. But in any event on January 18, 1888 the *SDE* confirmed that the FA's Executive Council had endorsed its Commission's recommendations, an appeal by SAFC having failed.

A week later, on January 25, 1888, the *NDL* noted that there was 'dissension' both in the Sunderland Committee and between the Committee and 'some supporters' over the disqualification and: 'There is talk of a pretty lively time at the next half-yearly meeting, when the officials were to receive a "bit of the mind" of some at any rate of the members.'[6]

The Meeting

The *SDE* for May 4, 1888 contains the minutes of the 1888 half-yearly meeting of SAFC ominously prefigured above. But that is not the only reason those minutes are of interest. For they also:

(1) contain a lengthy summary of James Allan's last report as club Treasurer before his departure from the club and his creation of Sunderland Albion.[7] Indeed he is replaced as Treasurer by Samuel

---

the final tie of the 'northern region' competition and thus much was at stake in winning it.

6   *NDL*, January 25 1888, p. 7.

7   He was almost certainly not present. The minutes state that he 'submitted' his report, not that he presented it, and all the exchanges over its contents are between club members and the chairman, Robert Thompson (see later), which they surely would not have been had its author been there. Indeed given what was to happen

Tyzack at this meeting, although there is no mention of his re-signing.[8] As we shall see, Allan had been active in organising the new club long before his formal departure from SAFC.

(2) show the considerable income and expenditure of a successful late-nineteenth-century football club even before its professionalisation, and

(3) provide dramatic evidence of SAFC's concern with what would now be called its 'public image', especially as this was conveyed in the local press.

We will first take points (2) and (3) first. Point (1) will then be the main focus of the rest of this chapter.

SAFC's Finances in 1888

James Allan's report shows that in 1887–8 SAFC had a turnover of nearly £1,000 (about £112,000 at current prices). This was a full two years before it joined the Football League and became a professional club. It also shows, however, that the club actually made a loss on this turnover of over £50.

By far the largest items of SAFC expenditure in season 1887–8 involved payments to visiting teams. This included their share of home gates, plus the cost of their rail fares to Sunderland and their accommodation and entertainment while there. In total this expenditure (£471 16s 2d) equalled almost half the club's annual turnover of £998, or more than 60% of its gate receipts. In the 1887–8 season the most noteworthy of these expensive visitors had been

---

immediately after the meeting, it would have been extraordinary if Allan had been present. For more details see, p. 135 and note 38 below.

8   Born in Adelaide in 1854, Samuel Tyzack was part-owner of the Monkwearmouth Ironworks and of a number of local collieries. In 1886 he and his wife had narrowly escaped death when explosives were planted outside their house by some militants during a strike at one of his company's pits. For the colourful Tyzack family, see 'Tyneside Tyzacks' at <http://www.tyzack.net/>.

Blackburn Rovers, Blackburn Olympic (twice), London Corinthians, Derby Junction, Cambuslang, Renton and Partick Thistle (all from Glasgow) and Sheffield FC.

However the full import of these figures only emerges if they are put in comparative perspective. Allan's Treasurer's report for 1887 showed that SAFC's turnover in that year was about £400, less than half of what it was to be just a year later.[9] Moreover by the end of the 1889–90 season, just before the club's election to the Football League, it had quadrupled again, to £3,900 – about £430,000 in current values.[10] In other words, between 1886 and 1890 SAFC's turnover increased tenfold! The club was *deluged* in money in a very short space of time, and this seems to have produced ever-rising suspicions about the use of that money, and especially about the club Treasurer's behaviour. These suspicions emerge clearly in some letters sent by disgruntled club members to the *SDE* immediately following the 1887 AGM, as well as in the section of the 1888 minutes discussed immediately below. Moreover comments on the letters by the *SDE's* 'Athletics' correspondent ('Football') suggest that such suspicions went back even further – to 1886 or earlier.[11]

9   *SDE* May 6, 1887, p. 3.
10 All figures for the present value of money magnitudes found in this chapter are derived from the calculator at <https://www.measuringworth.com/calculators/ppoweruk/> and use the simplest 'purchasing power' measure – that is, the current value of an historical figure obtained by multiplying the original sum by the rise, over the intervening period, in the retail price index of a 'fixed' bundle of goods. This always gives the lowest possible 'present' figure. For details, and other methods of calculating present worth, see the website above.

Despite this stupendous rise in its income the club was still reporting a net loss of over £200 in 1890. See *SDE* June 24, 1890, p. 4. This pattern was to continue even after SAFC's first league championship and the national domination of 'The Team of All the Talents'. In fact high turnover loss-making has remained a standard feature of football club finance to this day.

11 *SDE*, May 10, 1887, p. 4 ('Notes on Athletics' by 'Football'). 'Football' noted that "as usual … perfect harmony had not reigned supreme" at the AGM and he had received "a large number of letters commenting on the proceedings and complaining about the extravagant expenditure during the season". One of these letters, from 'A Retiring Member', could not be printed because it had 'insulted' those 'officials' "who have borne the brunt of the battle when the club was not so popular

'Too much ... has come out.' The Press and SAFC's Public Image

The 'explosive' section of the 1888 GM minutes bearing on the club's public reputation appears immediately after James Allan's financial report, and is worth quoting at length:

> 'THE CHAIRMAN ... moved the adoption of the financial statement. – Mr JOHNSON THOMPSON seconded the motion. –
>
> A MEMBER: I ask for some particulars with respect to the Middlesbrough pro-test. (Applause) – THE CHAIRMAN: Well, if you will be guided by me, I think the least said the soonest mended. (Hear, hear) – Another MEMBER here moved that the financial statement be printed and circulated for the information of the club. – THE CHAIRMAN: The only thing is that if you print the statement it will go broadcast (*sic*) to the whole world. Too much about the affairs of the club has come out, and things have been published that ought not to have been made public. I mean in reference to the teams that we were playing, and such like. – THE MEMBER: Seeing that the report and treasurer's statement are so satisfactory to the club there can be no harm in having them published. (Hear, hear.) – A show of hands was taken on the amendment and the CHAIRMAN said; I should say it is against it. – the original resolution was then put and carried. – Addressing the Chairman, the mover of the amendment said; I think you hardly gave me fair play. You should have allowed me to say what I was going to say. – THE CHAIRMAN; I cannot allow you to speak twice. (Hear, hear and applause)"[12]

Although this section makes it clear that there was a deal of conflict and ill-feeling around, it leaves the reasons almost entirely opaque. For ex-ample, what prompted Robert Thompson's interventions from the chair?

---

as it is now." 'Football' went on though to recommend greater 'Economy' to the club, particularly instancing the amount spent on entertaining visiting clubs, on SAFC's own travelling expenses, and on team uniforms and boots. In particular the £12 2s 0d spent on uniforms and boots was "one of the nearest approaches to professionalism I know of." One cannot help wondering whether 'A Retiring Member' had accused Allan (and others?) of appropriating some of SAFC's hospi-tality expenditure, either in cash or kind.

12   *SDE*, May 4, 1888, p. 4.

He did not want any more 'particulars' of 'the Middlesbrough protest' discussed. But *what* 'particulars' and why? Also, was 'least said soonest mended' a criticism of the conduct of 'the Middlesbrough protest' or an attempt to quieten that criticism? *A propos* of publishing the Treasurer's report, the only explicit example he gives of 'things … [being]… published that ought not to have been made public' is 'the teams we were playing, and such like'. But in itself this makes little sense. In 1887–8, just as in previous and subsequent seasons, SAFC spent a great deal of time and money *advertising* the teams it was playing, so he can hardly have been this, in itself, to which he was objecting.

It is also unclear why another member wanted Allan's report 'printed and circulated for the information of the club'. Did he want suspicious irregularities brought to the attention of club members, or to assure them that there were none?[13] His second intervention suggests the latter, but it is not entirely unambiguous – 'so satisfactory to the club' may have been intended ironically.

Allan's report certainly showed that the club had spent £81 9s 2d – about 10% of its entire 1887–8 gate receipts – on its appeal against disqualification, or well over £9,000 at current prices. Some of this money must have been spent on legal and travelling expenses for the Darlington hearing, and legal, travelling and accommodation expenses for the London appeal. But it is hard to see how these costs alone could account for this extraordinarily large sum.

Moreover another section of Allan's report showed that, whereas SAFC had received about £27 in gate receipts for its 'ordinary' matches, the figure for FA Cup ties was £38 2s 6d, that is, each 1887–8 cup tie had brought in roughly 30% more per match than all other first team games. SAFC's disqualification in the fourth qualifying round meant that it had certainly lost next round revenues, and might have missed out significant later round revenues too. At this date the FA Cup was by far the most lucrative football competition in England, and, just as today, its later rounds were dominated by bigger clubs who could guarantee large gate receipts,

---

13   Reading these exchanges in the pages of *SDE* makes this objection seem especially odd. The report *was* published, at least in part.

whether ties were home or away. It is almost certain therefore that had Sunderland proceeded to the first round proper and beyond that £38 figure would have risen rapidly.

So SAFC had been disqualified from the country's most prestigious and lucrative competition and failed in its appeal. But *why* had it been disqualified and *why* had its appeal failed? These – surely – were 'the particulars' the recalcitrant member was asking for. But the minutes do not provide them and neither does any of the *SDE's* or *NDL's* coverage. In fact, and predictably, the nearest one gets to an answer to either question is in a Middlesbrough paper, *The North-Eastern Daily Gazette*. In a brief report of the FA meeting of January 14, 1888 (at which Sunderland's appeal was heard), the paper said:

> The Sunderland Club to-day submitted that the decision of the Commission was arrived at, not on the ground of disqualification urged by Middlesbrough – viz., illegal professionalism – but on an irregularity in the constitution of the Sunderland Club which came to the knowledge of the Commissioners in the course of their scrutiny of the books laid before them. A question altogether outside the ground of objection was, the Sunderland representatives maintained, outside the jurisdiction of the Commission, but it was urged in (*sic*) behalf of Middlesbrough that the Association had the right to exclude from the competition any club which was detected in violation of the Association's laws. The disqualification of Sunderland was confirmed.[14]

Putting this report together with some puzzling remarks in the *SDE* of December 29, 1887 concerning the Commission chairman's 'reading of the Challenge Cup competition *(sic)*, which bears upon the general enrolment of members'[15] begins to throw some light in the darkness.

14 *DG* January 14, 1888, p. 5. This is an example of what was to become a common pattern in the North-East (and no doubt elsewhere) – where 'it's' club is seen to be the innocent or offended party in a dispute a local paper would report that dispute openly and impartially (as does the Middlesbrough newspaper here). When however 'it's' club can be seen as the guilty or offending party the local paper would generally remain silent or taciturn (as does the *SDE* in this case).
15 *SDE*, December 29, 1887, p. 4. The *DG* for December 28, 1887 (p. 4) tells us that the Commissioners were "Messrs Jope of Wolverhampton; Bellamy of Lincoln; and Craven of Darlington" but it does not say which of them chaired.

It seems that for some reason SAFC's rules did not require the club to enrol all its members. In particular six players – Hastings, Richardson, Monaghan, Ford, Gloag and Halliday – had not been enrolled as members at the time of their playing against Middlesbrough. Without access to Sunderland club records for this period (which no longer exist) it is impossible to say more than this factually, but one can make a logical observation. If these players were not enrolled as club members and SAFC's rules allowed this – in direct contravention of FA rules – then either (a) the club did not know the FA rules, or (b) it did, but preferred to follow its own, assuming that it would not be found out. In other words, some officials of the club were either incompetent or mendacious. (Incompetence is perhaps the more likely explanation here, since the offending rules on enrolment were in the club 'books' that the Commission examined, which they surely (?) would not have been had the illegality been intentional).

These events occurred right in the middle of the transitional 'shamateurism' period of FA history. In this period – which lasted just four years from 1885 to 1889 – clubs were allowed to register players as professionals and pay them match fees, but the FA also tried vigorously, in a kind of ideological balancing act, to police amateurism more forcefully, both on entirely amateur clubs and on amateurs playing for clubs with professional players. This meant not only forbidding all kinds of expenses payments but also enforcing its residence and enrolment requirements for *bona fide* club members. At the same time it was continually tinkering with these expenses and membership rules, both in response to club objections and to take account of the fact that an increasing number of formally amateur clubs were recruiting players nationwide. It was therefore very common in this period for clubs to be caught out by some recent tinker and very difficult to distinguish – even at the time, let alone a century later – advertent from inadvertent contraventions.

There is a further point about all this though. The Commission of Inquiry formally found SAFC not guilty of professionalism in paying three newly acquired Scottish players – Hastings, Richardson and Monaghan – their rail fares from Dumfries to Sunderland for the Middlesbrough replay. But despite this verdict being lauded in the Sunderland press, all it really meant was that the SAFC representatives *claimed* that SAFC did not know that paying such fares was illegal, and, having no evidence to the contrary, the Commission was forced to 'believe' them. However, its chairman then immediately examined the club's books and found the enrolment infractions.

So again, some of the club's officials were guilty either of incompetence or mendacity, and in this case mendacity is surely more likely. (Is it really conceivable that the club did not know the FA's latest professionalism rules, given the constant high-profile squabbles about them at this time?) But having 'got away' with a confession of ignorance in regard to professionalism, the club was then caught by an enrolment infraction it could not deny since it was contained in its own rule book! So it seems that, overall, SAFC was guilty of both mendacity and incompetence. It had been mendacious in contravening the professionalism rules in the first place, mendacious in claiming ignorance of them at the Commission, and incompetent in leaving itself open to disqualification anyway on a technicality!

But whether these explanations are true in whole or part, it is clear that James Allan became embroiled in the 'dissension' within the club arising from them. Indeed so embroiled that, well before the AGM took place, he had already decided to resign and to create a competitor club – Sunderland Albion. But *how* precisely was he embroiled? Did he object to the mendacity and incompetence which had led to SAFC's ejection from the FA Cup, or, on the contrary, was he to blame for them and being held responsible for them?[16] Did he object to SAFC's ever-increasing 'shamateurism' or was he the prime author of it? Trying to answer these questions requires us to cast our net still wider and consider the history of SAFC from its formation in September 1880 until James Allan's resignation in May 1888, a period of less than eight years.

---

16   We know from another *DG* report that "Messrs Allan and Woodward" (the latter being SAFC's Secretary at the time) represented SAFC at the appeal, assisted by 'Mr Trewitt' a solicitor, so clearly one or both of them would have borne the brunt of member disappointment at its failure. *DG*, January 7, 1888, p. 3.

The SAFC Split and the Creation of Sunderland Albion

Formed by Allan himself, on his arrival from Glasgow,[17] as the Sunderland Teachers Association Football Club and based at an Elementary Board School in Hendon in the south of the town (where Allan taught), SAFC was the first, and for some three years, the only association football club in the town. It began, like all such clubs, as a purely recreational organisation of football enthusiasts and players, and James Allan was not merely its founder but its outstanding player. Known as 'Bendy' Allan because of his resilience to injury and ability to ride the toughest of tackles, he appears to have been a skilled and tricky left-winger who both scored goals and created them. But as well as starring for the team on the pitch, Allan also filled major administrative roles on the club committee, beginning as Secretary in 1880 and serving as club Treasurer from 1884 until his resignation in 1888.

Over the period of James Allan's domination SAFC progressed rapidly from total obscurity to the most successful and popular football organisation in the town. Between 1880 and 1883 the town's major newspaper, though very briefly noting its founding,[18] did not deign to report SAFC's AGMs and ignored most of the club's matches. Yet by the time of Allan's resignation, the club had won the Durham FA Challenge Cup three times (1884, 1887 and 1888) and been defeated in the 1885 final. It had gone from playing sparsely watched games on a field in Hendon to entertaining 'big-name' opponent clubs from Lancashire, Scotland and the Midlands at its well-equipped ground in Newcastle Road. By 1887 the club was regularly attracting crowds of 8–12,000 to high-profile matches and was widely recognised as 'the premier club of the North of England'.[19] It had overtaken

17   He probably arrived from Glasgow. He had certainly trained as a teacher there, but may have been teaching elsewhere in Scotland immediately before coming to Sunderland. For details see the 'Ryehill Football' entry on Allan at <http://ryehillfootball.co.uk/>.

18   *SDE*, September 27, 1880, p. 3.

19   To quote a boast from 'The Ball', a correspondent to the *SDE* of January 19, 1888, p. 3.

Middlesbrough FC (which was certainly the best north-eastern soccer club in the early 1880s) and had also outstripped the two major Newcastle soccer clubs of this decade (Newcastle East End and West End). Indeed so indubitable was SAFC's leading status in north-eastern soccer by 1887 that it was simply treated as a given by all the sports correspondents of Newcastle's three major newspapers.[20]

However, despite its local dominance and the size of its popular support, in May 1887 SAFC was still a soccer 'minnow' in national terms. Though it could dominate the Durham Cup and usually beat its local rivals in Northumberland and Durham, it had never progressed beyond the third qualifying round of the FA Cup, and would not have been taken seriously as a candidate for membership when the English Football League began in September 1888.

The principal reason for this was that, up to 1887, SAFC recruited almost all its players from the town and its immediate surrounds. In these respects it remained an amateur football club in reality as well as in name. It employed no registered professionals, its first team players genuinely satisfied the FA's residence rules, and, if they received any 'under-the-counter' payments at all, it was for minor travelling expenses to matches within the region, and travel and accommodation expenses for the club's – rather rare – matches outside it. As James Allan's Treasurer's reports for 1887 and 1888[21] testified, SAFC *did* spend large, and ever-rising, amounts of money on 'big-name' visiting teams, and these payments could be seen as funding 'disguised' professionalism. But even if they were, up to 1887 the professionalism being funded was that of other clubs, not of SAFC.[22]

---

20   See, for example, *NDL*, March 13, 1889, p. 7 and September 28, 1891, p. 4.

21   *SDE* May 6, 1887, p. 3. Allan's treasurer's report for 1887 showed that, in that year too, the club spent nearly half of its turnover on teams visiting Newcastle Road, including paying for their travelling expenses and entertainment.

22   This raises the broader question of the existence of *de facto* professionalism in elite football in England and Scotland *before* its formal legalisation (1885 in England, 1892 in Scotland). The matter is discussed at length in the concluding chapter of this book, but suffice to say here that footballers were paid to play from the moment that soccer attracted significant numbers of spectators – that is, from the late 1870s onwards. Professionalism was legalised by the FA as a pragmatic

It is *this* however which changes in the 1887–8 season. At the beginning of that season, Robert Thompson JP, owner of the shipbuilding firm of Robert Thompson and Sons of Southwick, prominent local magistrate and President of the town's Liberal Association, took over the club's presidency. He seems to have immediately determined that SAFC should progress from a locally dominant club to a genuinely national force and do so by the method standard at that time, the recruitment of outstanding Scottish players. Such players had made Lancashire clubs like Blackburn Rovers, Blackburn Olympic, Bolton Wanderers and Preston North End into FA Cup winners and three of them into Football League founder members. So in 1887–8 SAFC set out to use its own position close to the Scottish border to follow the Lancashire example.

It is important to note that doing this did *not*, at this time, require spending large sums of money, at least not directly. There were no formal transfer fees for players as yet, and even registered professionals were paid a fee per match rather than a wage or salary. So had this been all that was required to 'professionalise' SAFC's playing staff it could probably have been done from the club's rapidly rising gate receipts.

But outstanding young Scottish footballers (indeed outstanding young footballers of this time from *any* UK region) were invariably from working-class backgrounds, and, in the early part of their football careers, continued to combine playing with waged work. Moreover if they agreed to play for a club outside their home region, they needed to pay for accommodation, food, wives, dependents, etc. So even when they were recruited as registered professionals, they invariably also demanded a job in the area to which they were moving, and a job which an eighteenth century observer would have called a 'sinecure' – that is, one which they held formally but which allowed

---

recognition of this fact, and in the hope of eliminating shamateurism by making open what had been nominally hidden. But legalisation did *not* eliminate shamateurism (see Chapter 5) and in itself did nothing to solve the major problem created as soon as footballers were paid (openly *or* clandestinely) for playing – the extraordinary bargaining power of the best players and its effect on football competition. Hence the introduction of the maximum wage (1901) and the 'retain and transfer' system (1904) by the Football League in an attempt to attenuate that power.

them unlimited time to train, practice and play football. Shipyards were perfectly positioned to provide such work in a variety of trades.

We certainly know that SAFC assiduously courted Robert Thompson to become its president. In the 1886–7 season he was regularly invited to matches, and even kicked off a match against a 'Sunderland and District' side in February 1887.[23] His election to the presidency at the 1887 AGM was said to be 'unanimous' and followed an effusively flattering motion in support by one of the club's oldest members, the Rev W. A. McGonigle.[24] In short, there is no evidence that Thompson's ascent to power was in any way a 'coup', or opposed by anyone on the club's committee. In addition, a member of another prominent local shipbuilding family, 'Mr Pickersgill', was elected to the SAFC executive committee in May 1888.

So in one season – 1887–8 – SAFC went from having ten local players in its regular first eleven to seven of those eleven being Scots imports. The club did *not* however register these imported Scottish players as professionals, preferring to remunerate them by sinecure employment and through expenses. The major reason for this (apart from 'sinecurism' being almost impossible to prove and the ease of hiding illegal expenses in club accounts or explaining them as an 'error' if discovered) was that, under FA rules, registered professional players could not play in FA Cup ties against purely amateur clubs and teams. Thus, given the ubiquity of 'shamateurism', clubs that registered their professionals properly often had to play cup ties against *de facto* professionals without their *de jure* ones![25]

23 *SDE*, February 28, 1887, p. 4.
24 *SDE*, May 6, 1887, p. 3.
25 Technically the rule was that registered professionals could not play in cup ties unless they had been born within 6 miles of the club for which they were to play or had been resident there for two years (Percy, *op cit*, pp. 173–4). The FA's recognition that its rules on fielding *de jure* professionals in FA Cup ties had provided a perverse *incentive* to shamateurism, especially in 'aspirational' clubs like SAFC, is what decided it to embrace fully fledged professionalism in 1889. It had legalised clubs paying players in 1885 in order to regularise and control 'shamateurism' but had done so in a qualified form which had backfired. In 1889 therefore it recognised reality and abandoned the qualifications. It is no coincidence that the Sunderland/Sunderland Albion split occurs right in the middle of this brief period of 'hedged' or 'qualified' professionalism.

Nonetheless, this adoption of 'shamateurism' by SAFC did not occur without resistance within the club. In January 1888 there was an attempt to create what was – explicitly and significantly – described as a *'bona fide'* Sunderland Association Football Club – 'Sunderland Rovers'. Rovers was to be a Sunderland club fielding only players long-time resident in Sunderland and District, that is, a club functioning as SAFC had done until 1887. It appears to have been an initiative of disgruntled playing members who saw their chances of appearing in the club's first XI disappearing in the flood of Scots imports. It quickly came to nothing, at least as an attempt to replace SAFC. In less than a season Sunderland Rovers declined into one of a host of local 'minor' or 'junior' teams. It then played in a couple of local Sunderland leagues before disappearing in 1894.[26]

But Sunderland Rovers was not the only expression of 'localist' opposition to the sudden influx of Scots imports to SAFC. It also appears in the intra-club 'dissension' after Sunderland's FA Cup disqualification. For some members clearly felt that not only was the club's culture being changed, but that 'outsider' players had been recruited in an incompetent way that had cost the club money and brought it into disrepute. It is also possible that the weakening of Allan's position as a result of the FA Cup disqualification gave his opponents among the committee and membership the opportunity to oust him. As we have seen, there may have been doubts about his financial probity as well as about his recruiting of fellow Scots.

At any rate it was against this background that James Allan resigned from the club he had founded and brought to prominence, and created a local rival – 'Sunderland Albion'. And unlike Sunderland Rovers, this rival had – or initially *seemed* to have – a serious chance of 'smashing the Newcastle Road club'.[27] The main reason for this was that 'the Albion' *was* Allan's creature. He had been SAFC's founder, leading light and best

---

26 I hope to tell the fascinating tale of Sunderland Rovers elsewhere, but for the main references see *SDE*, January 12, 1888, p. 3, January 14, p. 3, January 17, p. 4, January 19, p. 3, January 25, p. 2 and for the apparent demise of the club, *SDE*, June 13 1894, p. 4 and June 18, 1894, p. 4.

27 This was the ambition attributed to the Sunderland Rovers in a letter written to the *SDE* by one of their opponents – a correspondent calling himself 'National'. *SDE*, January 27, 1888, p. 2.

player, still had friends and admirers among the members and on the club committee and enjoyed similar admiration among supporters at large. But despite all these advantages Allan failed, and failed fairly rapidly. It was clear by 1890 that Sunderland Albion could not seriously compete with SAFC, let alone replace it, and when it was finally wound up, in 1892, Allan had abandoned it. So why did Sunderland Albion fail? And what was James Allan aiming to do in creating it?

SAFC v Sunderland Albion 1888–1892

Sunderland Albion failed because it was never able to match SAFC either in support or finances. From its first competitive season (1888–9) onwards its gates were always a fraction of SAFC's and it rarely succeeded in attracting opposition clubs of the quality regularly entertained at Newcastle Road. But in addition, from the closed season of 1888 onwards (i.e. from the time of Albion's creation) SAFC's committee began a sustained campaign to get their club into the Football League. And just two years later, after a very successful 1889–90 season (in which they had defeated several Football League teams in friendly matches home and away, and had dominated the newly created Northern League) they were admitted to the Football League in May 1890, playing their first League season in 1890–1.

But even during SAFC's last two seasons as a non-league club (1888–9 and 1889–90) Sunderland Albion struggled to meet the costs of competing with their Newcastle Road rivals, especially the substantial costs of attracting 'big-name' opposition teams. They did compete, very successfully, in the Football Alliance in the 1888–9 and 1889–90 seasons, and in 1890–1 they replaced SAFC in the Northern League and competed well in that competition too. But neither Football Alliance nor Northern League matches could match the 'pulling power' of Football League fixtures once SAFC was elected to the League.[28] Albion themselves tried three times – in

---

28   In addition Football Alliance matches involved Albion in expensive travel outside the region often to clubs attracting quite small gates. It also involved Albion in

1890, 1891 and 1892 – to gain election to the Football League, but without success.[29] That failure made their demise almost certain, especially as SAFC competed well from the start in the country's premier football competition, finishing in a respectable seventh place in 1890–1 and winning the League championship the following season.[30] Over that championship-winning season the gap in gates and revenues between the two clubs became cavernous.[31] Thus, deeply in debt and unable to raise further capital, the Sunderland Albion company was wound up in May 1892.[32]

However, a rapid synopsis of this kind fails to capture the significance of short-period events. And it is those events which really shed light on Allan's motivation in forming Albion and on the contradictions he confronted from the moment of its formation. As we shall see, those contradictions did not make his – and Albion's – failure inevitable, but they certainly made it highly likely.

The first point to note is that on Saturday, May 5, 1888, just two days after the SAFC half-yearly meeting at which he disappeared as Treasurer, James Allan reappeared in the pages of the *SDE*. But now he was the 'hon sec' of 'Albion FC', assuring readers of the paper, in a brief official letter, that a planned first match between the new club and Shankhouse FC *would* 'come off' on that day, despite some 'doubts ... expressed' and that

---

paying three quarters of the travelling expenses of Alliance opponents coming to Sunderland. *SDE*, May 11, 1891, p. 4.

29 *SDE*, May 3, 1890, pp. 3&4, April 27, 1891, p. 3, May 14, 1892, p. 3. Albion applied for admission in 1892, but withdrew their application at the Football League AGM, having been wound-up as a football company the day before the League meeting. (In a further irony the 1892 AGM was held in Sunderland to mark SAFC's first championship.) The early Football League rule that there should be only one FL club per town or city must have told heavily against Albion, since it could only have been admitted by evicting SAFC.

30 Albion became a Limited Company in March 1890 with the aim of being better-equipped financially for Football League entry. But even by the time of the company's first AGM, in June 1891, it was already making heavy losses. *SDE*, June 16, 1891, p. 2.

31 See Chapter 3, note 27, for figures on Albion attendances in comparison with SAFC's.

32 *SDE*, May 13, 1892, p. 3.

a telegram had been 'received from London' (presumably from the FA) confirming this.[33] And the match did 'come off', as did a further fixture a week later against Newcastle West End.

The *SDE* previewed the Albion-Shankhouse match on the very same page on which it reported the 'dissension-ridden' SAFC meeting of May 1888. It is inconceivable that whoever wrote this preview did not know that James Allan was already acting as the new club's Secretary. Indeed the preview told *SDE's* readers that, among those who would take the field for Albion the following day, were none other than the three infamous Scotsmen whose train fares from Dumfries had brought SAFC such grief five months earlier – viz. Hastings Richardson and Monaghan![34] In the event Richardson and Monaghan, but not Hastings, appeared for Albion against Shankhouse, being joined by another recent SAFC Scots' recruit – Gloag.[35] In the following game, against Newcastle West End, these three were joined by a further two ex-SAFC Scots, Strachan and Kilpatrick.[36] In the *SDE's* report of the West End game it also emerged that Albion's home was to be 'the Blue House Field, Hendon', the very same ground on which SAFC had begun eight years earlier. The same report also claimed that 'notwithstanding rumours to the contrary ... we understand that the club will be run on amateur lines'. However this assurance hardly gelled with six of SAFC's Scots imports having been persuaded to defect to Albion *en bloc*,[37] since they must have received some material incentives, or promises, for doing so.

It was impossible that all this could have occurred without considerable preplanning, indeed pre-plotting. In fact from a truly extraordinary article which appeared in the *SDE* on December 1, 1888 we know that Sunderland Albion had been formed nearly *two months* before SAFC's

---

33   *SDE*, May 5, 1888, p. 2.

34   *SDE*, May 4, 1888, p. 4. Although I have no proof, I think it very likely that Allan himself wrote the preview.

35   *SDE*, May 7, 1888, p. 4.

36   *SDE*, May 14, 1888, p. 4.

37   By the time SAFC played Albion in the first of two friendly matches, in December 1888, the total had grown to eight – Stewart, Monaghan, McLellan, Kilpatrick, Hastings, Richardson, Moore and Gloag. See *EC*, December 1, 1888, p. 6.

half-yearly meeting – on March 13, 1888 – and that Allan had been elected
as both its Secretary and Treasurer.[38] So everybody attending that SAFC
meeting on May 3, 1888 knew that Albion was already well established and
that Allan was its prime mover. They also knew that Albion's first match
against Shankhouse was immanent – because SAFC attempted to use an
obscure FA rule to stop it.[39]

These events show unequivocally that the motive for James Allan's
resignation from SAFC was *not* any kind of protest against shamateurism.
On the contrary, he was almost certainly the prime mover in recruiting
Hastings, Richardson and Monaghan *et al* to SAFC in the first place, paying
their train fares and finding them jobs in Sunderland. He was probably also
the person whom unhappy members blamed for the failure to enrol these
players properly and for the expensively failed appeal against FA Cup disqualification. In addition, and perhaps most divisively of all, he was almost
certainly the prime target of the 'localist' sentiment within the club that
lay behind the Sunderland Rovers initiative, with some notion abroad that,
as a Scot, he was flooding SAFC with fellow countrymen.[40] Certainly if

38   *SDE*, December 1, 1888, p. 4. In this extraordinary report the *SDE* finally re-
     vealed, more than *nine months* after the fact, that Sunderland Albion had been
     formed at a meeting at the Empress Hotel, Sunderland on March 13, 1888, and that
     Allan had been appointed as both its Secretary and Treasurer. It also revealed that
     six of Allan's Scots imports to SAFC were at that founding meeting, including
     Richardson and Monaghan! Everything in the report suggests that Allan had
     been planning the new club's formation even earlier – possibly as early as February
     1888. And since the mentions of 'dissension' over the club's FA Cup disqualifica-
     tion date to late January 1888 this makes perfect sense.

39   *SDE*, May 4, 1888, p. 4.

40   Criticism of 'foreign' imports to English football clubs were common in the 1890s,
     at least among enthusiasts for football amateurism. It is unlikely though that such
     criticisms found much echo among fans. See the lengthy discussion in the conclu-
     sions to this book. Certainly hostility to Scots players seems to have been concen-
     trated among SAFC playing and non-playing *members* rather than supporters and
     exacerbated by doubts about Allan's financial probity as treasurer. *A propos* of the
     latter, in August 1888, just four months after he left SAFC, an autumnal meeting
     of the club applauded the reading out of the club's rule 7, "that the accounts be au-
     dited annually by a professional auditor to be elected by the committee." It is hard
     not to think that this refers to previous financial irregularities. It is certainly odd

all this were the case it would explain the emotional intensity of the split and, as we shall see, the bitterness with which Allan pursued it through the following two seasons. To be seen as some kind of 'traitor' to a club he had created and turned into a powerful local force, and for which he had still greater ambitions, must have been galling in the extreme.

The Matches

During the period of Allan's close association with the club, Sunderland Albion played two 'friendly' matches against SAFC – on December 1, 1888 and January 12, 1889. Both matches were played at the Newcastle Road ground and both resulted in SAFC victories. The first attracted what was said to be the largest football crowd in Sunderland up to that time – 14–15,000 people – and the second, though not nearly so well attended, (about 9,000), ended in a riot. The proximate cause of the riot was a controversial decision to award SAFC a late winning goal, a decision which led to vociferous protests by Albion's supporters, and the departure of the Albion players from the pitch in protest. Moreover, after the match there was a stone-throwing assault by SAFC supporters on Allan and

---

for a meeting to be 'applauding' the reading out of a standard procedural rule *and* for this applause to be noted in the minutes.

There may have been other issues too. In the minutes of SAFC's AGM for the following year – August 30, 1889 – there is the following tantalising passage:

"The Rev W.A. McGonigle said that last year he had almost decided to sever his connections with the club because of some disgraceful scenes which took place. Things he believed had altered for the better. The new captain, Auld, had never tasted drink in his life, and several other members, he was informed, could say the same. If the committee were to import men who had so much influence as football players, it was their duty to bring respectable men. (Applause.) He hoped none of the members would tempt the players to drink. In bringing such men to the town Mr Watson and Mr Tyzack had made the best temperance lecture ever delivered in Sunderland. (Applause.) Personally, the speaker said, he was thoroughly satisfied. It rested with the members to make the ground a place of real recreation, and to discountenance betting, which he regarded as worse than drinking." *SDE*, August 31, 1889, p. 3

some Albion players as they left the Newcastle Road ground in a horse-drawn carriage or 'brake'.[41]

There was also a moment during the match itself when Allan – who acted as Sunderland Albion's umpire – was photographed threatening a young SAFC supporter with a stick. He claimed that he only did this after mud was thrown at him by the boy and some friends (a claim disputed by other witnesses at a subsequent FA inquiry).[42] But nonetheless in January 1889 the man who had created SAFC was photographed threatening with a stick the fans of the club he had created. This was probably a simple product of the high emotions the match had occasioned. But even before the matches a series of events involving the two clubs meant that they would be played in bitterness.

We have already seen that once Allan had formally split from SAFC, the club tried to use an FA rule to prevent Albion from playing its first two matches. Then, at the beginning of the following season, Southwick (a junior Sunderland club) appealed their defeat by Albion in a first round Durham Cup tie, an appeal in which SAFC were clearly complicit.[43] When a Durham Football Association inquiry dismissed Southwick's appeal, SAFC scratched from the competition rather than play Albion in the second round. And if this were not enough, later in the same month (November 1888), Albion were drawn against SAFC in a FA Cup qualifying round. Once more, and sensationally, SAFC refused to play, and scratched from the country's premier football competition rather than do so. The reasons that SAFC's chairman, Robert Thompson, gave for this latter decision were so obviously specious that even the normally pro-SAFC 'Sunderland Correspondent' of the *NDL* could not take them seriously. According to a letter Thompson sent to the press 'explaining' his club's decision:

> … in the past Cup Ties have done much to create public interest in the game and to make it popular …[but]… having reached almost its height in this town we submit they have answered a good purpose and may now be safely abandoned in the interests of the game.[44]

---

41   *NDL*, January 14, 1889, p. 7.
42   The inquiry is reported in an *SDE* for February 1, 1889, reproduced in Days, *op cit*.
43   *NDL*, November 5, 14 and 16, 1888.
44   *NDL*, November 28, 1888, p. 7. An *EC* summary of the same letter has Thompson saying that "Cup competitions import into the game unhealthy excitement and

'The writer …,' says the Sunderland Correspondent, 'goes on to speak' of 'these never ending protests' as sources of trouble, and concludes 'these are our most important reasons.' Manifesting considerable self-control, Sunderland Correspondent suggested: 'This letter needs no comment. The supporters of the club will form their own conclusions upon it.' A few lines later however, screwing up his courage, he added:

> I cannot help thinking that the main question is one of 'gate'. As is well known, in these ties each club takes half the receipts after the payment of expenses and it looks to me very much as if the Sunderland club begrudged their younger rivals a share of the pudding.[45]

The incredulity with which even its own supporters greeted its explanations/excuses for not playing eventually led SAFC to propose a compromise to Albion. The two clubs agreed, sometime in late November 1888, to play two friendly matches in place of the FA Cup tie. In one the gate receipts would be divided equally between the two clubs, in the other they would be divided between two nominated charities. But the *EC* thought that there was an altogether sleazier reason for SAFC's wanting to replace a cup tie with a friendly match. In its match report on the first SAFC v Albion clash, the *Chronicle* said:

> Had this game been played under the original arrangements, it must have resulted in a win for the Hendonites, because at the present time, Sunderland have only six first team men who are qualified to play in Cup ties, whereas the Albion Club could put out their full strength, all their players being available. As it was however, Sunderland were enabled to place an exceedingly strong eleven upon the field and both clubs felt certain of success.[46]

---

tend to diminish the high quality of the play" and the paper's correspondent expresses similar doubts about its honesty. *EC*, November 28, 1888, p. 4.

45   *NDL*, November 28, 1888, p. 7.

46   *EC*, December 1, 1888, p. 3. As always this assertion was challenged by two SAFC partisans in letters to the *Evening Chronicle*, but the most they were able to claim was that SAFC had nine qualified players. *EC*, December 3, 1888, p. 4.

The Wider Effects of the Split

Though there is much to be got from detail, there is always a danger of insight turning into myopia, so we may leave the dishonesty, partisan spite and bad temper surrounding the SAFC v. Albion matches there.[47] Because all it really reveals is that, if the creation of Sunderland Albion was certainly not an attempt to resuscitate SAFC's amateur past, neither was 'the senior club's' response to it. Despite the new Treasurer's high-sounding assertion in July 1888 that 'the team which will represent the club … [in 1888–89]… will be almost entirely different from that of last season, and not one of the Scotchman who then appeared in the ranks will be seen in the red and white striped jersey'[48] this was simply an acknowledgement of the *fait accompli* created by the wholesale desertion of these players to Albion, not an amateurist manifesto, nor even a localist one.[49]

In fact under the leadership of Thompson and Tyzack, SAFC simply continued down the 'shamateurist' Scottish road which Allan had followed, but with more money at its disposal from still rising gates and the new Chairman and Treasurer's abundant resources. In addition, in

47 More dispiriting evidence of all three can be found in the witness statements to the FA Council hearing into the second match (held after an Albion protest over the crowd's behaviour) and in the letter exchanges between SAFC's Secretary, W.T. Wallace, and Allan immediately after the match. The letters appeared in the *SDE* for January 17 and 19, 1889 and are reproduced in full in Days, *op cit* along with an account of the hearing. Allan's letter is especially interesting because in it he denies Wallace's 'charge' "that I have during the last few months done my best to break up the Sunderland club", saying instead that "My action has only tended, as I hoped it would, to cause the Sunderland committee to exert themselves to get talent to raise the game in the North of England." *There is however no such 'charge' in Wallace's letter!*

48 *NDL*, July 25, 1888, p. 7.

49 In fact in the very same interview with the *NDL* in which Samuel Tyzack made the statement about dispensing with the previous season's Scots players, he also told his interviewer that the club had acquired "Raylton and McDermott, late of West End Newcastle and McKie of Cambuslang". And by the time of SAFC's first prestige match of the new season – against Blackburn Rovers – they had also acquired "Dickson, the celebrated Scottish international", whom they had pinched

mid-1889, the club appointed the Novocastrian Tom Watson to be its 'football secretary'[50] Watson was one of the first club secretaries to play a quasi-managerial rather than a simply administrative role, taking charge of player recruitment, selection, training and (to a degree) team tactics. He had built his reputation in Newcastle on his detailed knowledge of Scottish soccer clubs and players. It was Watson above all who created SAFC's 1890s 'Team of All the Talents', made up overwhelmingly of Scotsmen.[51]

In other words, from the moment of the split SAFC entered a race with Sunderland Albion to be the first to bring 'national' football success to the town – which meant either winning the FA Cup or being elected to the Football League. For this was what Allan was aiming at too. Indeed Albion could only have displaced SAFC by doing either or both of these things. Winning any number of Durham Cups or north-eastern 'friendly' fixtures would not suffice, because Allan himself had taken SAFC too far beyond purely local domination for this to be adequate. In effect the situation in which the split occurred immediately placed both clubs on the same 'national prominence' treadmill. 'Back to the future' was simply not an option. In fact Allan's own success at SAFC made his failure at Albion all the more likely, because it required the newly formed club to 'vault' immediately to competitive levels it did not have the resources to attain.

But that is just one of the ironies of the situation. Another was that had the Albion split not occurred, SAFC might have pursued the patient localist agenda that the Sunderland Rovers enthusiasts supported. Because when one of those enthusiasts – 'Wearside' – said that 'if those in command had been content to make haste slowly there is no reason why, in a year or two, we might not have had a team of whose performance in the English

---

from under the nose of Bolton Wanderers to whom "he had given a promise ... but afterwards withdrew it." *NDL*, July 25, 1888, p. 7.

50   *NDL*, October 16, 1889, p. 7.

51   There is a mass of internet and other sources on Watson, who enjoyed considerable success at Liverpool as well as at Sunderland. A good starting place is "The greatest football manager you've probably never heard of" at <http://www.victorianfootball.co.uk/>. He also has a Wikipedia entry.

Cup tie we as Sunderland men might have been legitimately proud',[52] he was not just being a wide-eyed optimist. SAFC *had* won three Durham Cups and become the best team in the North-East fielding entirely local players. Had they used their prestige to recruit more outstanding local talent from the amateur clubs that were mushrooming all around them in the late 1880s, they probably could have fielded a 'local' team capable of winning the FA Cup or even gaining League status – eventually.

But SAFC simply could not afford to 'make haste slowly' because Allan and Albion were intent on making haste rapidly through acquiring ready-made Scottish talent, and failing to win that race would have been disastrous. So Thompson and Tyzack simply 'stepped on the gas'. Between May and July 1888 SAFC invested massively in the Newcastle Road ground, turning it into what was regarded, at least until the early 1890s, as the best football venue in the region.[53] From the beginning of the 1888–9 season they also set about paying 'guarantees' to high profile clubs – including existing League clubs – to play there. These guarantees were 'attendance independent' (i.e. they were not shares of gate monies but pre-agreed sums that had to be paid 'up front' whatever the actual match crowd.) They therefore carried greater risk, but it was a risk that had to be taken if Albion were to be beaten. And the risk paid off, for large crowds invariably turned up to the 'guarantee' fixtures, and in 1890 SAFC won League status, and two years later, under Watson's guidance, the League itself. But in doing all this Thompson and Tyzack were simply 'out-Allaning Allan' – flattering through emulating.

There were other paradoxes too. When James Allan left SAFC it had never attracted a crowd exceeding 12,000 people. We have already seen that the first SAFC-Albion match drew the first 15,000 football crowd in the town's history. In fact between 1888 and 1890 the SAFC-Albion rivalry was the main factor building further interest in football in the town and its surrounds. James Allan also adopted – or readopted more effectively – the 'Sunderland Rovers' tactic of using his Hendon base to appeal to a 'south of the River Wear' localism, and in this he was at least partially

---

52   *SDE*, January 12, 1888, p. 3, letters to the editor.
53   The improvements are reported in detail in *NDL*, July 25, 1888, p. 7.

effective.[54] Although it could never match Newcastle Road attendances consistently, Albion did occasionally attract 8–10,000 crowds to the Blue House Field (in which it also invested) when it had attractive opponents and the 'senior club' had no fixture or was playing away. So the net result was that when, in 1890, SAFC was elected to the Football League it became heir to a considerably expanded support base, which it then inherited *in toto* when Albion wound up in 1892. That support base then helped drive SAFC's famous 'Team of All the Talents' to still more success.

It is unclear what James Allan made of all this, but I doubt whether he would have appreciated any of these ironies, or taken pleasure in any of them. The rift with the club he had founded had been too bitter, and the defeat of Albion too total for that.[55]

Synthesis, Inevitability and the Transition to Professional Football

Everybody in the field of sports history knows that Britain in the Victorian period produced a variety of professional sports out of what had once been popular recreations. Association football is a classical case, and in that case the transition took the form of football clubs transforming from voluntary organisations for amateur recreation to commercial organisations paying professional players to entertain large crowds of paying spectators. This transition began in Scotland in the late 1870s, and

54   It seems that both the Sunderland Rovers initiative and Sunderland Albion's support base reflected a much older rivalry in Sunderland – between the church diocese of Bishopwearmouth, south of the River Wear, and Monkwearmouth, north of it. However, I have not investigated this systematically.

55   Allan's involvement with Sunderland Albion appears to have decreased markedly after the end of the 1890–1 season, when the company was in severe financial difficulties and it was already clear that it would never displace SAFC. His departure allowed relations between SAFC and Albion to improve sufficiently for the two clubs to play a third friendly match – in April 1892 – and to split the gate proceeds. However, this was all too late to help Albion. They lost the match 8–0 and were wound-up less than a month later.

was essentially complete across England, Scotland and Wales by the late 1890s, that is, it took about twenty years.

But in fact this is not what happened. There was no 'transition', no 'transforming' or 'transformation'. The 'Victorian period' did not 'produce' professional sports and 'Association football' is not a 'case' of such 'production', nor did 'it', or 'its' clubs 'transform' into anything. Rather specific *people* in the football clubs of Victorian Britain *did* things, and their doing things gradually produced states of affairs which, looking back, historians can summarise using terms like 'transformation', 'transition', etc.

But the only way to remind ourselves that the above are not just irritating banalities but profound historical truths – to observe people actually *doing* the specific things which culminated in a retrospectively characterisable 'transformation' – is for the historian to work in very short time periods (sometimes a handful of years, not infrequently a mere handful of months or even weeks) and in very localised contexts. We have to observe particular people doing particular things in particular years – or even on particular dates – in particular places. And in the case of football clubs that is often difficult. Most of them do not care about history so have left no archives worth speaking about. In addition all the witnesses to these events are now long dead and were not, generally, the kind of people who left diaries or masses of personal papers. So that leaves one with the local press, and, as we have seen, it often had an agenda or agendas of its own, not always compatible with being a rigorous, or even reliable, reporter of fact.

But when such detailed local research has been done the old problem remains. Knowing in detail what the leaders of SAFC and Sunderland Albion got up to between 1880 and 1890 provides a much more nuanced and humanly rich account of these extraordinary changes than any synthetic overview. But nonetheless it is only a local monograph. Synthetic overviews are still required for a range of quite proper explanatory purposes and can only be written in broad generalisations and passive forms of the verb. So 'transformation' and 'transition' and 'production', etc. must make a comeback, even if now 'illustrated' with the new monographic material. The discipline of history has never solved the problem of integrating the synthetic with the monographic, and it never will, because these are two different accounts of reality informed by quite different (but equally legitimate) purposes. That is to say, they are *not* like small jigsaw pieces that one puts together to make 'a bigger picture'. That is simply a false analogy.[56]

So we can never replace synthetic overviews with detailed monographs, or *vice versa*. But that leaves a problem. Because, however unavoidable they may be, the very language in which synthetic accounts are cast leaves the impression that, in general terms, (always 'in general terms') what happened is the only thing that could have happened. After all, if there is a 'transition' or a 'transformation' going on, the only question is how long such 'processes' take to 'complete', not whether they will be completed. Of course they will be completed. Transitions 'complete', that is what *makes* them transitions. So even if we do not intend it to, this kind of terminology smuggles in apparent inevitabilities.

But actually nothing that happened in the past 'was inevitable'. Because to say that anything 'was inevitable' is merely to say that it happened. Indeed, the *only* evidence anyone can ever adduce for something having been inevitable *is* that it happened. So past tense assertions about inevitability are just logically empty.[57] Nonetheless, many past events, if not inevitable, could be judged, even at the time, as 'highly likely' to happen, and sometimes we find contemporaries making just such judgements. But if we don't there is a major psychological problem in making them with hindsight. Because in assessing *how likely* something was to happen, it is very hard for the historian to disregard what she or he knows *did* happen. In the conclusion of this chapter I illustrate all these difficulties in regard to the professionalisation of soccer in Sunderland.

---

56   This does not mean that one cannot use monograph material to 'illustrate' and 'enrich' synthetic, longer-period overviews. One can, and historians do, all the time. It only means that, when they do, they must shorten and simplify those monographic accounts and relate them to whatever 'general themes' they wish to 'illustrate'. But doing that requires them to remove or condense a lot of the short-period detail that make monographs so rich. In other words, the *purposes* for which accounts are composed shape *how* they are written.

57   Present tense assertions about the inevitability of future events are *not* logically empty, but that is another matter which need not concern us here.

Conclusions: Amateurism, Shamateurism and the Coming of Professional Football to Sunderland

SAFC did not have to professionalise. By this I mean that, logically, it could have remained an amateur football club if the club members and/ or the people of Sunderland had wanted it to. But why would they have wanted it to? According to Victorian 'amateurist' ideology they should have wanted it to, because (a) playing football is better for people than spectating it – far better for their physical fitness particularly, and (b) being paid, directly or indirectly, to play football undermines the fun and pleasure of playing, and, especially where payment is in any way linked to results, inculcates an 'ungentlemanly' 'win-at-any-costs' attitude. In fact one of the primary arguments for amateurism in the Victorian period was that winning *replaced* playing as the primary point of any sport for both 'shamateurs' and professionals.[58]

I cannot say that there was nobody in late-nineteenth-century Sunderland who believed such things.[59] But I can say that in the course of my research, I came across nobody there articulating such beliefs. Why?

58 Standard texts on Victorian amateurism include J.A. Mangan, *Athleticism in the Victorian and Edwardian Public School*, (Cambridge: Cambridge University Press, 1981) and J. A. Mangan and Mike Huggins, *Disreputable Pleasures: Less Virtuous Victorians at Play* (London: Frank Cass, 2004). For a classic contemporary text see Shearman, *op cit*. But the issue is ubiquitous in the football history literature. See, for example, Taylor *op cit*, pp. 48–52, 63–4 and especially 82–5, Wray Vamplew, *Pay Up and Play the Game: Professional Sport in Britain 1875–1914* (Cambridge: Cambridge University Press, 1988), 191–5 and 197–8, Nicholas Fishwick, *English Football and Society 1910–1950* (Manchester: Manchester University Press, 1989), 20–1 and 85, Young, *op cit*, pp. 183–7 and Brian Dobbs, *Edwardians at Play: Sport 1890–1914* (London: Pelham, 1973), 46–7. For the issue in the north-east specifically, see Huggins, *op cit*, p. 313 and Alan Metcalfe, 'Football in the Mining Communities of Northumberland, 1882–1914', *IJHS*, 5 (3), 1988, 284–5.

59 If there were any they were probably associated with Sunderland's major rugby club – 'the Sunderland football and cricket club', as it was referred to, based (as it still is) at Ashbrooke in the south-west of the town.

In the first place, the vast majority of the people watching SAFC play football from (about) 1883 onwards[60] were manual workers. So, while they may have lacked good nutrition, decent housing and adequate health care, they did *not* lack physical exercise. On the contrary, most of their waking hours were filled with such exercise in the form of manual work, and that was as true for the relatively few women spectators as for the men. That being the case they were highly likely to have thought that point (a) in the amateurist ideology did not apply to them. And it did not. It was formulated with the new rising class of 'sedentary' white collar workers in mind, and at this period these people were far more abundant in the south of England than in the north.

In the case of point (b), in the 1880s there was a rapidly growing number of young men in Sunderland and its surrounds who *did* play football for pleasure (although they also played to win). And there are still thousands of such men playing in north-eastern football clubs today. However most of them think now, and most of them almost certainly thought then, that if they were 'good enough' they could play for pleasure *and* for money, and that the pleasure would not be any less if they got the money too. So they simply would not have accepted the antithesis – the 'either/or' – of point (b).[61] They might have been wrong in this of course. (They might have

---

60   The earliest account I can find of an entrance charge (3d) being made for an association football match at Hendon Blue House field is for November 1881, but this was not an SAFC match but a representative fixture – 'Probables v Improbables' – to select a Durham team for a forthcoming county match against Northumberland. But there were a "large number" of spectators for a Sunderland v Haughton-Le-Skerne match in February 1883, and the club was certainly charging for admission for some matches from the 1883–4 season. *SDE*, November 10, 1881, p. 4 and February 5, 1883, p. 4.

61   Alan Metcalfe simply notes in passing that "the word amateur was rarely used" in the mining communities of late Victorian East Northumberland and that "truly amateur teams were noticeable by their absence" from the beginnings of organised football there. (Metcalfe, *op cit*, 284–5). The matter is discussed at length in my conclusions, but suffice to note here how important this observation is. Association football players in the north-east regarded themselves as footballers rather than as amateurs *or* professionals. They played the game because they enjoyed it but, from the very beginning, hardly any of them could afford to play

found that playing for money *did* reduce the pleasure of playing in some way). But again, up to 1890 at least, I have found nobody playing football for SAFC as a 'shamateur' saying so. Thus when, from 1885 onwards, the number of people watching SAFC play football increased rapidly the club used the flood of money from 'gates' to move to a second stage of commercialisation. It found 'shamateurist' ways to pay players and to attract better players by offering considerable under-the-counter payments.

So there was no 'amateurist' resistance to SAFC's commercialisation of football. But there was a quite strong 'localist' resistance to it. Neither the members of SAFC nor its supporters had any objection to its players being shamateurs, but a significant proportion of *members* anyway objected to using local gate money to recruit and pay 'foreign' shamateurs from Scotland. How far that objection was sheer ethnic prejudice, how far simply the *schadenfreude* of second or third rate local players, and how far a contingent response to events leading up to a bitterly disappointing FA Cup disqualification, it is difficult now to judge. But it seems that James Allan experienced it as anti-Scots prejudice and bitterly resented it. Indeed he resented it so bitterly that he set out to destroy the club he had created, but which had turned on him as an incompetent/corrupt 'outsider'.

But he failed, and I judge that he was very unlikely to have succeeded. Indeed many informed observers at the time thought him very unlikely to succeed. Why? Because to do so he had to create Sunderland Albion as a 'shamateur' club from the beginning (there could be no period of amateur build-up) and Albion had to field better players and be more nationally successful than SAFC immediately. And Allan and Albion simply did not have the resources to do that.[62] Moreover, it was very likely that SAFC

---

seriously without some form of monetary or other remuneration. Hence the best of them were 'always' paid to play and thus their being 'formally' or 'legally' paid to play (becoming 'professionals') was far less of a change in their eyes than it was in the eyes of football administrators. Hence, when in 1974, the FA simply abolished the distinction between amateur and professional players it acted far more in accord with the world view of those who played the game, than it had (oddly enough) when it legalised professionalism.

62   Sunderland Albion's main financial backer was James Hartley Jr., owner of the Wear Glass Works in Monkwearmouth. Days, *op cit*, suggests that a long strike at the Works in 1891–2 (1892 was a year of considerable economic distress in

would respond to Albion's challenge by intensifying its own shamateurism because, *given* the attitudes of people in late Victorian Sunderland, the challenge could only be met that way. Had those people had different attitudes SAFC could have made a different response, or no response at all, to Albion's challenge. But the people of late Victorian Sunderland had the attitudes they had, and for good reasons.

However, whilst given the attitudes and characteristics of the town's population SAFC was highly likely to become a shamateurist and then a professional football club, it could, I think, have chosen to recruit its shamateurs locally and still been successful. Certainly (1) such a strategy would have been popular in the town, and (2) SAFC could probably have become a League club by using it, although it would have taken longer. However, I can make these judgements now because I know something that nobody knew then – that in the near century that followed, not only Sunderland but the entire North-East (from Ashington in the north to Middlesbrough in the south) would become one of the great soccer 'nurseries' of England, a 'hotbed of soccer'.[63]

I conclude then that the professionalisation of football in Sunderland was 'highly likely' to happen, and that people *at the time* could have known that it was. Indeed some of them clearly did. (See the previous chapter on 'Mercutio'.) I also conclude that the professionalisation of football in the town could have taken a 'localist' rather than a 'Scottish' form. But it would probably only have done so had the SAFC/Albion split not occurred – which means, had James Allan not reacted to events at SAFC by forming a rival club.

Note however: saying that SAFC could have done local shamateurism and professionalisation more slowly but just as successfully takes no account of the fact that had James Allan not recruited the dreaded Scottish trio

---

Sunderland), and Hartley's inability or unwillingness to further bankroll the Albion Company's debts, led to Albion's wind-up in May 1892. But whether this is true or not, it is clear that in Thompson, Tyzack and Pickersgill, SAFC had the bigger economic guns throughout the four years of the rivalry.

63   Appleton, *Hotbed of Soccer*. Though nearly sixty years old, Appleton's book is still the best general introduction to the subject.

of Monaghan, Hastings and Richardson in November 1887 SAFC might have *lost* that vital, last-qualifying-round FA Cup replay to Middlesbrough. And that was probably his major – perhaps sole – consideration at the time. Truly a case of butterfly wings and storms!

Appendix: A Postscript

In 2004 SAFC celebrated the 125th anniversary of its foundation in 1879.[64] As part of those celebrations the then club chairman, Niall Quinn, led a bevy of dignataries out on to the pitch of the Stadium of Light at the beginning of an evening match. I was at the match. Among the dignataries, and directly following Niall on to the pitch, were some grandchildren and great-grandchildren of James Allan. The announcement of their names and identities was greeted with a roar, and they all waved delightedly to the crowd.

Though I didn't think so at the time, that moment now seems to me deeply ironic. Leaving aside a small minority of club history enthusiasts, the *only* name among the Victorian leadership of SAFC known to today's fans is James Allan's. Thompson, Tyzack, McMillan, Kidson, Marr, Woodward, Wallace and many others have disappeared into the historical ether, but 'Jimmy' Allan is remembered and revered as the founder of the club they love.[65] And indeed he was. But he was also the man who, for two or more years, bent all his energies to trying to destroy it. But this fact has been expunged – not from history – but from SAFC's historical mythology, as indeed it has to be if its founder is to be suitably reverenced.

But if today's fans were told that the club's founder was also its would-be destroyer, they would surely, after they got over the shock, want to know *why*. And if told – as I believe they should be – that the most likely explanation is that he felt himself to be the victim of anti-Scots prejudice, I can only imagine that they would be totally bewildered. Or rather, I'm sure they would have been totally bewildered in 2004. But in 2020, post-Brexit and its still rumbling ramifications north of the border – perhaps not!

---

64   Wrongly, so far as I can judge. Like Paul Days I can find no mention of the club pre-dating the late summer of 1880. For Days' view see the *Sunderland Echo* article of February 18, 2016 at <http://www.sunderlandecho.com/news/sunderland-afc-were-formed-a-year-later-than-believed-says-author-1-7739198>.

65   Indeed he is now a member of the club's official 'Hall of Fame'.

CHAPTER 5

The Curiously Contorted Class Struggle: Crook Town FC, the Durham Football Association, and the FA, 1927–1933

Introduction

Like David Johnson, the only other person (so far as I know) to have written about the matter at length[1] I first read about 'the so-called Crook Affair' in Harry Pearson's wonderful book, *The Far Corner*. In the little over six pages he devotes to the matter, Pearson focuses on two issues, one rather conventional, the other less so. In his first four pages, Pearson offers a powerful, but conventional, denunciation of the class-based hypocrisy of the English Football Association (hereafter 'FA') in enforcing its amateurist ideology on an area and a people (Durham miners and other manual workers) whose economic circumstances bore no relation to those for which that ideology had been developed. But in his last two pages Pearson focuses on the much less discussed, and, in my view, much more interesting issue – the dominance of amateur football clubs and players in County Durham, not only in the 1920s, but in the entire period from the turn of the twentieth century to the FA's abolition of the amateur/professional distinction in football in 1974.

[1]   David Johnson, *A Storm in a Teacup: The Durham Sham-Amateur Affair of 1928* (Beeston: SoccerData, 2009), 77 pp. Mike Amos devotes six pages to the affair, (also under the heading 'Storms in a Teacup') in the official history of the Northern League; Brian Hunt, compiler, and Mike Amos, editor, *Northern Goalfields Revisited*, privately published and printed (Shildon, Co.Durham, 2000).

For after all the Crook Town Affair could not have arisen in Durham if the majority of its hundreds of football clubs had not *claimed* to be amateur clubs in the first place. Because, given that their players could not play (or at least would not play) if they did not receive some payment, the most prominent of those clubs were effectively forced to adopt 'under-the-counter' ways of paying them, ways that left them wide open to exposure as 'cheats' and 'shamateurs'. Yet it can seem that they did not have to do this, that they could have opted to employ their players openly as professionals. After all, when the Crook Town Affair began in 1927, professionalism in association football had been legal for forty-two years.

So why didn't more Durham football clubs opt to professionalise? The answer, according to Pearson, was 'financial expediency':

> County Durham, with a population of around half a million, was already heavily burdened with full and part-time professional clubs. Sunderland, Gateshead, Hartlepool and Darlington played in the Football League; Spennymoor, Durham City, Chester-le-Street, Horden and Consett in the North-Eastern League. And Newcastle and Middlesbrough were each just a few hundred yards across the county borders. As the likes of Darlington and Hartlepool knew only too well, there were hardly enough supporters to sustain the professional clubs already present, without adding a further dozen. Top Northern League clubs such as Stockton, which did turn professional, soon found themselves returning to the amateur ranks.

> Conversely, the county was … incapable of sustaining a fully amateur league. The amateur game was reliant on players whose employment left them with weekends free. In an era in which men who worked in industry invariably put in a five and a half day week which included Saturday mornings, this effectively meant those who were self-employed, who worked in one of the professions, or who were so financially secure that going without a half-day's pay didn't matter to them. There simply weren't enough such players in the North-East to furnish sufficient teams for a league, let alone one of any sort of quality.

> Faced with a choice between foundering as professionals or sinking as mediocre amateurs, many of the Durham clubs opted to steer a slightly different course. They held on to amateur status, and while those who wished or could afford to play without pay did so, those who couldn't were compensated, either through payment in kind via friendly shopkeepers, or by the practice known as 'boot' money. 'When you came out of the bath', an ex-foundryman who'd turned out

in the Northern League in the thirties told me, 'there'd be a few shillings tucked in the toe of your shoe.'[2]

In the rest of what follows I am going to assume that this explanation is correct, and that it was valid, not only in the late 1920s, but for the entire period from the turn of the century until at least the 1960s. I am also going to assume that those who ran the Durham Football Association, (hereafter 'DFA') both before and after the 1920s, knew that it was valid.

But if this is true, it immediately raises another puzzle. If the DFA's General Council in the 1920s knew that the economic situation facing all its major amateur clubs was as Pearson outlines, then why did it simply not operate a conspiracy of silence in which, as it were, everybody's shamateurism was nobody's shamateurism?

For it was only because it didn't operate such a conspiracy, or at least not consistently, that 'the Crook Town Affair' occurred at all. It began in July 1927 when the FA received an anonymous tip-off about illegal payments made to Crook Town players during the 1926–7 season (in which Crook had won both the Northern League and the Durham Challenge Cup.) This tip-off certainly came from within the Durham County football establishment and probably from one or more members of the DFA Council. (The Crook Town club, at least, was convinced so.) But whatever its origins, in response to its allegations the FA requested the DFA to set up a Commission of Inquiry (into Stockton FC as well as Crook Town), and so the first stage of the convoluted 'Crook Town Affair' began.

So why couldn't a conspiracy of silence be maintained? An ambiguity in Pearson's own account provides a first clue. According to him, the problem was not simply lack of sufficient 'well-off' players to maintain an amateur league in County Durham. It was the lack of enough such players to maintain a league 'of any sort of quality', a league that was not 'mediocre'. Logically therefore, if the DFA, or the people of County Durham, had been content with a small, mediocre amateur football league, they might have been able to find enough players from 'financially secure' or 'professional'

2   Harry Pearson, *The Far Corner: A Mazy Dribble through North-East Football* (London: Warner Books, 1994), 221–22.

backgrounds to staff a handful of genuinely amateur football clubs. But as it was the Northern League of amateur clubs in Northumberland, Durham and North Yorkshire was neither small nor mediocre. Formed in 1889 it is 'the second-oldest surviving football league in the world after the English Football League'.[3] Currently divided into two divisions, each of 22 clubs, it rarely had less than 20 members even when constituted – as it was over most of the twentieth century – as a single division.

More importantly, up to 1974 the Northern League was arguably the most successful amateur football league in England. Between 1894 and 1974 its clubs won no less than 24 of the 71 English Amateur Cup finals contested, or nearly 34% of the total. A remarkable 15 of those 24 victories were achieved by just two Durham clubs – Bishop Auckland (10) and Crook Town (5) – whose grounds lay a mere 5 miles (or 8 kilometres) apart, in the centre of Durham County and its coalfield, and who enjoyed a fierce rivalry from the earliest days of the league[4] As we shall see, that rivalry also played its part in both the onset and continuance of the Crook Town Affair.

The men (they were all men) who ran the DFA – many of whom also held executive positions in Northern League clubs – were fiercely proud of the number and quality of the amateur and professional clubs they super-intended. They also shared the deep local loyalties that fuelled, not merely the Crook/Bishop Auckland rivalry, but the fiercely competitive Northern League generally. And it was that competitiveness which, in turn, main-tained high standards of play in the league and made its clubs nationally successful for over six decades. So 'shamateurism' in north-eastern amateur soccer was part of a determined pursuit of playing excellence, an excellence driven and maintained by local rivalries which were just as intense *within* the counties of Northumberland and Durham as between them. And the men who ran the DFA and the Northumberland Football Association (hereafter 'NFA') took pride in that excellence and were participants in the loyalties and rivalries which produced it. As we shall see, it was the

3   Wikipedia entry for 'The Northern League' at <https://en.wikipedia.org/wiki/Northern_Football_League>.
4   "List of FA Amateur Cup Finals" at <https://en.wikipedia.org/wiki/List_of_FA_Amateur_Cup_finals>.

intensity of those rivalries which made it impossible for the region's football administrators to maintain a conspiracy of silence consistently.

But the contradictions did not end there. For the leaders of the NFA and DFA were also representatives of the FA in the north-eastern region, and therefore charged with maintaining the norms and standards laid down by the national body. Those norms included the strict distinction between 'amateur' and 'professional' players, and the 'allowable expenses' receivable by the former, laid out in the FA's famous, or infamous, 'Rule 29' (of which more below). They therefore had to find a way of enforcing those standards locally while allowing shamateurism to continue. And they did so. But not without a considerable amount of doublethink and hypocrisy.

But that is just what makes the Crook Town Affair so fascinating for the historian. For at its climax it produced a rare, and almost total, breakdown in the façade behind which shamateurism in County Durham football was conducted, and of the hypocrisy and doublethink that sustained it. Yet that breakdown did not reveal any great iniquity or evil. On the contrary, all it revealed were the harsh realities of life for many north-eastern working men and their families in the continually difficult inter-war decades. In fact, the Crook Town Affair only revealed the positive, even admirable, way that scores of football clubs in the county made life a little easier for the young men who played for them. Yet, as we shall also see, nobody involved in the affair could quite *say* that openly, even if everything they did say showed that they knew it and felt it.

But that is for later. For the moment all that needs to be understood is that the men who served on the 'General' (or Executive) Councils of the DFA and NFA in the 1920s were required to serve three masters – the local clubs and leagues from which they came and which elected them to the Councils, the interests of north-eastern football as a whole, as those interests were understood and interpreted by the two county associations, and the rules of the national Football Association to which they were formally subordinate. Much of the complexity of the Crook Town Affair is explicable in terms of the 'cross-pressuring' experienced by men trying to play these different roles at different times and even at one and the same time. But even this was not all. Further levels of complexity were added by the fact that, in the end, such men were individuals – people of varying views and temperaments – who thus responded to those cross-pressures in different ways. In particular some were much less willing than others to engage in doublethink or hypocrisy.

But enough of generalities. It is now time for the convoluted train of events that was the 'Crook Town Affair'.

The Crook Town Affair Part One: The First Commission

The DFA's decision to create a Commission of Inquiry into Crook Town and Stockton FC was taken at its summer meeting in early July 1927 in response to a request from the FA.[5] That request derived, as we have seen, from some anonymous allegations made to the FA about illegal activities in both clubs. In the case of Crook, the allegation seems to have been that 'not all gate-money was being recorded in the club's accounts and that this surplus was being utilized to pay amateur players far more than their legitimate expenses'.[6]

However, although set up at the beginning of July, the Commission did not formally meet (at Darlington) until the 20th of the month. Little more than a week after that meeting though, on Friday, July 29, came the sensational news that the Commission had suspended Crook Town forthwith (which meant that the club would be unable to play the 1927–8 Northern League season). According to the Hartlepool-based *Northern Daily Mail* this 'drastic action' had been taken because Crook had failed

---

5   *NDM*, July 9, 1927, p. 7, *SDN*, July 29, 1927, p. 6. There is some confusion about this matter though. Both these press sources are unambiguous in saying that the initial 'tip off' was to the FA who then asked the DFA to investigate, and this is confirmed by Amos (*op cit*, p. 484). But Johnson (*op cit*, p. 22) claims that the tip-off was to the DFA. There are no records remaining with the FA or DFA to clarify the matter, but it is almost certain that the initial anonymous allegation *was* sent to the FA but originated from within the DFA Council. The latter then used the FA request to legitimate a pre-planned local action.

6   Johnson, *op cit*, p. 22, Amos *op cit*, p. 484.

to furnish the Commissioners with some 'additional information' required to forward its investigation.[7]

The *Northern Daily Mail* did not say what this 'additional information' was, but a story in the *Shields Daily News*, just two days earlier, threw some light on the matter. It appeared that, when the Commission met, it had been supplied with a 'cash book' by Crook, but that this:

> was not the proper cash book, but one prepared for submission to the commission or for some other purpose.

Also, the Commission had discovered that:

> Newcastle United F.C. sent Crook Town cheques for £125 and £250 in respect of two players, J. Little and J. Wilkinson, and whereas … the club secretary Mr. E.F. Peart, in his first statement intended the commission to believe that only £225 was received from Newcastle United, the commission came to the conclusion that the secretary had in his possession about £570 belonging to the club of which the committee had denied knowledge, and they ordered Crook Town to obtain from Mr. Peart the money held by him and belonging to the club within 21 days: failing payment legal proceedings would be taken. Mr. Peart has been suspended from taking any further part in football for all time.[8]

A number of things should be noted about this. Firstly, the *Shields Daily News* story claimed that these allegations were in a 'report' issued by the Commission sometime between July 20 and 27. But the DFA Commission of Inquiry did not issue its formal report until almost a month later (on August 24, 1927) so in fact this was an orchestrated press leak. Secondly, the Commission seems to have decided extraordinarily quickly that the cash book submitted to it on the 20th was a fake, and to have had very detailed knowledge of the financial affairs of Crook Town from the very beginning. It felt able, for example, to state publicly that the club's secretary was illegally in possession of a precise sum of the club's money (despite the entire Crook Town committee denying this) and even to say where he got it from.[9] And thirdly, if the *Shields Daily News* story

---

7   *NDM*, July 29, 1927, p. 7.
8   *SDN*, July 27, 1927, p. 6.
9   *NDM*, July 29, 1927, p. 7.

is accurate, the Commission had already decided to suspend Fred Peart as Crook's Secretary, even before it suspended the entire club. In fact, all that happened between the Commission's suspension of Peart and its suspension of the club, was that Crook formally stated (sometime between July 27 and 29) that they had no 'additional information' to provide to the Commission other than what it had seen on the 20th, and which it had already dismissed as incomplete or fraudulent.[10]

Given the speed at which all this occurred, and the fact that throughout this period, and indeed right up to the August 24, little or nothing was heard of the supposed parallel inquiry into Stockton FC,[11] it is hard not to think – as Crook Town clearly did – that the whole thing was a 'fit-up'. In other words, the DFA Council, or some of its members, had known in detail about events inside the Crook club well before the inquiry, those same people were almost certainly responsible for the anonymous 'tip-off' to the FA, and they knew what action they intended to take even before the Commission met. If that was the case it becomes important to know who the DFA's Commissioners were. The Commission was chaired by Thomas Dowling, President of the Durham Football Association, of the Northern League and of Bishop Auckland FC. He was assisted by four Vice-Presidents of the DFA, Arthur Stephenson of West Hartlepool, Harry Askew of Spennymoor United, Joseph Bennett of West Stanley FC and William Fortune of Ryhope.[12]

Predictably therefore when the Commission of Inquiry finally published its findings they were damning, and much more damning of Crook Town than of Stockton. The Secretary, Treasurer and Chairman of the club were all suspended, *sine die*, from taking any part in football administration, the entire Finance Committee of the club was suspended until

---

10   *ibid.*

11   An *SDN* story of July 30, 1927 (p. 6) claimed that "The illness of Mr R. Shields, the Stockton secretary, has caused some delay in the inquiry into the affairs of the club. Mr Shields ... was taken ill while on holiday, and although he is now out of danger it will be three weeks or more before he can resume his normal duties." But however that may have been, (and the report of the Commission also excused Shields for his non-attendance at its hearings "owing to illness") when the DFA Commission finally reported its punishment of Stockton was significantly less than that of Crook. See note 13 below.

12   *NM*, July 21, 1927, p. 10.

the end of the 1927–8 season 'owing to neglect of duty in the office which they held', and the General Committee of the club was 'severely cautioned' and one of its members suspended *sine die*.

The General Committee of Crook Town was however given permission to 'reorganise the club and to carry it on' subject to eight conditions. These were:

'(1) That proper Minute books of the General Committee and of any sub-committee be kept.

(2) That the Minute Books of the Finance Committee or that of the General Committee must contain each week a record of the attendance at matches played on the ground of the club; the figures for the turnstiles or tickets; the total amount of the gate receipts; and details of all accounts and of payments which are authorised to be made.

(3) That all money shall be paid each week into the banking account of the club and cheques must be drawn each week for all accounts and general expenditure.

(4) That the club must obtain from E. F. Peart, the amount of money in his possession belonging to the club and receipt of same must be reported to the Durham Football Association with a statement showing how the amount is made up. Should the club fail to receive this money within fourteen days legal proceedings must be instituted against Peart.

(5) That the club be fined £25.

(6) That the players in future shall be required to sign only for the actual money paid to them, and that payments for taxi-cabs, etc., used by players must be paid for by the club and entered through the ordinary accounts of the club.

(7) That all books of the club must be submitted to the Durham Football Association once per month during the ensuing season.

(8) That the club must keep such books as are required by the regulations of the Football Association and the Durham Football Association relating to the club's finances.'[13]

---

13   *NM*, August 25, 1927, p. 7. The same story reported that Stockton FC had been found guilty of keeping a defective 'gate admission book', for which they were

It will be noted that the Commission's report on Crook (and indeed on Stockton) is almost entirely concerned with irregularities in records and account keeping, not with illegal payments to players. Even in point six, where players are mentioned, the implication is that it was the club's officials who were at fault in allowing players to 'sign for' money that they had not actually received. What this means is rather unclear, but the most obvious interpretation is that the players' signatures receipted 'reimbursements' of expenditures that they had not actually incurred but that Crook *claimed* to have made on their behalf. However, the Commission could find no evidence of these expenditures in the club's accounts.

If this interpretation is correct, it strongly suggests that Crook Town's players were not in fact 'signing for' money 'not paid to them'. On the contrary, they were receiving sums of money as 'reimbursements' of expenditures ('for taxi-cabs, etc.') that neither they *nor* the club had incurred. It is therefore surprising, to say the least, that the Commission did not make more of this. But it didn't. In fact, in a very carefully worded final sentence, it said:

> The commission … decided that they were not justified in taking any action against any of the players as it was not found that any payment to players had been made.[14]

As the *North Mail's* sports editor pointed out at the time, the Commission saying it had 'not found' that players had been paid was not to say that they had not been paid. 'It savours …', said 'Criticus', '… of the Scottish verdict "Not proven", and leaves a certain amount of doubt.'[15]

Before coming to the Crook Town club's response to these findings, it is worthwhile to look at little more closely at the origins of the inquiry itself. Since the anonymous letter seems to have disappeared from the FA's archive, its content will never be known, but there are enough clues in local press sources from earlier in 1927 and in the reporting of the inquiry itself, to allow for some informed guesses as to what may have motivated it.

---

    fined £25, but there were no suspensions of club officials and no demand that the club be 'reorganised'.

14   *ibid.*

15   *NM*, August 26, 1927, p. 11.

Crook Town had enjoyed an extraordinarily successful season in 1926–7, winning the Northern League itself for the first time since 1915. And they won it resoundingly, losing only one match, scoring 79 league goals, conceding a mere 32, and clinching the title by a five-point margin at the end of April 1927 with a 4–0 home win over Loftus Albion. They also won the Durham Challenge Cup, beating West Stanley 4–2 in a re-played final at Bishop Auckland. They rounded off their season, on May 7, by beating Stanley United 5–0 in the final of the Crook Nursing Cup.[16]

In addition, during that same season Crook transferred no less than five of their players – Hope, Nelson, Little, Brown and Wilkinson – to professional clubs; Hope and Nelson went to Derby County, Little and Wilkinson to Newcastle United and Brown to Huddersfield Town. All these players had played for Crook Town for only very short periods before being transferred. Johnny Wilkinson, for example, a 19-year-old centre forward, had been with Crook for just one season (during which he scored 43 goals!) before joining Newcastle, and Nelson and Hope had been transferred to Derby in January 1927, having only joined Crook (from West Auckland and Bishop Auckland respectively) at the beginning of the 1926–7 season.[17]

In other words, Crook Town were not only being very successful on the pitch, they were also developing a profitable 'throughput system' of young players, attracting them to the club from local rivals then selling them on rapidly to professional clubs for very lucrative (for the time) transfer fees.[18] But the question, of course, was *how* these players were being attracted to Crook. All these young men were formally amateurs so they could join

---

16   *Northern Goalfields Revisited, op cit*, pp. 130–2, John Phelan, Michael Manuel and
      Alan Stewart, *The Story of Crook Town Football Club* (Crook: Linton Printers,
      2001), 29–30.
17   *SDN*, January 14, 1927, p. 8 and May 18, 1927, p. 6.
18   Since all these players were technically amateurs, their registration papers could
      not be transferred, so these were not legally 'transfer fees'. In reality, however,
      Crook Town did receive payments for them from the professional clubs involved –
      de facto transfer fees – which was precisely what was alleged by the DFA. As noted
      in my final chapter, such payments went back to the very beginnings of commer-
      cial soccer in Britain in the 1880s, well before their legalisation by the Football
      League in 1904.

and play for whatever football club they wished, subject only to residence requirements. In reality, however, all would have been receiving 'expenses' at their previous clubs, so they must have joined Crook on the promise of remuneration above what they were already receiving. That in turn raised the question of how Crook were funding those extra payments. It is entirely unsurprising therefore that the primary focus of this first DFA Inquiry was on financial matters – gate receipts not recorded in Crook Town's accounts, and transfer fees under-recorded in its accounts and finding their way into the club Secretary's personal possession.

The Crook Town Committee's first response to all this was to try to circumvent the Commission's eight conditions by winding-up the club and forming a new one ('Crook FC'). This tactic, and a related attempt to join the new club to the Northern League, resulted only in the General Committee itself being suspended (in early September 1927). Moreover, all its attempts to register the new club with the DFA or to join the Northern League were firmly blocked.[19] So, in mid-September 1927, left with no alternative if they wished their club to play the new season, and with just a week to go to its opening matches, the Crook Town General Committee commenced frantic negotiations with the DFA to have the suspension lifted.

In the course of these negotiations, all of the Commission's conditions for 'reorganising' Crook were quietly dropped, and instead the Commissioners insisted only on receiving a 'satisfactory financial statement' from the club. This was delivered to them on September 17, and the suspensions of the club and all its officials – save Fred Peart – duly lifted. Five days later Crook played their first game of the new Northern League season against Cockfield.[20]

Just as we do not know what was in the anonymous letter to the FA, so no evidence remains in the DFA archives of what was in Crook's 'financial statement', but one must assume that it dealt with gate receipts or transfer fees, or both. But though it appears to have satisfied the Commissioners sufficiently for them to lift the other suspensions, it did not persuade them to reinstate Fred Peart, who was not only Crook Town's Secretary, but the

19   *NM*, September 2, 1927, p. 11 and September 6, 1927, p. 11.
20   *NM*, September 19, 1927, p. 11 and September 24, 1927, p. 11.

club's prime mover and power broker.[21] He remained suspended *sine die* from all involvement in football administration, a fact that was soon to have further dramatic consequences.

For Crook Town's return to respectability and the football pitch was short-lived. Less than four months later, on January 11, 1928, the same DFA Commissioners suspended the club again, and in so doing produced a series of events which threatened, briefly, to bring an end to organised association football in County Durham. But before coming to that, we should note one other small incident in this first stage of the Crook Affair, an incident which shines a narrow but penetrating light on the hierarchy of power in north-eastern football.

We have seen that the DFA's Commission of Inquiry suspended Crook Town from all involvement in football competition in late July 1927, just over a week after its first meeting, and almost a month before it issued its formal report. However, just three weeks later, on August 18, the Commissioners suddenly lifted the suspension. They did so because, although Newcastle United had secured the transfer of Wilkinson and Little from Crook in May, they had still not registered them as Newcastle players. Therefore, still being Crook players, they too were suspended from playing, for Crook or any other club. So, the suspension of the club was lifted, (not that of the officials) and forty-eight hours later, with Wilkinson and Little now registered with the Magpies, it was reimposed.[22]

This little side-story hardly needs comment. What can be said of Newcastle United in 1927, could be said of them (and Sunderland FC and Middlesbrough FC) for decades before and afterwards. The three great white sharks of north-eastern football would tolerate any amount of squabbling among the smaller fish, and between them and the football associations that controlled them, but they did so only so long as such

21   For some background on Fred Peart Sr., at this time head teacher at Crook Junior School, see Johnson, *op cit*, p. 22. (His son, Fred Peart Jr., played for Crook Town briefly as a wing half, before going on to a successful career in politics. He served as Minister for Agriculture in the first Wilson Labour government before becoming Lord Privy Seal.)

22   *NM*, August 19, 1927, p. 11.

squabbles did not compromise their own voracious chomping further up
the local football food chain!

The Crook Town Affair Part Two: The Second Commission and the 'Great Outing'

On Saturday, January 7, 1928 Crook Town defeated Bishop Auckland
2–1 in an English Amateur Cup tie.[23] Just four days later, on Wednesday,
January 11, the DFA's Commission of Inquiry reconvened. According to
the *North Mail* it:

> … had again had [Crook Town's] affairs under review, and … the club and all
> players who took part in the match last Saturday were permanently suspended.

The newspaper then listed five reasons which the Commission had given
for its decision to 'wipe out' the Crook club again:[24]

' (1) The members of the Commission are satisfied that the player
Arthur Stephenson, 2, Sandringham Road, Fulwell, Sunderland
has received from Crook Town … remuneration above his hotel
and travelling expenses actually paid and therefore, in accordance with Rule 29 of the … Football Association, he is declared
a professional.

(2) The members of the Commission are further satisfied that the
player, Arthur Stephenson, would not play for any club without
payment for lost time or a fee for playing. This decision is based
upon correspondence written by the player.

---

23   For details on the match and its aftermath, most notably Bishop Auckland's secretary – John 'Kit' Rudd – launching an immediate appeal to the DFA on the
grounds that Crook were "not a properly constituted amateur club", see Johnson,
op cit, pp. 27–8.

24   The headline of the *NM* story reporting the new suspension was "Crook Town
Club Wiped Out." *NM*, January 12, 1928, p. 11.

(3) In view of the payment made to the player ... Crook Town ... have violated the regulations relative to amateur clubs.

(4) The members of the Commission are also satisfied that people have been admitted to the ground and grandstand of the Crook Town club without tickets and the money thus obtained is not accounted for in the books of the club.

(5) The members of the Commission are also satisfied that Mr E.F. Peart has been actively engaged in the affairs of Crook Town in violation of previous decisions of the Commission.'[25]

The most important point to note here is that, in contrast to its first suspension, the DFA Commission explicitly mentions a player receiving payments beyond the expenses allowed under the FA's Rule 29.[26] In other words, the Commission abandoned its earlier attempt to 'shield' (to use *Criticus's* word) Crook's players and to confine the blame to corrupt or incompetent club officials. It even claimed to have a written statement from the guilty player confirming that he was a *de facto* professional.

The Commissioners almost certainly came to regret this change of tactic. Because it unlocked a Pandora's box which Crook Town then proceeded to throw wide open. To the Commission of Inquiry's single written statement from a single player confessing to professionalism, Crook Town were to respond by circulating a mass of written statements from a mass of Crook Town and other players confessing to professionalism. Also, in explicitly instancing Arthur Stephenson's violations of the FA's Rule 29, the Commission directly implicated the national body in the affair, a move which it also came to regret.

---

25 *ibid.*

26 For the full text of Rule 29 as it related to expenses and other payments to amateurs, see Appendix 2 to this chapter. The rule defining amateurism had been around, under various numberings, since the 1880s. Brian Dobbs quotes an 1882 FA rule under which "Any member of any club receiving remuneration or consideration of any sort above his actual expenses and any wages actually lost ... shall be debarred from taking part in either cup, inter-Association, or International contests ..." Dobbs, *op cit*, p. 41.

But if the three of the five reasons that the DFA Commission gave for suspending Crook anew marked a departure, the fourth and fifth signalled continuity. For, whatever it may have undertaken to do in its September 1927 'financial statement', in January 1928 Crook Town was once again accused of receiving gate monies not properly accounted for, and of allowing its supposedly suspended *eminence gris* – Fred Peart – to continue running the club, including masterminding its dodgy accounting practices and under-the-counter player payments.

If the Commission changed tack in Crook's second suspension so did the club in responding to it. This time there was no attempt to evade it by administrative manoeuvres, but an immediate decision to fight tooth and nail. Moreover, Fred Peart now openly and aggressively led the campaign against the Commission, rather than directing operations surreptitiously through front men. In fact, in the same *North Mail* story which recounted the club's second suspension, it was also reported that 'one prominent member of the Crook Club' (probably Peart himself) had said, ominously, that:

> Crook were less guilty than numerous clubs in Durham County, and if the Commission were desirous of cleansing football in the county then it behoved the Crook Club officials to assist them.[27]

Despite this initial pugnacity, Crook flirted, briefly, with the less dramatic option of a formal appeal to the FA. But when told that it would cost a non-refundable ten guineas even to have an appeal heard, they decided to set about 'cleansing' Durham football in a different way, even if it meant:

> the exposure of the practices of other amateur clubs in their methods of recouping (*sic*) players who in these days of depression cannot afford to lose work for the sake of the game.[28]

So, on February 2, 1928 Crook Town FC forwarded to the FA, the Welsh FA, the DFA, the Lord Lieutenant of Durham County, the Bishop of Durham, FIFA, the Chairman of the Northern League, various county

27   *NM*, January 12, 1928, p. 11.
28   *NM*, January 16, 1928, p. 11.

football associations, several MPs and the local and national press, a dossier containing sworn statements from 36 County Durham footballers, making reference to 20 different clubs for which they were currently playing or had played. In those statements, all the players alleged that they had received, or were still receiving, payments which were clearly illegal for amateur footballers under the FA's Rule 29.

The dossier was accompanied by a covering letter from Peart himself. In it, he said, *inter alia*:

> the decision of the Durham FA Commission left Crook with no other course than to show that they were not alone in making breaches of the said rule, and that were Crook Town and other clubs within the county unable to continue their prior working practices they "cannot hope to achieve even a small amount of success"... The club were not acting out of vindictiveness but in order that they be allowed to continue in the sport ...[The club]... also felt unfairly treated owing to Colonel Dowling acting as chairman of the commission ... [given that]... his club, Bishop Auckland, had been implicated in the charges made against Crook.[29]

In Appendix 1 to this chapter the reader will find, reproduced verbatim, the statements made by the 36 players. They are quite informally written, and in reading them it is not difficult to hear the voices of a range of ordinary County Durham men. However, from the point of view of the subsequent development of 'the Affair', the most important point is that the statements can be divided into two broad groups. In a little less than half (17 of the 36) an amateur player admits to receiving supposed 'expenses' well in excess of his actual match-related costs. In slightly more than half however (19 out of 36) a player admits to receiving undisguised match fees without *any* regard to his actual expenses. In other words, more than half of these statements are frank admissions of professionalism in its most

---

29   As summarised in Johnson, *op cit*, p. 31. Amos, *op cit*, p. 486, has Peart's letter saying that "Football in Crook is an asset to the town, and tradespeople as a whole have been hit hard owing to the suspension of the club. The club and its players have not taken this action out of vindictiveness but to show that the football authorities have left no other course open, and also to show that they have a right in being allowed to participate in our national sport."

direct and unmediated form, not simply admissions to breaching the FA's expenses rules.

The news of Crook's 'sensational' dossier broke in the local press on February 3, 1928. Less than a week later the club received a letter (immediately released to the press) from Frederick Wall, the influential Secretary of the FA. Wall informed Crook that 'There will ... be an investigation into the matters which you have brought to our notice.'[30] Despite this undertaking, the FA's Commission of Inquiry into Crook's allegations was not actually appointed until late April and did not meet until May 2. This three-month delay is one of the most interesting, and difficult to investigate, aspects of the whole story. One of its effects was certainly to condemn Crook to football inaction for the rest of the 1927–8 season. However, given that the club had openly admitted, in its dossier, to significant breaches of Rule 29, (including making payments for 'lost time')[31] it would not have had its suspension lifted by the FA Commission whenever the latter had met.

It is unlikely therefore that the FA's delay was motivated by any particular animus against Crook. The most likely explanation is that it signalled divisions, both within the FA, and perhaps between the FA and the DFA, over how to act and when. For in effect Crook had backed both bodies into a corner. If the allegations in the dossier were true, a positive mass of Durham clubs, officials and players were in flagrant breech, not just of the expenses provisions of Rule 29, but of the FA's distinction between professional and amateur players on which the rule was based. That being the case any FA investigation would *have* to result in wholesale punishments of those players and those clubs. The only way such an outcome could be avoided would be for the Commission to find that all the statements in Crook's dossier were false. But it could hardly do this without looking mendacious, ridiculous, or both. In fact, the only courses practically open to the FA, once Crook had sent it the dossier, were either to ignore it, or to delay an inquiry in the hope that something might 'turn up' to get it (and the DFA) off the hook.

Certainly, Crook suspected that the delay represented an attempt at column dodging, either by the FA or the DFA, or both. For in March and

30   *NM*, February 10, 1928, p. 11.
31   Johnson, *op cit*, p. 31.

April Peart addressed irritated letters to the FA querying the delay and con-
trasting it bitterly with the alacrity with which the original DFA Commission
into Crook had been set up and acted.[32]

In late April 1928 however, a meeting of the Emergency Committee of the
FA finally announced the appointment of a seven-man Commission of Inquiry
'into alleged breaches of the rules of the Association by officials and players
of clubs in the county of Durham'. The Commission consisted of the Vice-
Chairman and Treasurer of the FA, and the Chairmen of the Nottingham,
London, Lancashire, Birmingham and Lincolnshire football associations.[33]

In the event, C. E. Sutcliffe, Chairman of the Lancashire FA, became
ill and, in his place, Frederick Wall attended the Commission's hearings,
held in the DFA headquarters in Durham, on May 2 and 3, 1928 (although
his name is not appended to its report).

The FA's dilatoriness in convening it was more than made up for by the
speed with which its Commission acted once convened. In just two days
of hearings it found enough evidence to 'be satisfied' that 427 players from
12 different clubs in Durham had received payments 'above their expenses
actually and necessarily incurred', declared them to be professionals, and
suspended them 'from taking any part in football until the 31st December
1928'. In addition, 28 players from 12 different clubs had actually 'admitted
receiving payment contrary to Rule 29'.[34] They too were declared professionals and were 'suspended from taking any part in football during the

32   See, for example, *NM*, March 16, 1928, p. 13. By May the football season was over,
     which may have been another reason for the delay. Punishing clubs in the off-
     season, and particularly if one was doing so *en masse*, allowed time for negotiation.
     And as a new season approached there was growing pressure on all sides to com-
     promise. That was certainly how things worked out in the first DFA inquiry into
     Crook, and how it was to work out with the FA inquiry.
33   *NM*, April 26, 1928, p. 13.
34   This a significantly smaller proportion than I calculated from the Crook dossier.
     It is difficult to know what accounts for this discrepancy. Perhaps the FA simply
     baulked at too frank a recognition of the extent of *de facto* professionalism in
     Durham. Perhaps the players who appeared before the Commission in Durham
     had been advised to 'back track' on some of their claims. Also, the distinction be-
     tween being paid 'expenses' well in excess of those incurred, and simply being paid
     to play was a difficult one to draw and might not have been clear to many players.
     After all, what was the difference in practice between being paid (say) 13s 6d in

season 1928–9'. Finally, 61 officials from 18 different Durham clubs were suspended (usually until June 30, 1929) and hundreds of others warned about their future conduct. All these clubs also received fines varying between £10 and £50, with the majority receiving £25 fines.

The following were the clubs affected by these measures: Bishop Auckland FC, Ferryhill, Willington, Consett, Cockfield, Spennymoor Utd, West Stanley FC, Annfield Plain, Chilton Colliery, Durham City FC, Craghead, South Shields, Hartlepool Utd, Stanley Utd, Langley Park, Esh Winning, Darlington and Shildon.[35] This list overlaps almost perfectly with the clubs mentioned in the player statements in the Crook dossier. In fact, the only two clubs whose names appeared in the dossier but *not* in the FA Commission report were 'Darlington Railway Athletic' (a different club from Darlington FC, and a minor club in the town) and Consett Celtic (also a minor club in the iron and steel town of Consett.)

The Commission presented its report to the summer meeting of the FA in Blackpool and formally published it on Saturday, June 30 to a positive storm of publicity in the national press, both sporting and non-sporting.[36] In fact, it was at this point (mid-summer 1928) that the 'Crook Town Affair' became a fully fledged sporting scandal.

Panic and Scandalised Unity: The Dilemmas of the DFA

If, during the three months between Frederick Wall promising Crook a Commission of Inquiry and its actual convening, the Durham FA *had* attempted to collude with the FA or to influence its actions, that attempt

---

'expenses' when you had not incurred any, and being paid 13s 6d 'on top' of your expenses?

35   The Football Association, *Report and Recommendations of the Commission appointed to enquire into alleged Breaches of the Rules of the Association by Officials and Players of certain Clubs in the County of Durham* (London: 42, Russell Square, June 18, 1928) (8 pp).

36   See, for example, *Athletic News*, July 2, 1928, pp. 10–11 and *NM*, July 2, 1928, p. 10.

had clearly been a complete failure. Because, just four days after the 'sensational' report was issued, on Wednesday, July 4, 1928, the DFA Council called a 'special meeting' in Durham. It consisted entirely of bitter denunciations of the FA's Commission and all its doings and findings, and culminated, after a unified chorus of outrage, in the unanimous passing of an extraordinary motion, moved by Colonel Dowling himself:

> That the Council of the Association has been guilty of paying a flat rate for tea money in their cup finals equally with the various clubs who have been dealt with by the Commission and hereby suspend themselves for the same period as the officials of the various clubs.[37]

The passing of this motion was widely taken to mean that there was no longer a football association in the County of Durham, which raised some tricky questions about how the game was to be carried on in the county in the following season. Since all football competitions on the territory of a county had to be sanctioned by the county association at the beginning of each season (including Football League fixtures) the DFA Council's 'self-suspension' raised the alarming possibility that Sunderland, Gateshead, Hartlepool Utd, South Shields and Darlington would not be able to play 'legal' home games in 1928–9. The FA disputed this interpretation, claiming that the DFA *Council* suspending itself did not mean that the DFA *itself* had ceased to exist, especially since its only full-time paid officer (its Secretary, William Spedding) remained in post.[38] Since the Council de-suspended itself five weeks later, and association football in Durham County went on almost as normal in 1928–9, these legal issues were never put to the test. But nonetheless between the beginning of July and the end of September 1928 the fate of association football in County Durham – and especially amateur association football – seemed to hang in the balance and was the focus of continued excited attention in the football world.

If Fred Peart of Crook Town FC had been the prime focus of that attention up to early July, Lieutenant-Colonel Thomas Dowling, OBE, TA,

---

37   *NM*, July 5, 1928, p. 7.
38   For discussion around these issues, *NM*, July 7, 1928, p. 1 and July 16, 1928, p. 10.

President of the DFA, President of the Northern League and President of Bishop Auckland FC, now took centre stage.[39] Dowling's long speech at the July special meeting – in which he eloquently denounced the FA Commission's entire proceedings (and especially the role of Frederick Wall), passionately defended the 'fixed' expenses procedures of his association and its clubs, and differentiated their behaviour firmly from Crook Town's illegalities – was widely and sympathetically reported in the local and national press. One passage in particular was reproduced over and over again:

> All that the majority of these clubs have done is a more or less recognized custom, and they make a man a professional because he has probably received 2s 6d or 5s for his lunch and tea, and he has spent practically the whole of it. Some of the poor beggars in the County of Durham at the present time would be absolute brutes if they spent that money on themselves, when they had wives and children starving at home. I cannot conceive how, because a man who receives a legitimate sum for his expenses, prefers starving himself and feeding his wife and children or his mother, he should be made a professional.[40]

Given the widespread economic depression and high levels of unemployment in the North-East at this time, it is hardly surprising that these emotive appeals received widespread sympathy, including from other football associations outside the region.[41] However, in fairness to Frederick Wall and the FA, it must be said that the emotive force of Dowling's speech can easily distract attention – and perhaps was meant to distract attention – from a number of highly dubious assertions in it.

Dowling said, for example, that:

> nine-tenths of the charges made against the clubs were for paying a flat rate for tea money ....I see from the evidence that 90 per cent, at least, of the suspended players were so dealt with for receiving payments varying from 2s 6d to 5s, as tea or lunch money at the matches in which they took part.

39 For some biographical details on Dowling, a founder member of the Bishop Auckland Church Institute Club of 1882, a decorated World War I soldier, and an enormously respected solicitor and civic figure in Bishop Auckland, see Johnson, *op cit*, p. 21.
40 *NM*, July 5, 1928, *op cit*, p. 7.
41 See, for example, the *Athletic News*, July 9, 1928, p. 12.

And that:

> not a single one of those players who have been suspended has been asked for or
> proved to have received one halfpenny more than he spent.

Also that:

> Crook are alleging that their case is the same as the cases that have been dealt with
> by the F.A ....[but]... The Crook case is entirely different. We recognized in the
> case of Crook payment of tea-money. What the Crook club was suspended for was
> for not keeping proper books and for not showing what their gate returns were –
> financial arrangements of the F.A.[42]

Yet:

(1) If the evidence that the Commission heard in Durham was anything like that contained in the Crook dossier, (and another
section of Dowling's speech suggested that it was)[43] then it would
have heard players stating that they received 'expenses' payments
greatly in excess of any expenses actually incurred (whether for
'tea' or anything else); others stating that they received monies
not provided as 'expenses' at all; and virtually all of them alleging
that the payments they received were rarely if ever 'fixed', but
highly varied. Moreover, since one of Dowling's major complaints
was that neither he, nor anyone at the DFA, had been provided
with copies of the evidence heard by the FA Commissioners it is
unclear how he could have 'seen' anything from it.[44]

42　*NM*, July 5, 1928, *op cit*, p. 7.

43　*ibid* "Colonel Dowling went on to explain that the only persons present at the inquiry were a number of players who had signed statements and representatives of
clubs."

44　*ibid* "Colonel Dowling explained that a representative of the Durham Association
was entitled to be present at the Commission's meetings in Durham, but owing
to his holiday he was unable to be present and Mr W. Spedding, the County secretary, attended. At the request of the Commission, Mr Spedding took notes and
at the close he asked Mr F. J. Wall ... if he could send a copy to him [Colonel
Dowling]. Mr Wall said he could not. I did think, he [Dowling] said, that as your

(2) All the 36 player statements in the Crook dossier flatly contradict
     Dowling's statement that they received not 'one halfpenny' more
     than they spent. (At least if by 'spent' he meant money that the
     players spent *before* receiving their expenses). A lot depends on
     what Dowling meant by saying that such allegations had not been
     'proved', but it is difficult to know what proof the Commission
     could have acquired beyond the players' own statements.

And:

(3) Dowling's statement about Crook is debatably true of Crook's
     first suspension, and completely untrue of the second. Indeed,
     the primary reason given for the second suspension was that
     Arthur Stephenson had 'received from Crook Town … remu-
     neration above his hotel and travelling expenses actually paid
     and therefore, in accordance with Rule 29 of the … Football
     Association, he is declared a professional'.[45] Moreover, even in
     the case of the DFA Commission's first suspension of Crook, its
     sixth condition of 'reorganisation' (that: '… the players in future
     shall be required to sign only for the actual money paid to them,
     and that payments for taxi-cabs, etc., used by players must be paid
     for by the club and entered through the ordinary accounts of the
     club.') surely implied that there *were* issues with Crook's expenses
     procedures.[46]

---

representative on the Football Association I was entitled to see these notes and to
know what the charges were and what evidence had been given before I went to
the meeting at Blackpool."

45 This was not to be Arthur Stephenson's last involvement in the Affair. See
    Appendix 1.

46 Indeed, the DFA Commission's closing words to its first report came back to
    haunt it when, in late August 1928, the FA refused the DFA's request to rescind
    the mass suspensions of Durham club officials and players. Responding to this
    request, the FA said: 'In reply to a suggestion by the Durham Association that the
    Football Association had knowledge, in August 1927… of a "flat rate" being paid
    in Durham, the Commission regret that the attention of the Football Association

The truth of the matter was, that in paying so-called flat rate expenses, Crook Town had not been different from any other County Durham club, including Dowling's Bishop Auckland. In fact, the original objection of Dowling, Askew and the others to Crook Town's activities had nothing to do with expenses as such, but with the conviction that the club was pursuing financial practices that allowed it to pay 'expenses' (or, simply, to pay players) more than competing clubs.

Unfortunately however, even the first Commission did not stick strictly to Crook's gate money and transfer fee infractions but dragged in expenses misdemeanours by officials as additional ammunition. Then, when Crook failed to abide by their 'financial statement' and mend their ways re. gate monies and unaccounted transfers, Dowling and others decided to 'get them' through a second inquiry. And this time the charge sheet featured, as its major count, a named player's written allegations of 'excessive' expenses payments contrary to Rule 29. Crook then responded in kind by publishing a raft of similar allegations against other Durham clubs, and the FA's Commission of Inquiry accepted those allegations as true and acted accordingly.

Faced with the FA's official endorsement of Crook's allegations – and thus hoisted, in effect, with their own petard – Dowling and the rest of the DFA Council were then forced to claim that:

(a) They, unlike the FA, had never suspended Crook for its expenses procedures (which was not true), and

(b) that, unlike Crook Town, all Durham's other amateur clubs, and its professional clubs playing amateurs, operated within the spirit of Rule 29, because they only paid 'reasonable' fixed rates for very basic player expenses – the oft-evoked 'tea-money'. But this was also not true.

---

was never drawn to the fact. On the contrary, the Commission of the Durham F.A. in their findings in the cases of Crook Town and Stockton F.C., reported that "the Commission cannot find that any payments have been made to players other than reasonable out-of-pocket expenses, and therefore they are not justified in taking any action against them" '. *NM*, August 28, 1928, p. 11.

One point of fact is particularly vital here. The FA's Rule 29 did *not* require amateur players to incur expenses before they were reimbursed. All it required was that players be provided with a 'receipt' by the club. This 'receipt' listed items of expenditure which the players *claimed* they had incurred or would incur, in playing a match. They then signed that 'receipt' as evidence that what they had *claimed* was true. Then, having paid those expenses, the club was required to keep those 'receipts' and enter them and their totals in its accounts.

In effect then, Rule 29 allowed clubs to accept, unquestioningly, what players claimed and 'signed for' as allowable expenses. It did not require them to demand *real* receipts from players for payments already made – to railway companies, bus companies, canteens, etc.[47]

Thus, if the rule was being properly followed, 'receipted' amounts would vary from match-to-match, depending on what expenses an individual player said he had incurred or would incur, for that match. So obviously, in paying 'fixed rates' for expenses, Durham clubs were either assuming that all their players incurred the same expenses for every match, or they were paying the players the same amount irrespective of their (claimed) expenses. In the latter case of course, we are dealing with payments for play thinly disguised as expenses.

But in addition, as will readily be seen from the statements in Appendix 1, players were mostly not paid fixed amounts at all, whether as 'expenses' or no. An individual player might receive a payment fixed for a match or a run of matches. But payments also varied markedly, both between players and between matches, depending on:

(1) a player's worth to the team (skill level, goal-scoring ability, etc.);
(2) the particular match he was playing in (reserve or first team, home or away);
(3) the match result;
(4) the importance of a match, and/or;
(5) the level of gate receipts.

---

47   See Appendix 2 to this chapter for the FA's attempt to further clarify for clubs the 'allowable expenses' of Rule 29 in the light of the Durham inquiry.

In other words, payments to players varied in ways which had nothing to do with their 'expenses', claimed or real, and everything to do with general 'footballing' and/or commercial considerations.

In short then, all the major Durham County amateur clubs in 1927–8 were simply finding a way to pay young men to play football for them. Moreover, just as professional clubs would, they were paying those players differentially depending on a variety of factors. For the reasons suggested by Harry Pearson, these Durham clubs were operating, in fact, as quasi-professional organisations, with the 'quasi' consisting mainly in disguising professional payments as expenses.

If all this be the case, then two further questions arise:

(1) What difference did such payments make to the young men who received them and to their families? Were they mainly used to keep 'starving' wives, children and mothers alive, or was the truth a little more complex than this?
(2) Why did nobody involved in the affair say publicly what the Durham clubs were actually doing?

In the next two sections of the chapter we will take these questions in order.

Starving Mothers or Something More? Assessing the Magnitude of Durham Football Shamateurism in the 1920s

From the 36 player statements in the Crook dossier it is possible to derive rough calculations of the mean minimum (7s 3d) and maximum (17s 4d) amounts that those players claim to have been paid per match. It is also possible, from the same data, to work out their median payment per match (12s 3d).

Obviously though, such amounts mean very little in themselves. They must be compared with the wages that these players would have earned in their 'non-football' occupations. And here we encounter a number of difficulties. For a start, only 19 of the statements give occupations at all, and they give a slightly more varied picture than might be expected. Thus six of these 19 players *were* miners, and five others appear to have been iron-and-steel workers, but the other eight are quite varied, featuring two school teachers, a boot maker, a printer's apprentice, a corporation clerk, an unspecified 'railway employee', a 'fitter' and a 'labourer'. This variation obviously makes it difficult to know what comparative wage data to use, and, in addition, such data for County Durham in the 1920s are quite fragmentary anyway. However, one must do one's best.

In 1927 and 1928 economic and social conditions in the Durham coalfield, although not in some respects as bad as they were to become in the 1930s, were nonetheless dire. Nearly 20% of the county's mining workforce was unemployed, real earnings per shift were 20% lower than they had been at the outset of the 1914–8 war, and over 58,000 unemployed people in the county were in receipt of Poor Law relief, which meant that they had either exhausted their unemployment insurance entitlements or never had any. About the only positive development in these years was that the return of Britain to the Gold Standard in 1925. For whilst it rendered a number of Britain's export industries (including coal and shipbuilding) uncompetitive, it also reduced import costs, including prices for both food and clothing. This meant that those people who retained their jobs in the late 1920s and early 1930s found their wages going further, even if they were reduced in money terms.

Having said that by way of introduction, the following tables provide some illuminating comparisons.

'Shamateur' Football Earnings 1920s (Crook Dossier)

Mean Minimum	Median	Mean Maximum
7s 3d	12s 3d	17s 4d

Money Wages (various occupations) 1920s

Miners' wages Per Shift, Durham Coalfield (1928)	8s 1$^{1/2d}$ (c. 44s weekly)
Shipwright weekly wage (1925)	55s 7d

Money Wages (various occupations) 1920s

Shipyard labourer's weekly wage (1925)	38s 5d
Railway engine drivers' weekly wage (1925)	72s–90s
Railway porters' weekly wages (1925)	47–51s
Dock labourers' daily wage (1925)	11s–13s 6d (c.55s–65s weekly)
Tram driver's weekly wage (1925)	59s 2d
Book Binders and Machine Rulers (1925)	73s 4d
Agricultural Labourers' weekly wages (1925)	28s–42s

Unemployment
Insurance benefit (weekly), single man, 1928   17s 0d

Dole received (weekly) by unemployed miner, wife
and six children in Crook (1927)   36s 0d[48]

Cost of Living Indicators, 1920s

Weekly house rent in Crook (1927)	8s 6d
Pint of milk (1926)	3d
White loaf (1926)	4 1/4d

48   Sources for 1920s wages and dole data:
1.   *Hansard*, July 30, 1925, (answer of Sir W. de Freece, Minister of Labour, to a question about average rates of wages in twelve chief industries) at <http://hansard.millbanksystems.com/written_answers/1925/jul/30/average-weekly-wages>
2.   *Daily Telegraph*, 'A taste of Life in Britain in 1925' at <http://www.telegraph.co.uk/news/uknews/1491140/A-taste-of-life-in-Britain-in-1925.html>
3.   'Average salary for a female clerk in England in 1925?' at <http://www.rootschat.com/forum/index.php?topic=679283.0>
4.   W. R. Garside, *The Durham Miners 1919–1960* (London: Allen & Unwin, 1971), chapter VII, 274, 284 and Appendix II, 314.

1lb sugar (1926)	3 ^{1/2d}
Pint of beer (1925)	5d
Twenty 'Craven A' cigarettes (1928)	1s 0d[49]

As in all exercises of this type, there is no pretence of providing anything more than rough orders of magnitude, since the welfare of individuals and families could be significantly impacted by a host of variations not captured in these sorts of crude statistics. In a situation where small differences mattered greatly, variations in earnings due to illness, injury, or other factors, the differing policies of Poor Law Guardians from place to place, and variations in rental costs from place to place or even from dwelling to dwelling, could impact human welfare disproportionately.

Having said that, it will be seen that the median weekly earnings reported by players in the Crook dossier (12s 3d) was equal to a shift and a half of a Durham miner's wages in 1928 (or about twelve hours of work). Put another way, it was equal to about 28% of a miner's weekly wage. It was also the equivalent of nearly a third of a shipyard labourer's weekly wage and a quarter of a railway porter's. On the other hand though, one of the dossier informants was a 'printer's apprentice' and another was a 'corporation clerk'. Though I have not been able to find wage figures for these precise occupations in the North-East in the 1920s, all print workers seem to have been paid relatively well (over 73s weekly in 1925), and a clerk in a large wholesale firm in Manchester in 1925 earned no less than 110s per week in that year. In other words, for such relatively well-paid workers 12s 3d would have been equal to just 17% and 11% respectively of their weekly earnings – a welcome supplement but not much more.

That is the matter seen from an earnings perspective, seen from an expenditure perspective the results are rather more striking. For example, it appears that a player living in Crook in 1927 and earning the median amount weekly from playing football, could have paid his house rent and had a bit less than 4s left over to live on, that is, he could just about have survived on his football earnings alone even if (as was in fact very unlikely)

---

49   Sources for cost of living indicators, *Daily Telegraph, op cit*, Garside, *op cit*, p. 284 and Amos, *op cit*, p. 486.

he had no other monetary income. In fact, this median amount is equal to 72% of what he would have received in dole as a single man in 1928 (17s) and were he lucky enough to have been earning the mean maximum (or better) from football, he would have actually earned more in ninety minutes (17s 4d) than he would have got *in toto* from the dole. This assumes that he had no dependents. If he had dependents, it appears from the figures provided by Garside that he would have received an additional 10s or so weekly for his wife, and between 2s and 6s per child, depending on their age.[50] But even so his football earnings would still have constituted between a third and a half of his total income depending on the number of his children.

Summing all this up, it appears that the 'shamateurist' earnings from football reported in the Crook dossier would have constituted a considerable addition to the incomes of ordinary County Durham working men in 1928, raising their real incomes by something between a quarter and a third in most cases, and by at least 10% even in the case of players in better-paid occupations. There is no way of knowing from the player statements in the dossier how many were unemployed in 1928, but even if, like Durham miners generally, 20% of them were out of work, it seems that they, a wife and one or two children, could just about have survived on their football earnings.

But if they were among the highest earning players, they could have done much better than that. Eight of the 36 players in the dossier reported having been paid over £1 a match, and four said they had received payments of over £2, and in a world in which a large number of workers earned little more than £2 for working a five-and-a-half-day week, these were considerable sums.[51] As we have seen, even the average maximum earning (17s 4d), was more than the dole paid to a single man in Durham under the 1927 Unemployment Act.

In short then Colonel Dowling's impassioned statement about starving wives and mothers, however sympathetically received, was misleading at almost every level. For,

---

50   Garside, *op cit*, p. 278.
51   This assumes of course that players earned these sums regularly, and that was certainly not always the case. The earnings of shamateur players could be disrupted by injury, loss of form and selection decisions, and unlike properly professional players shamateurs earned nothing when not playing.

(1) had the majority of players actually just been paid 'tea money' of between 2s 6d and 5s such payments would barely have prevented the players themselves from starving, let alone their wives or mothers. But if the Crook dossier statements were typical, they were not, in the overwhelming majority of cases, receiving payments anything like this low. However,

(2) the payments the players were receiving would have prevented both their own starvation and that of at least a small number of dependents. In fact, they would have done this and a little bit more, even if the players had no other sources of income. But in reality,

(3) the majority of Durham shamateur footballers were in work in 1928, and since they were, and their football earnings constituted in most cases a substantial addition to their income, such players were undoubtedly among the better-off workers in County Durham in the terrible years of the late 1920s.

Silent Collusion as Class Hegemony? The FA, the DFA and a Century of Shamateurism

'The ruling ideas of every epoch are the ideas of its ruling class,' said Karl Marx famously.

In early 1927, as Crook Town were carrying all before them in the Northern League, one of his most well-known disciples, the Italian Communist Antonio Gramsci, had just been incarcerated in a fascist jail. While there he attempted to elaborate this idea of Marx for twentieth century societies that maintained order more by consent than coercion. In one of his *Prison Notebooks* he identified what he called 'two major superstructural "levels"' of capitalist society. [These were]... 'civil society ... the ensemble of organisms commonly called "private", and ... "political society" or "the State".' He went on,

> These two levels correspond on the one hand to the function of 'hegemony' which the dominant group exercises throughout society and on the other hand to that of 'direct domination' or command exercised through the State and 'juridical' government. The functions in question are precisely organizational and connective. The

intellectuals are the dominant group's 'deputies' exercising the subaltern functions of social hegemony and political government.

The first of these functions, 'social hegemony', was defined by Gramsci as:

> The 'spontaneous' consent given by the great masses of the population to the general direction imposed on social life by the dominant fundamental group; this consent is 'historically' caused by the prestige (and consequent confidence) which the dominant group enjoys because of its position and function in the world of production.[52]

According to Gramsci, among the 'intellectuals' exercising 'social hegemony' throughout society on behalf of the ruling class were, 'the must humble "administrators" and divulgators of pre-existing, traditional, accumulated intellectual wealth' (i.e. teachers).[53] It is unclear whether Gramsci would have considered William Pickford, Arthur Kingscott, Wilfred Bellamy, Charles Sutcliffe, Albert Hines, Henry Huband and William Hart (the seven original members of the FA Commission of Inquiry) as 'intellectuals', though I suppose they were classical functionaries of English football's 'democratic-bureaucratic system'. He might well, however, have considered Frederick Wall (its entirely unofficial, but most influential member) a *bona fide* part of England's 'dominant fundamental group'.

But whatever Gramsci would or wouldn't have said, it is certainly striking that, even at the height of the Crook Town Affair, when elite amateur football in County Durham stood pretty unambiguously revealed as professional football on the cheap, *nobody* involved – not even Fred Peart – was prepared, publicly, to describe it (let alone defend it) as such. In the case of the DFA, its public defence was that it did not condone paying players for 'lost time' from work, and if any of its clubs had followed Crook in doing this they should indeed be punished.[54] But otherwise it insisted that all its clubs were just

---

52 Antonio Gramsci, *Selections from the Prison Notebooks*, edited and translated by Quintin Hoare and Geoffrey Nowell Smith (London: Lawrence & Wishart, 1971), 12.

53 *ibid*, p. 13.

54 Bishop Auckland, for example, officially held that, unlike Crook, they did not pay for lost time. But see the statements by Francis Smith and Arthur Stephenson in the Crook dossier (Appendix 1).

paying small amounts of 'allowable' expenses at a 'flat' or 'standardised' rates, and that this practice was both widespread in the country and condoned by the FA (or so it had genuinely believed).[55]

Even Fred Peart, though gratified by the FA Commission's 'sensational' outcome and revelling in the DFA's (and especially Thomas Dowling's) squirming disingenuity, did not directly challenge the rationale for the punishments dished out. His response was not to say, 'we all do it and it's right that we should', but 'we all do it, and if it's wrong for Crook, then it's wrong for everybody.' In fact, the main thrust of virtually all his public statements after the Commission reported and the DFA Council suspended itself, was to pour scorn on Dowling's assertions about minimal 'tea money' and to reiterate that there was nothing Crook had done (including paying players for lost time) that other clubs had not done as well.[56]

But why this silence? Why this universal failure to challenge the FA's amateur/professional distinction directly? Why, most especially, was there no public attack on the governing body's conception of 'allowable expenses' as a piece of class legislation illegitimately exported from the playing fields of Eton to the altogether tougher and grimier playing fields of County Durham? Was this self-censorship a classical example of subordination to Gramsci's intellectually mediated 'social hegemony'?[57] The answer is no.

---

55   *NM*, July 5, 1928, p. 7.
56   See, for example, Johnson, *op cit*, pp. 52–5 and Amos, *op cit*, pp. 488–9. It is striking, in this context, how similar were the actions of Fred Peart Sr., to those of William Suddell, (chairman of Preston North End) forty-four years earlier, in the dispute with the FA which led to the legalisation of professionalism. Suddell, like Peart, openly admitted to infracting the FA's (then) rules against profession-alism, claimed that many other clubs (especially in Lancashire) were also guilty, and simply defied the FA to do its worst. Such tactics could hardly have been suc-cessful, however, unless many other people already *knew* what Peart and Suddell 'admitted'. In effect they both played on a widespread awareness of hypocrisy and used it to undermine the force of amateurist strictures. See Chapter 6 for further thoughts on this.
57   The nearest approach to such an attack was a statement made to the *Northern Echo* by R. W. Harrison, BA, captain of Cockfield. "The amateur who sports plus-fours and knows the best people, travels in comfort, lunches before the match, dines after it and stays at the best hotels keeps his status. The stocky built,

These silences were *not* expression of ideological subordination to some ruling class 'hegemony'. Rather, every Durham football official knew that an explicit or 'head-on' attack on amateurism as a class ideology would put the FA in a difficult position and the DFA in a completely impossible one.

To take the FA first, its legalisation of professionalism in 1885 had, from the first, been hedged around with various conditions designed to assuage the suspicions of a number of genuine (because socially elite) amateur clubs in London. The most significant of these conditions was the firm distinction, which came to be embodied in its Rule 29, between amateur and professional players, and the insistence that any player 'receiving remuneration … of any sort above his necessary hotel and travelling expenses actually paid, shall be a professional'. When, in 1888, the Football League began, its creation allowed the FA to largely delegate governance of professional players' employment to a parallel organisation, whilst it remained the custodian of the amateur game and the guardian of its purity.[58]

The problem was, however, that, from the 1880s on, association football, both amateur and professional, became dominated by players from working-class backgrounds. In fact, given the social structure of Britain at that time (and for almost a century afterwards) this was an inevitable consequence of the game becoming the country's most successful spectator and participation sport.

In the case of amateur football, the effect of its working-class colonisation, not only in Northumberland and Durham, but all over the country (with the only partial exception of London and the home counties) was the manipulation of the 'expenses' provisions of Rule 29 to find ways of paying players. Indeed, of the FA's original seven-man Commission of Inquiry into the Crook Affair, four members (Charles Sutcliffe, Wilfred Bellamy, Albert Hines and William Hart) headed county football associations (Lancashire, Lincolnshire, Nottinghamshire and Birmingham

---

bow-legged Durham pit lad goes without lunch, crowds into a United bus, receives five shillings for tea, contents himself with a pie or a snack in a side street and consequently, is a professional." Quoted in Amos, *op cit*, p. 488.

58   For this, see, for example, Richard Holt, *Sport and the British: A Modern History* (Oxford: Clarendon, 1989), 106.

respectively) in which such practices were probably as widespread as they were in Durham or Northumberland.

It is possible therefore that, as Thomas Dowling suspected,[59] Bellamy, Hines and Hart were dragooned into endorsing the draconian punishments handed out by the Commission by Frederick Hall (perhaps supported by William Pickford and Arthur Kingscott). But it is much more likely that *all* the members of the Commission simply felt that, in the light of the Crook dossier, they had no choice but to dish out a mass of suspensions. After all, these were thirty-six statements made under oath to a solicitor, and (so it seems) repeated at the hearings in Durham and amplified there by similar or identical statements made by other players. Under such circumstances, failure of the Commission to act would have amounted to a public confession that the expenses provisions of Rule 29 were a sham.

In other words, Crook's dossier represented a kind of sin against the ark. The FA could hold the official position that it was the proud custodian of a predominantly working-class amateur game (i.e. that there was no contradiction hidden in that description) so long as that assertion was never publicly challenged. Frederick Wall may or may not have known that the description slurred over a contradiction, Bellamy, Hines and Hart almost certainly did. But just because they did, they would have been even less inclined than Wall to accept (let alone welcome) its 'outing' by Crook. For both they and their associations would face an identical situation to Thomas Dowling and the DFA should Crook's brutally honest precedent be taken up in Lincolnshire, Nottinghamshire or Birmingham.[60] It is important to understand precisely why this was – why virtually all English football associations were as vulnerable as Durham to having their expenses procedures 'outed'.

'Shamateurism' in association football was made possible through a simple but significant linguistic manoeuvre, a manoeuvre which had been

---

59   *NM*, July 5, 1928, p. 7.
60   An unnamed 'director' of Hartlepool United, when interviewed about the results of the FA Inquiry by the *NDM*, said, "If anybody was to blame for the position that has arisen … it was the amateurs themselves, who seemed never satisfied with the amounts allowed them as reasonable expenses." *NDM*, July 2, 1928, p. 4. For the distinctly vague descriptions of the expenses practices of Birmingham and several other English regional FAs at this time, see *Athletic News*, July 9, 1928, p. 12.

employed by virtually every county football association and the national body since the beginning of the twentieth century. It involved interpreting the crucial Rule 29 phrase 'necessary hotel and travelling expenses actually paid' as 'necessary hotel and travelling expenses *claimed to have been* paid'. Understanding the phrase in this way allowed football administrators to accommodate working-class realities by dropping the requirement that clubs pay expenses only as genuine reimbursements of properly receipted expenditures previously incurred.[61] For taken at face value the latter was certainly what the words 'expenses actually paid' seemed to imply. But they could *not* be taken at face value because, if they were, working-class amateurism would have been impossible. In fact, amateur football would have reverted to a monopoly of the middle and upper-middle classes.

But this linguistic manoeuvre, while it made working-class amateurism possible, entailed an obvious logical fudge – that claiming to have paid something is not the same as having 'actually paid' it. Thus, paying player expenses claims could simply be used as a way of paying them to play. And the FA itself, a mass of local football administrators, and a raft of middle-class critics, knew this. After 1885 it led the latter in particular to argue that such 'dishonest' *de facto* professionalism should be replaced everywhere by 'honest' *de jure* professionalism. But that demand too had to be avoided or evaded, because for the mass of English football clubs, 'proper' professionalism was just not economically sustainable. Therefore the fiction had to be maintained that paying expenses claims was the same as reimbursing expenses incurred. And the fiction *was* maintained, but only by observing an absolute silence about the obviously flawed logic at its centre.

In short, what Gramsci would have called the 'dominant' and 'subaltern' groups in football administration silently united to operate the only system which could square the circle, which could allow poor men to be paid for playing football without making them professionals. In so doing

61   Significantly, in its survey of the expenses procedures of other county associations ('What is Done in Other Parts'), carried out as part of its response to the Crook Town scandal, the *Athletic News* could find only one Association (Surrey) where accommodation expenses were only paid *after* receiving hotel-issued receipts from players. *Ibid.*

they allowed tens of thousands of working men to play the game they had come to love. 'Shamateurism' in association football therefore transcended class divisions by recognising and allowing for them but doing so in a way which could only operate so long as its fudges were not 'called out'. Crook Town's sin, therefore, consisted in calling them out and revealing what paying players 'expenses' for expenditures not 'actually paid' really amounted to.[62]

How one evaluates the FA's official position on amateurism between the end of the nineteenth century and 1974 depends, it seems to me, on how one weights intellectual honesty against social sympathy. It can be condemned as 'rank hypocrisy' if one thinks logical consistency is some kind of supreme moral virtue. But if one thinks that understanding the economic circumstances of others more disadvantaged than oneself is itself a virtue, and administering rules in a way which allows those people some latitude in accord with their disadvantage is another, then one will see, not hypocrisy here, but an unavoidable and socially compassionate compromise.

So much for the FA. What about the DFA? Was the DFA's, and even Crook Town's, unwillingness to shatter the silence by challenging the FA's conception of amateurism head-on an expression of ruling class 'social hegemony'? Were working-class football administrators in Durham publicly endorsing amateurist values they did not believe in out of a 'subaltern' ideological subordination to a hegemonic 'dominant group' – the Council of the FA?

Again, I don't think so. I think Dowling, Askew, Stephenson and others in Durham may have been endorsing a set of values that did not believe in, but not in submission to the FA's 'social hegemony'. On the contrary, they did it out of economic self-interest and social understanding and compassion, an understanding and compassion which was shared by the FA. In other words, it was not just the 'subaltern group' of county football administrators who were operating a strategically compromised conception of amateurism, so were the 'dominant group' in the national

62   One might ask why the recognition of class differences in football had to be elliptical and fudged and not direct and open. And the answer to that *is* a Marxist answer. In class societies the recognition of class is *always* elliptical and fudged, that is the essential mark of their being class societies!

association, and for precisely the same 'socially empathetic' reasons. So if the dominant group in football was exercising 'social hegemony' it was doing so through the values that it *shared* with the 'subaltern' group, not through values it was imposing on them.

At bottom in fact the whole situation was the precise reverse of that postulated by Gramsci. The 'subaltern' groups running the majority of county football associations were exercising a 'social hegemony' *over* the 'dominant group' because they represented the class interests of the mass of working men – the interests that had come to dominate association football as a sport. A minority of workers wanted to play football and benefit from doing so if they could,[63] and a much larger group wanted to watch the best possible 'amateur' football they could. In the conditions prevailing between the turn of the century and the 1960s only 'shamateurism' could bring both these things about, and the men who ran the FA knew that as well their 'subordinates'.

Conclusion: Retreat and Strategic Forgetting

Having said all that, we may now return, for one last time, to the Crook Affair, and consider its denouement. For once the FA Commission had issued its punishments, and the DFA had added to them by suspending itself, the issue inevitably arose of what was to happen next.

Logically, all the clubs suspended, along with Crook, could have opted to professionalise, as could the Northern League itself (and the Council

---

63   It is important to understand what this means. Matthew Taylor cites an FA estimate that "a few years before the 1st World War" there were 12,000 amateur football clubs in Britain, fielding between 300,000 and 500,000 players. (Taylor, *op cit*, p. 76) The vast majority of these men (they were all men) probably received little or nothing for playing – in that sense they were amateurs, 'working-class' amateur footballers. However, the vast majority of them would have accepted remuneration if offered, and many may have harboured ambitions of becoming professional players. Again, see Chapter 6 for a discussion of the broader significance of all this.

of the League seriously considered that.[64]) But such a course immediately encountered 'the Pearson problem'. Because, apart from anything else, once their shamateur players had become full-fledged professionals they had to be given season-long contracts, rather than being paid match by match. This meant that they had to be paid whether they were playing or not, and, in some cases at least, they also had to receive a wage in the off-season. And it is quite clear that, at least in the 1920s and 1930s, the income of even the most successful and well-supported amateur football clubs in Durham could not have funded that level of expenditure.

Another possibility was for the Durham Football Association to disassociate from the FA and create its own 'amateur' and 'expenses' rules, more openly reflecting working-class reality.[65] But doing so would have meant its ejection from all FA-controlled competitions, including the English Amateur Cup, by far the most lucrative competition in which its clubs competed. It would also have meant that outstanding young players from Durham would have been barred from joining Football League clubs, and from playing for any club, amateur or professional, in any league or competition still affiliated to the FA. And that last fact would surely have spelled doom to an independent Durham Association. Why would any ambitious and talented Durham footballer play for a club, or association of clubs, whose competitions were a guaranteed career dead-end?

To repeat then, the draconian outcome of its inquiry had put the FA in a difficult position and the DFA in an impossible one. Thus the 'sensational' events of June 30 and July 4, 1928 had no sooner occurred than both parties were scrambling – in the DFA's case desperately scrambling – to backtrack from confrontation and return to the *status quo ante*. Both parties had a motive (stronger in the DFA's case than the FA's, as we shall see) to 'close the waters over' as soon as possible, to restore the congenial silence, the silence which allowed shamateurism to be both known about and not known about. But how?

---

64   For discussions around professionalising the Northern League, see, for example, *Athletic News*, July 9, 1928, p. 12 and Johnson, *op cit*, p. 56.
65   For some discussions about this, see, for example, *NM*, July 6, 1928, p. 15 and July 7, 1928, p. 1.

A first attempt at rapprochement was made at a special meeting of the FA Commission, held in Sheffield on July 28, to which – after correspondence between the DFA Secretary, William Spedding and the President of the FA, Sir Charles Clegg – Dowling, Stephenson and Spedding were invited. At this meeting, the Commission agreed to reduce – from six months to one month – the suspension of a small group of Durham players who had been registered or signed as *de jure* professionals prior to its hearings in May. However, it refused to reconsider the generality of its suspensions, and Dowling expressed himself 'very disappointed' with this minimal concession.[66]

Nonetheless William Spedding remained in regular contact with the FA, and a fortnight later, on August 11, 1928, another 'special meeting' of the DFA was held in Durham, with Wall, Harry Walker (the vice-President of the FA), William Hardisty and Phil Bach attending as national representatives. Some progress seems to have been made, because the meeting 'unanimously' decided to 're-elect' the members of its self-suspended Council. Moreover, the tone of newly restored-President Dowling's remarks, (in reply to a question about the suspended players), was now decidedly upbeat:

> the chairman said that Mr. Spedding had made representations to the FA with regard to suspended amateur players of which he (the chairman) had great hopes. The matter was now *sub judice* and it would be indiscreet to say anything which might prejudice the discussion or affect the amateur players whose interests they all had at heart. If they took his advice they would let the Association deal with it.[67]

But Dowling's hopes were to prove illusory, at least initially. At its annual summer meeting, (held just three days after lifting its self-suspension) the DFA instructed its Secretary to write to Frederick Wall requesting an 'amnesty' from the FA for all the players suspended by the Commission for receiving 'fixed rate' expenses.[68] The rationale for this was that, without it, it would be impossible to begin the football season in Durham (due to start on August 25). This was because:

66   *NM*, July 28, 1928, p. 11.
67   *NM*, August 13, 1928, p. 9.
68   *NM*, August 16, 1928, p. 11.

In accordance with the definition applied to Rule 29 by the members of the Commission, the members of our Council have been compelled ... to advise all clubs and players in the county that they are liable to protests being lodged against them if a 'flat rate' has been paid for refreshment allowances – such allowances being 'irrespective of the amount disbursed by the players'. The decisions arising from such protests must be in accordance with the decisions of the FA Commission, and such procedures will not only affect our own clubs and players, but those affiliated to other associations. At the moment no other course is open to the governing bodies of the associations, and we, therefore, solicit immediate consideration of these ... facts in order that football may be successfully and harmoniously pursued on August 25th.[69]

In other words, the DFA argued that the practice for which the FA Commission had suspended the bulk of Durham players and officials was so widespread that its outlawing would make football impossible, not only in Durham but all over the country. For any club which had lost any match could immediately protest the result on the grounds that opposing players had been paid 'flat rate' expenses, and such appeals would always have to be upheld.

If the DFA thought that it had obtained the FA's tacit consent to an amnesty on these grounds, (if indeed Spedding's letter to Wall had been written on that assumption) it was to be sorely disappointed. Because, on August 28 the FA Commission, having considered Spedding's request, 'declined to vary their previous decisions' and recommended the FA Council to adopt their findings unchanged.[70] Once again, the DFA held Frederick Wall responsible for holding this hard line and for bullying others at the FA into accepting it. (They thought he did so because the FA was involved in a dispute with FIFA about the latter's willingness to allow 'lost time' payments to amateur players in Olympic football tournaments, and so had to appear 'whiter than white' on the issue domestically.)[71]

But whether that was true or not, the FA Council, while adopting its Commission's report, simultaneously offered an escape clause. Because:

69   Spedding's letter to Wall as reproduced in *NM*, August 28, 1928, p. 11.
70   *ibid*. It was in this reply to Spedding that Wall also denied the DFA's claim that the FA had knowledge of the paying of 'flat rate' expenses in Durham in 1927. See note 46 above.
71   See, for example, the story "Harsh FA Ban on Durham Clubs: Clubs Demand Its Removal" in *NM*, July 7, 1928, p. 1. "Mr H. Askew, Spennymoor, a vice-president

... in deciding that the report be adopted, [the FA Council] also decided that each player be given an opportunity of making an individual appeal for the removal of his suspension, and if possible reinstatement of his amateur status.[72]

Imposing multiple suspensions and then allowing individual appeals against them was a practice commonly employed, not only by the FA, but by all its member associations. It was an invariant practice of both the DFA's and NFA's player 'disciplinary committees', for example. And it was usually a prelude to generosity, even indulgence. If a player was punished (suspended and/or fined) for a playing or behaviour offence, but came before his association's disciplinary committee in person, appeared genuinely contrite and promised not to do it again, he usually had his punishment rescinded or reduced.

And so it proved this time. An FA minute for October 5, 1928 listed 59 Durham players who, on appeal, had had their suspensions reduced by two months, and four by one month[73] And the minutes of an FA Emergency Committee meeting of December 1928 had a similar list of Durham club officials having their suspensions reduced by a month.[74] In January 1929 the FA Council also extended the period for the payment of club fines – to March 1929 – in view of 'the industrial position in Durham'.[75] So it went on for the next four years, with one set of largely successful appeals succeeding another, until, in 1933, the very last of the player and official suspensions were rescinded. And because the FA Commission had suspended players and officials but not the clubs (which still had the bulk of their officials in place – despite most of them having been 'warned'), they

---

of the Durham FA ... said 'I am perfectly sure the Commission's findings is (*sic*) intended merely for Continental consumption. Those who have been following ... will know the acute situation that has existed for a considerable time between our own FA and the continental associations, in connection with the definition of an amateur." See also Johnson, *op cit*, p. 55.

72   *NM*, August 28, 1928, p. 11.
73   *FA Council Minutes*, October 5, 1928, p. 53. There also seem to have been further suspensions lifted on October 15. See Amos, *op cit*, pp. 489–90.
74   *FA Emergency Committee Minutes*, October 9 to December 3, 1928, p. 83.
75   *FA Council Minutes*, January 29, 1929, p. 94.

were all, including Crook, able to field teams from the beginning of the 1928–9 season.[76]

That said, the DFA never got its amnesty from the FA, despite a further campaign in late 1928 (led not by Dowling this time, but by William McKeag, the suspended chairman of Durham City FC) to try and obtain one.[77]

But if the amnesty did not materialise, neither, of course, did the torrent of match protests over fixed rate expenses. On the contrary, there were no such protests, clubs went on paying expenses and issuing 'receipts' for player claims, and no further questions were asked. In short, the waters *were* closed over, the soothing silence *was* restored, and although their continued to be inter-club spats over match results, player behaviour, and even, sometimes, the dubious amateur status of one or other player, no club ever again 'outed' its neighbours *en masse* the way Crook Town had done. For the Crook Town Affair had shown definitively that, whatever its momentary temptations and satisfactions, the dangers of this kind of whistle blowing were too great and the benefits too negligible for everybody involved. In essence, in 'the Crook Town Affair' an inter-club vendetta (between Crook and Bishop Auckland) had been allowed to get out of hand and to embroil football's ruling class (or caste) in a way which could only have one outcome. In football manager speak, Crook Town 'had given the ref no choice'. And that was never to happen again.

---

76   Crook, understandably enough, were denied entry to the Northern League for 1928–9, but having played that season in the Durham Central League, were readmitted in 1929–30. Amos, *op cit*, p. 490. That the FA's punishments were formally draconian but their practical effects minimal, might lead a cynic to see the whole Crook Town Affair as nothing more than an orchestrated 'ritual dance' between the FA and the DFA, designed to obscure, through a 'storm in a teacup', the tacit acceptance of shamateurism by both bodies. But I think that in this case such cynicism would be unjustified. It ignores, for example, the real differences between Peart and Dowling (and others) over what precise forms of 'shamateurism' were acceptable, and the FA's need to maintain control over the northern game while also keeping London elite amateur clubs onside.

77   See, for example, *NM*, September 1, 1928, p. 11.

Finally, and *a propos* of varying individuals, silence, doublethink, (and perhaps even ideological hegemony) one last incident is worth recording. Nearly a decade after the above events, in June 1937, there was a public meeting in Spennymoor to decide whether the town's football club, which was in severe financial difficulties, should continue as a professional club in the North-Eastern League or turn amateur. William Spedding, the DFA's long-serving secretary was present, and at a certain point addressed the meeting. According to the *North Mail*:

> Mr Spedding ... opened by saying that that he must disagree with Mr Askew's [the President of Spennymoor United's] statement ... that amateurs in Durham would not play for nothing. There were about 700 clubs in Durham ... and if you deducted the 50 professional clubs and the 50 top amateur clubs that left about 550 minor clubs, representing about 5,500 players, who, he was sure, played for the love of the game.

> The players who did not were the cause of the trouble, and the remedy lay in the hands of the clubs.

> If, when a player came along to an amateur club and demanded payment for his services, that club would report the player to the association, he could assure them that he would be satisfactorily dealt with.

Unfortunately the *North Mail* report does not tell us what, if any, response Harry Askew made to these admirable sentiments, although it is perhaps significant that, after quoting Mr Spedding's words, the reporter simply concluded his report with:

'It was decided to form a Spennymoor United Supporters' Club.'[78]

---

78 *NM*, June 2, 1937, p. 11.

Appendix 1

Player Statements in the Crook Town Dossier to the FA, February 2, 1928[79]

Voluntary declarations and statements in support of the contention of the officials and players of the suspended Crook Town AFC that certain other clubs are no less guilty of violating Rule 29 have been made before Mr. Joseph J. Devey, a solicitor and Commissioner for Oaths. Briefly, they are as follows:

John Ayre of 31, Unthank Terrace, New Brancepeth, coke oven worker, declares that he played for Shildon in the NE League in 1923–24 and received 10s per match although actual expenses only amounted to 3s. That he played for West Stanley in 1926–27 and was paid 10s a match although expenses only amounted to 3s 6d.

Thomas Anderson, of 19 Third Street, Delves Lane, Consett, coal filler, declares that playing with Ferryhill Athletic in the present season he was paid 8s 6d a match when his expenses were 2s 6d. When playing with Esh Winning previously he received 12s 6d for a match when his expenses were only 2s 6d.

George Benson, Byers Green, miner, declares that when playing with Willington in 1920–21 he received 7s 6d a match in addition to travelling expenses and during the succeeding seasons he was paid 10s a match in addition to travelling expenses. He further states that whilst playing with Spennymoor United in 1923–24 he was paid 13s 6d a match with the first team and 8s a match with the second eleven. In addition he was allowed travelling expenses.

Frederick Bissett of 27 Middle Street, Blackhall Colliery, miner, states that when playing with Hartlepools United in season 1925–26 he was paid 5s a match in addition to an average of 7s 6d for loss of work.

Fred Brookshank, of Witton-le-Wear, declares that playing for Bishop Auckland in season 1925–26 he received 5s and expenses when playing for the first team and 3s and expenses when playing with the second eleven.

79   Reproduced from Johnson, *op cit*, pp. 32–7.

William Richardson, 30, First Street, Delves Lane, Consett, a hand putter, states that during the season 1927–28 he played for Ferryhill Athletic Club, and that every match he played he was paid the sum of 8s 6d, although his out of pocket expenses only amounted to 2s 6d or thereabouts. He further states that an official of the Ferryhill Club told him that he would have been paid more, 'if the gates they were getting were anything like'. In the season 1923–24 Richardson states that he played for Consett Celtic FC and that for every match he played he was paid 5s, although his actual out-of-pocket expenses were nil.

Francis Smith of the Constitutional Club, Church St, Crook, states that during the season 1914–15 he played for Stanley United FC and that he received 7s a game in addition to tea, although his actual travelling expenses to Stanley from Crook were about 6d. During the season 1921–22 he played for Willington and states that he was paid 12s, which included his travelling expenses to Willington. During the season 1923–24 he played for Bishop Auckland FC and he alleges that for the first match at Scarborough he was paid £1 5s which included loss of work for the Saturday and Monday after the match. Smith further alleges that playing for Bishop Auckland against Stockton in the Benevolent Bowl Competition he received the sum of £2, and that in other games in which he played for Bishop Auckland he was paid the sum of 5s and expenses.

Thomas Wilson, of 10 Station View, West Auckland, a miner, states that when he played for Bishop Auckland FC against Scarborough several seasons ago he received 15s each time in addition to his travelling expenses. When on tour he was paid 21s in addition to all expenses "because everything was found." This was given as spending money. Wilson further states that during the season 1911–12 he played with Spennymoor United Football Club and received 15s for each game he played. During the season 1912–13 he further states he played with Willington FC and on one occasion he received the sum of £2 10s for playing against Crook Town in the Benevolent Bowl.

John Wallbanks, a miner, of 13 North Terrace, Chopwell, states that during the season 1926–27 he played as an amateur for Annfield Plain FC, and for matches which he played with the club he was paid 14s and on other occasions he was paid 10s. His actual travelling expenses amounted to 2s 4d.

Fred Colling, of The Holmes, Crook, states that he played for Darlington FC as an amateur in 1920–21, and was paid a minimum sum of 15s a match in addition to travelling expenses. In the same season he also played for Darlington RA and was paid from 7s 6d to 30s for a match.

Thomas Leo Duffy, 70 Eastbourne Rd, Darlington, Corporation clerk, states that he received from Bishop Auckland in 1924–25, five shillings a match in addition to travelling expenses, and an allowance for dinner. Playing for Ferryhill Athletic the following season he received 12s 6d a match when the team won, 10s for a draw, and 7s 6d for a lost game. All these payments were paid in addition to travelling expenses.

Edward Ellis, of 2 Lister Terrace, Crook, school teacher, states that he was paid 4s 6d for playing a practice match with Bishop Auckland at the commencement of the present season, and his expenses only amounted to 3d.

Alfred Elliott Hartford of 17 Ferndale Avenue, East Boldon, states that about three years ago he played for South Shields as an amateur. For each match in which he played he received £1, including travelling expenses from his home, which amounted to 11d. The same players states that in 1923 and 1924 he played for Durham City as an amateur. For each match in which he played with the reserves he received 15s in addition to his expenses. When he travelled with Durham City first team he was paid extra for loss of work. During 1926–27 Hartford states that he played for Ferryhill Athletic and received the following scale of payment – 12s 6d when they won, 10s for a draw, and 7s 6d when they lost. These payments were in addition to travelling expenses which were paid by the club, but in all cases the payments included remuneration for lost work.

Robert Jones of 6 Woodhouses, Grahamsley, Crook, states that that when playing for West Stanley in 1915–16 he was paid the sum of 10s in addition to expenses. In 1921–22 and 1922–23 he played for Willington and he received various amounts, ranging from 10s to £1 a match. During 1926–27 he played for Spennymoor United and received amounts varying from 10s to £1 a match.

John William Scott of Mafeking Street, Sunderland, a labourer, states that during the season 1926–27 he played for Craghead FC as an amateur. In some matches he alleges he was paid 7s 6d, whilst in other matches he was paid 9s – his actual expenses to Craghead being 2s 3d. On one occasion he played for Craghead against Stockton and was paid 12 6d.

Robert Thomas Mills, of 9 Derwent Terrace, Washington Station, states that in 1925–26 he played for Langley Park, and received 15s for one match, including travelling expenses, which amounted to three shillings or thereabouts.

Norman Marshall of Broad Oak Cottage, Hamsterley Colliery, says that he played for West Stanley and received 15s for each first team match in which he played, the 15s being in addition to travelling expenses.

George William Longstaff of 31 Carlton Terrace, Spennymoor, a school teacher, states that he played for Spennymoor United FC in the season 1924–25 and he received the sum of 10s for each match he played, and when playing at home his expenses were nil.

Robert Alderson Kipling states that during the season 1927–28 he received the sum of 15s for each game he played, in addition to his travelling expenses.

Robert W. Etherington, 7 Victoria Avenue, Crook, printer's apprentice, alleges that when playing for Willington in season 1925–26 he received 11s 6d for a Northern League game with Stockton. His expenses were sixpence. Playing for Shildon the following year he was paid 7s 6d a match in addition to travelling expenses. He also played with Stanley United during this season and received an allowance of 2s 6d a match, in addition to his expenses.

Arthur Stephenson, 1 Sandringham Road, Roker, Sunderland,[80] states that in August 1927 he played in a practice match for Bishop Auckland at Bishop Auckland. Afterwards he was asked what his expenses were, and he replied 3s 6d. That amount was handed to him along with 3s to pay for his tea. He then asked for payment for loss of work, but was told that the club would not pay anything for loss of work, but he alleges that subsequently the expenses amount was increased to 6s and he was given 3s for his supper. In all he received 12s although his actual expenses were 3s 2d (*sic*). Stephenson has signed a further statement in which he alleges that he was approached by Chilton Colliery RA Club and asked to sign for that club. He was promised payment for loss of work.

George William Munsey of 8 South Street, Langley Park, states that during 1927–28 he played for Consett and received 5s for signing. On one occasion he travelled as a reserve to Burnhope, and he was paid 5s, his actual out-of-pocket expenses being 1s.

Matthew Pears of Arthur Street, Crook, states that during the year 1890 or thereabouts he played for Bishop Auckland Reserves and received travelling expenses, pay for lost time, and 5s and sometimes 6s for playing.

---

80   The very same Arthur Stephenson who, just a month earlier, had "written correspondence" with the second DFA Commission attesting that he had "received from Crook Town … remuneration above his hotel and travelling expenses actually paid." One can imagine the pleasure with which Fred Peart included this statement in Crook's dossier, particularly since, this time, Stephenson's allegations concerned Bishop Auckland. (Probably the player himself did not think either statement a big deal!)

Frank Richmond of Queen Street, Witton Park, states that during 1923–24 he played for Bishop Auckland against Stockton. He travelled in a car sent by the club from Durham to Stockton and after the game was paid 7s 6d, although actual out-of-pocket expenses were nil.

John Watson Scott, 9 Glebe Road, Harrowgate Hill, Darlington, states that during the season 1924–25 he played for Shildon FC, members of the North Eastern League, and that against Workington at Shildon he received £1 for his travelling expenses, although the actual amount was 1s 9d. He signed for the payment of £1 and 1s 9d in two books.

Arthur Stallard, 73 Leybourne Road, Darlington, a fitter, states that when he played for Darlington Reserves he received 10s for each game in addition to travelling expenses, which were nothing. He further states that when he played for Consett during the present season he received £1 in addition to his expenses. For all other games he received 25s in addition to his expenses.

David Robson, of 24 Short Street, Shildon, says that he played for Bishop Auckland about 1924–25. He received 5s tea money and full third class rail fare from Kirkby Stephen and West Hartlepool, whenever it was necessary for him to travel from these places. As a railway employee his actual fare from Kirkby Stephen was about 2s 2d. He always had tea at home and his out-of-pocket expenses were only 2s 2d, although he received from the club the full railway fare – somewhere about 8s 6d – and 5s tea money in addition.

Stanley Edward Grieves, of 21 Violet Cottages, Sunderland, bootmaker, states that Durham City paid him 10s for each match he played over a period of three seasons in addition to his travelling expenses. On each occasion when he travelled as reserve he was paid £1, travelling and hotel expenses being paid for him. From Esh Winning in 1925–26 he declares that he received 10s a match plus travelling expenses. He alleges that he was approached by a member of the Bishop Auckland Committee at the start of the present season and an arrangement was made whereby he was remunerated for lost work.

Thomas Hall, 35 Sandringham Road, Crook, by-product worker, declares that when he played for Spennymoor United in 1907–08 he received 10s a match over and above actual expenses.

William Richardson, of 30 first Street, Delves Lane, Consett, says that in 1927–28 he played for Ferryhill Athletic and was paid 8s 6d although his actual out-of-pocket expenses amounted to 2s 6d. In 1923–24 he played for Consett Celtic and for each match was played 5s although his out-of-pocket expenses were nil.

Arthur Drury Sams, 6 High Hope Street, Crook, played for West Stanley FC in two practice matches in the season 1920–21 and alleges that he was paid 5s for each match, although his travelling expenses were nil. He also played for Annfield Plain FC as an amateur and for the first two matches he was paid 17s 6d per match. For all other matches which he played for Annfield Plain FC he was paid 17s 6d per match, with the exception of the last match which he played for this club, for which he was paid for loss of work, receiving £1 13s, his actual travelling expenses averaging about threepence.

David Rhees Thomas, of 6 Victoria Street, West Auckland, a miner, states that for four seasons he played for Bishop Auckland FC and that whenever he had to miss work to play football he was always paid for his lost work, in addition to his travelling expenses.

John William Hutchinson, 21 Whessoe Lane, Rise Carr, Darlington, iron worker, alleges that during the season 1922–23 Cockfield paid him £1 a match, which included travelling expenses amounting to about 4s 6d. The following season he received £2 10s, which included expenses amounting to about 5s. He further alleges that during the present season Consett have paid him £1, including travelling expenses.

Joseph Emerson Seymour, 24 Thirlmere Street, Milkwell Burn, Hamsterley Colliery, states that during season 1925–26 he played for Annfield Plain and that in each match he was paid £1 in addition to the usual hotel and travelling expenses. Seymour also played for Spennymoor United FC in a cup tie and was, he alleges, paid £1 although his travelling expenses were only about 3s or thereabouts.

Thomas Temple, 34 First Street, Horden, miner, states that when playing with Spennymoor United in 1925–26 he never received any less than 15s a match plus expenses. In the following season with Ferryhill he was paid 12s 6d in addition to expenses and during the present season Consett FC in the NE League paid him £2 10s for playing against Shildon, and in other games he has received 16s a match including expenses of 3s.

George Kirby of Albert Terrace, Peases West, Crook, alleges he received payment of 7s 6d in addition to expenses for playing in one game for Stanley United FC.

Appendix 2

Rule 29 of the Football Association on Allowable Expenses and other Payments to Amateur Players, as it was in 1927 and 1928

Players are either amateur or professional. *Any player registered with this Association* as a professional, or *receiving remuneration or consideration of any sort above his necessary hotel and travelling expenses actually paid, shall be a professional.* Training expenses of Amateurs other than the wages paid to a trainer or coach must be paid by the players themselves. *Amateur players receiving any payment must give a written receipt for the same, stating particulars of expenses, and secretaries must produce such receipts to the Council of this Association at any time if required to do so.* If an Amateur player is engaged by a Club in any capacity for which he receives remuneration, the Club may be required to prove, to the satisfaction of the Association, that his services as a player do not affect the amount of remuneration paid to him. A player competing for prize money in a football contest shall be a professional. When a player is registered as a professional he at once loses his status as an amateur. When an Amateur player is injured while playing football he shall, upon obtaining the consent of this Association, or the local affiliated Association, be entitled to receive his Doctor's fees, or the proceeds of any benefit match, subscription or collection, without losing his amateur status.

[Sections of particular relevance to the 'Crook Town Affair' are italicized.]

FA Communique to Clubs re. Allowable Payments to Amateur Players following the FA Commission of Inquiry into Durham Clubs, June 1928

An amateur may have paid to him or refunded to him:

1. Railway, motor, tram, boat etc. fares or other necessary expenses actually incurred by him in travelling from and to his home or work or for the purpose of playing a match.

2. Hotel expenses, that is, necessary meals during the day and sleeping accommodation if absent for more than the day during the actual and necessary absence from home for the purpose of playing in a match.

Extravagant or unnecessary expenses must not be paid by a club and every amateur player must give his club a detailed statement of expenses incurred with a receipt for the sums paid to him. It is the duty of a club's secretary to ask for such a statement and receipts, and to keep the same for production at any time if required.

Payment for loss of time, compensation considered or remuneration of any kind other than the items included in (1) and (2) automatically makes a player a professional and renders both him and his club liable to punishment.

Source for both passages: *NM*, July 2, 1928, p. 10

CHAPTER 6

Conclusions: Football as a Commodity

In the introduction to this book I said that my interest in my research project 'waned markedly once the North-East became recognisably the football region in which I had grown up' and that the main reason for that was 'my distinctly ambiguous attitude to the *commodification of football*'. It is now time for me to say what I meant by that, and doing so will require me to centralise my identity as a social theorist and philosopher rather than as a football fan (which I still am, despite everything) or as an amateur historian of the game (which is all I consider myself to be.) So this chapter will make use of ideas which are rarely explicitly encountered in the historical or contemporary literature on football. Nonetheless I will make continual reference to the earlier chapters of this book and to football history generally, as I develop them.

Commodification and Moral Qualms

In a capitalist economy nearly all material goods – cars, buses, screws, paint, steel, textiles, butter, pork, refrigerators, computers, sound systems, jewellery and a million other things – are commodities. That is to say, they are all *sold for money* (which is all that one means by calling anything a commodity). But commodities are not only sold for money, the vast majority are produced by means of money. In conventional economic terms the 'inputs' to such production (raw materials or components and production machinery in the case of physical commodities, the physical infrastructure used – buildings, equipment, etc. – in the case of services) are themselves commodities.

However, there is one type of commodity that is *not* produced monetarily but is still sold for money – human skills or abilities. And in so far as such skills and abilities are an essential input into the production of all other commodities, this commoditisation of human creativity was seen by Karl Marx, and is seen by many other people, as the most economically profound and the most socially and morally problematic aspect of capitalism.[1] But irrespective of whether one agrees with this last point or not, it is true that, if left unimpeded, capitalist or free market economies will convert an ever-greater number of goods, services *and* human abilities into commodities, and this is all I mean by capitalism's strong 'commoditisation' or 'commodification' tendency.

Although commodification is endemic to capitalism, moral and political doubts about it are most frequently expressed when either (a) certain human needs are supplied as commodities – housing, health care, education, water or energy, etc. – or when (b) things are bought and sold as commodities which it is thought should be outside 'the cash nexus' altogether. These include human beings themselves (slavery), sexual intimacy (sex work), or physical or psychological health and wellbeing (access to health professionals or lawyers).

That commodification is mainly objected to when supplying certain needs or when it demeans the people commodified, makes the commodification of sport a particularly interesting and complex case. For neither the playing nor spectating of sport seem to be essential needs, and the commodification of 'sports labour' surely does not demean the 'labourers' – the sports men and women – whose labour is commodified. Yet, in the case of football and of other sports there *were* people in Victorian England who objected to their commercialisation and professionalisation from the beginning. I mean those advocates of 'amateurism' who objected to commercialisation on the grounds that people should be playing health-giving

---

1   Skills and abilities can be improved by training, and if training labour is paid labour then, to that extent, skills and abilities can be monetarily enhanced. But enhancement is not production, and to date at least the biological and social processes that produce human beings with their numerous and varied abilities (and disabilities) are mainly *not* money-mediated. It follows that I think that most human abilities are innate, that though they can be improved by training and experience, their origin precedes both. For a broader discussion see my *Karl Marx and the Philosophy of Praxis*, (London: Routledge, 1988) especially 106–19.

sport rather than watching it, and to player professionalism on the ground that it encouraged a 'win-at-all-costs' attitude in place of the amateurist ideals of 'fair play' and pleasure in sport 'for its own sake'.

As already noted (see Chapters 4 and 5), Victorian amateurism has not, to put it mildly, had a good press in modern sports history. Apart from allegations of dishonesty and hypocrisy, (did amateurs really not play to win? Did they really always put enjoyment of the game ahead of its result?) the most common criticism has been that amateurism was a class ideology masquerading as a set of moral values. For in the conditions prevailing in Victorian Britain only a minority of middle and upper-middle class men could afford to play sport at an elite or serious level without payment, and, as we saw in Chapter 5, that remained the case well into the twentieth century. And I agree with all these criticisms. I have no doubt that Victorian amateurism *was* a class ideology and that its advocates rarely lived up to the values they espoused, that they were often guilty of hypocrisy.

And yet and yet; from the first both football professionalism and football 'shamateurism' *do* seem to have been driven by, and reinforced, a 'win-at-all costs' mentality. More importantly, from the moment good footballers were paid (openly or clandestinely) for playing, then, logically enough, they tended to want to play for those who would pay them *most*. Thus were planted the seeds of professional football as it is today – a game which, at its elite levels at least, tends to align competitive success very closely with wealth – with the wealth of football clubs and those who own them, but also with the wealth of players as individuals.

1. Commoditisation and contemporary football

The 2018–19 football season was witness to an astounding phenomenon. The finals of both Europe's premier club competitions – the Europa League and the Champions League – were played out exclusively between English clubs.

But this formally 'English' triumph had a marked downside. Because 'six of the ten richest clubs in the world' being members of the EPL,[2] whilst

---

2   A quotation from Barney Ronay, "European finalists deliver a very English great moment forged overseas" at https://www.theguardian.com/football/blog/2019/may/10/great-english-football-moment-champions-league-forged-overseas>.

it makes those clubs powerful international competitors, also severely distorts the national competition in which they play. As many people have noted, the EPL has become not one but three competitions; a largely fixed 'top six' group of clubs competing for the League title itself, a shifting middle group of six to eight clubs competing to be 'the best of the rest', and a fierce competition between a shifting bottom six or eight to avoid relegation. To put that more simply, at any given point in time, supporters of 14 or so of the EPL's 20 clubs are following teams which have *no* realistic chance of winning the competition of which they are formally a part.[3] In that respect at least, they are simply 'making up the numbers', and for the most obvious, most crude, most commercial of reasons. They simply aren't rich enough to recruit the quality of players (or more precisely the number of such players) necessary to win the EPL. And the same is true of all the other elite football leagues in Europe. They too – all of them – are divided between a small minority of clubs with a real chance of winning, and a majority of permanent 'also rans'. The only difference is that those leagues tend to be bifurcated rather than trifurcated, with the 'best of the rest' category little developed and the minority of potential league-winning clubs even smaller than in the EPL.

And here we come to the heart of the worry about the commoditisation of elite football – a worry not about lack of money leading to unfulfilled needs – but a worry about football *competition* itself. When struggling to resist the abolition of its maximum wage the Football League

---

3   "Forty-nine clubs have competed since the inception of the Premier League in 1992. Six of them (i.e. 12% GK) have won the title since then. Manchester United (13), Chelsea (5), Manchester City (4), Arsenal (3), Blackburn Rovers (1) and Leicester City (1)." Wikipedia entry at https://en.wikipedia.org/wiki/List_of_ Premier_League_seasons>. But this is actually only a continuation of a longer running trend toward ever-narrowing competition. "While eight clubs won the title [the English Division 1 title – GK] in the 15 seasons between 1947 and 1961 only 11 clubs were successful in the 34 seasons from 1961 to 1995 with just 5 of them, Liverpool (13), Manchester United and Everton (4), Arsenal and Leeds (3), sharing 27 of these titles … here is stark evidence of the revolution in English football that the changes of the early 1960s were to set in motion." Dave Russell, *Football and the English: A Social History of Association Football in England, 1863– 1995* (Preston: Carnegie, 1997), 126. See also Taylor, *op cit*, pp. 272–4 and 426–8.

warned that doing so would lead to a concentration of football talent in a handful of clubs,[4] and this argument turned out to be no less true for being self-interested. For this is precisely where unconstrained player wages have led, and there are two important questions one can ask about that.

The first, and more obvious, is whether any football competition as distorted as the EPL, will be able, in the long run, to retain the loyalty of its fans and spectators. And that question is even more pertinent in the case of that huge majority of English football fans who support clubs which cannot hope even to reach the EPL, let alone win it.

The second more profound question underlying the issue of competitiveness, concerns the nature of 'the football commodity' itself. What is it that people are *buying* when they watch professional football, either in person or through subscription media? Is it the beauty of the game? Is it the skills of the players? Or is it the competition among football clubs, and the 'hope eternal' which springs in the breast of every fan at the beginning of every season? For if it is the latter, then the appeal of professional soccer (and thus the monetary demand for it) will ultimately be vulnerable to what one might call 'the death of hope'. For if the vast majority of clubs and their supporters have no hope of winning football's 'glittering prizes' then either such supporters must be content with lesser successes – winning promotion to the EPL, or to the Championship or League 1, avoiding relegation from the EPL ('again'), winning the Checkatrade Trophy – or they must transfer their support to the tiny handful of clubs which have some 'realistic' chance of turning hope into supreme achievement.[5]

The possibility that the commoditisation of football – which means at bottom the commoditisation of *football players' abilities* – may destroy it as a hope and dream-fuelled competition in turn prompts wider reflections.

---

4   See the discussion in Leanne O'Leary, *Employment and Labour Relations Law in the Premier League, NBA and International Rugby Union* (Dordrecht: Springer, 2017), 28–9.

5   And that has indeed happened. There is even a name for it – being a "glory fan". You can just pick a team to support on the basis of its success or 'glory', or you can support a 'glory' club or team in addition to a less successful 'home' or 'native' one. For a discussion, see Taylor, *op cit*, pp. 372–5.

Earlier, I noted that the supplying of human needs as commodities was central to most moral and political reservations about commoditisation. However, I must now say that I do not believe in the distinction between wants and needs, at least not as some kind of 'universal' or 'essential' difference between types of human want. Therefore, I do not think that a coherent critique of commodification can be based on it. This is partly because there is no non-subjective way of making it. (In all times and places some peoples' wants *are* other peoples' needs, and *vice versa*). But it is also because which wants are classified as needs is itself something that changes over time. As many people acquire the money to satisfy ever more of their wants 'through the market', so some of those wants – like housing or health care or education – come to be reclassified as 'needs'. And the main point of that reclassification is to support the demand that all people – including poorer people who cannot satisfy them by paying – should nonetheless have them satisfied.

Moreover, I think that football is only one of several examples showing that the real reason people worry about commodification has nothing to do with the wants/needs distinction. Rather, commodification produces most moral qualms when it undermines or destroys something valued or essential in what has *been* commodified. When fine paintings are commodified, beautiful objects become 'investment vehicles' and appreciators of art are replaced as buyers by astute investors and /or hoarders of wealth. When housing becomes entirely commodified it becomes a route to homelessness. When education becomes commodified it becomes a means of acquiring valuable social contacts and social 'caché' as well as, or even in place of, education. When health care becomes commodified it becomes a route to perfectly avoidable sickness. And when football becomes commodified it replaces broad-based competition with oligopoly or (in extreme cases) duopoly or monopoly, which means it displaces the hopes and dreams of the majority by the monotonously repeated achievements of the minority. And note: all these concerns are valid irrespective of whether one defines fine art, or housing, or education, or health care, or the supply of clean water, or the watching of football, as a 'want' or a 'need'.

In the case of professional football however, it is highly unlikely that this trend – towards the ever-tighter alignment of competitive success with club wealth– will be changed unless it becomes unacceptable, either to a majority of players, to the most powerful football clubs, or to the majority of fans. What are the chances of any of these things happening?

Opposing Football Commodification? The Players?

I: The Professionals

In the case of professional footballers it might seem, at first glance, that it is hardly worth asking whether they might oppose, or even have reservations about, the commoditisation of football. For are they not its prime beneficiaries?

But things are not quite so simple, because the data also show that, while the real incomes of all football professionals have risen consistently since the 1960s, and have done so much faster than most other employee groups, the inequalities in earnings between the best-paid and worst-paid professional footballers have also risen sharply. Thus, in the most recent year for which figures are available, the average annual player salary in the EPL was over £2.5 million, while the figure for the Championship was £324,000, for League 1, £69,400 and for League 2, £40,350. Thus in 2018 the 'average' EPL player earned no less than sixty-four times the salary of his League 2 compatriot, and eight times more even than an 'average' player in the Championship.[6]

But also note two further complexities. First, the very best-paid players in the EPL in 2018 were earning at least seven times the league average (i.e. £350,000 a week or more), more than 450 times what the 'average' League 2 footballer earned! Second, although the League 2 footballer's average salary may appear (and is) a pittance in comparison with that of EPL 'stars', it was

---

6   All figures for footballer salaries are either from *Sporting Intelligence*, Global Sports Salaries Survey, 2019, https://globalsportssalaries.com/> or 'Lower league footballers' salaries', www.sportrac.com>.

still 22% more than the average male wage in England in 2018 (£32,960) and almost double the average female wage (£22,381).

Therefore, how likely the mass of professional footballers are to oppose this explosion in elite player earnings (and the narrowing of competition which has accompanied it), depends on how they weight their absolute privileges *vis-à-vis* the bulk of the working population against the ever-growing relative inequalities amongst them. All the evidence to date suggests that, whatever their feelings about the latter, it does not outweigh the former in shaping their attitudes and behaviour.

The main reason for that is that there are not only huge differentials between the best and worst player wages in the EPL, there are individual wage differentials at every level of the Football League, and indeed in every club. In all these contexts therefore, players can hope that, if they improve their performances, they can significantly raise their wages, either through bonuses, or improved terms when their contract is renewed, or (of course) by gaining a transfer to a club in a higher league or division. In fact, the average figures given above, although useful for making gross comparisons, actually serve to obscure the most important point about footballer wages – that these averages mean nothing existentially (as against statistically) because footballers live in a world of individual relativities, not of national, league or even club 'averages'.

The professional footballer is above all then an *individual* possessor (and seller) of a skill or talent, is treated as such by the club that employs him, by the manager and coaches who superintend him, and indeed by the fans who watch him. In that respect, he is exactly like an individual musician, or artist, or highly skilled artisan. And that individualism means that, economically at least, he is not like other 'workers' – not a purveyor of some quantum of undifferentiated 'labour time' which can, in principle at least, be readily supplied by some other worker currently in the dole queue or doing 'the same job' somewhere else.

And that has been true, it appears, from the very beginnings of professional football in Britain. Even before professional football was legalised in England, and long before its legalisation in Scotland, elite players were remunerated, in one way or another, for playing. As early the late 1870s (in Scotland) and the early 1880s (in England), the very best players could also raise their earnings well above their club compatriots, by demanding match and other bonuses, 'loyalty payments' for staying with a club, and 'signing on' fees when joining other clubs. It also appears that *de facto* transfer fees existed in football from the 1880s too – long before their formal legalisation by the Football League in 1904.[7]

Indeed, it was precisely to constrain the strong bargaining power of the best players (*vis-à-vis* the clubs for which they played) that the FA legislated a maximum wage for Football League clubs from the 1901–2 season on. But as Tischler emphasises, that innovation took fifteen or more years to enact and was profoundly controversial. Throughout the 1880s and 1890s it was the subject of agonised, and explicitly ideological, disputation among club chairmen and others. For most of these men were classical Victorian 'self-made' men and devotees of 'laissez-faire'. They were deeply committed to the notion that the price of anything – including the labour of workers – should be set by 'the free market', without 'interference' by governments or trade unions. But if they followed this conviction through into football, they simply legitimised the enormous bargaining power of those players with rare talent to sell. Faced with this conflict between an abstract principle and the reality of being 'on the wrong side' of a bargaining power equation, the majority of football club owners and administrators finally decided to ditch the principle and use legislation to control the 'free market' in footballers.[8]

However, the maximum wage, even when supplemented by the infamous 'retain and transfer' system, was still not enough to constrain the bargaining power of the best players.[9] During the sixty years of its operation

---

7   See Steven Tischler, *Footballers and Businessmen … op cit*, pp. 42–5. For the shadowy early history of transfer fees, legal, illegal and semi-legal, see Dobbs, *op cit*, pp. 54–5. It is unclear whether players received any part of these early *de facto* fees, and as far as I know this issue has never been investigated.

8   Tischler *op cit*, pp. 60–4.

9   On the maximum wage and its operation, see Tischler, *op cit*, p. 95, Taylor, *op cit*, p. 75, Vamplew, *op cit*, pp. 7–9, and, p. 224 and Russell, *op cit*, p. 49 and, pp. 145–6. See also Neil Tranter, *Sport, Economy and Society in Britain* (Cambridge: Cambridge University Press, 1998), 68–9 and Fishwick, *op cit*, p. 80. The problem, as all these authors stress, is that we simply do not know (since such practices were illegal) what proportion of players were remunerated, in cash or kind, *above* the maximum or by how much. The conventional wisdom is that

in England, ways, both legal and illegal, were continually found to circumvent 'maximum wage' restrictions for those players. Moreover, although
clubs could 'retain' players and even force them to play, they could not
force them to play *well*, so outstanding players had an obvious means of
obtaining a transfer if they really wanted it.[10] Indeed, all that happened
in the 1960s was that elite players realised that, with the enhanced revenue coming into clubs from mass media coverage as well from gates, they
could earn yet more by dispensing with the maximum wage entirely (and
weakening the 'retainer' powers of clubs in the transfer system) than they
could by informally circumventing these controls. And it was precisely because the PFA won the support of elite players in its campaign to abolish
the maximum wage that it was successful.[11] Because, once again and 'as

---

'flouting' of the maximum wage was 'widespread', that clubs "routinely broke the
rule, offering extra financial incentives to attract and retain the best players" and
that most such floutings went "undetected as it was neither to players' nor club
officials' advantage to report them." (Entry on 'Corruption' in Richard Cox, Dave
Russell and Wray Vamplew (eds) *Encyclopaedia of British Football*. London: Frank
Cass, 2002, 72.) Certainly, *all* the best-known maximum wage 'scandals' – the
Billy Meredith case of 1906, the Leeds City and Sunderland scandals of 1919 and
1957 – were revealed, not by unprompted investigations or monitoring by the FA
or FL, but as the result of power struggles or quarrels within the clubs involved
which led to leakings of corruption allegations and evidence. As shown by the
'Crook Town Affair' (Chapter 5), the FA (and the FL) infinitely preferred to turn
blind eyes to under-the-counter player payments unless absolutely forced not to.
But, for what it is worth, in 1910, 573 of an estimated 6,800 players in England (i.e.
just over 8%) were officially receiving the maximum £4 per week (Taylor, *op cit*,
p. 75 and Vamplew, *op cit*, p. 224). £4 was nearly double the highest weekly wage
in the top decile of workers' wages in 1906, so that footballers earning even half
that (£2 per week) were still very well paid in comparison with the bulk of people
watching them (Tischler, *op cit*, p. 95). By the 1950s some 30% of players were receiving the then maximum of £20 per week, but the disparity between footballers'
wages and those of other workers was probably smaller than in the Edwardian and
inter-war periods. (On this, see Russell, *op cit*, p. 145).

10   See Vamplew, *op cit*, p. 213 and, pp. 244–9, Fishwick, *op cit*, pp. 89–91, Taylor *op cit*,
      pp. 75 and 228–30.

11   See among a mass of references Vamplew, *op cit*, pp. 5, 8–9, 84, 224–5 and 246.
      Tranter, *op cit*, pp. 68–9, Russell, *op cit*, pp. 146–51. Fishwick, *op cit*, pp. 40 and
      89–90 and Young, *op cit*, p. 221.

always', withdrawal of labour by star players immediately threatened the revenue, and thus the financial viability, of the clubs for which they played.

In short, the 'banal' observation that I made earlier about Victorian Britain, 'the moment good footballers were paid (openly or clandestinely) for playing, then ... they tended to want to play for those who would pay them *most*' – turns out to be no banality at all. On the contrary, it encapsulates a logic and a practice based on it, which shaped the entire subsequent trajectory of the game. Football players operating that logic consistently over time gradually turned a 'workforce' into a minutely hierarchised set of individuals whose fate was entirely determined by the comparative rarity of their talent. By that I mean that talent differentials determined highly varied wages from the outset. But they also determined a player's ability to move club and to resist or circumvent the maximum wage and the retain and transfer controls while they existed. And 'in the end' their extraordinary abilities provided elite players with the power to remove all obstacles to the free working of 'demand and supply' in the market for their talent. So now, in the early twenty-first century, released from all regulatory constraints, an outstanding player's talent enables him to obtain huge 'media', 'commercial' or 'sponsorship' earnings in addition to massive wages – to become a millionaire, multi-millionaire, even a billionaire from his earnings.

II: The 'Amateurs'

'In 1974 the FA Council abolished the amateur/professional distinction in soccer.'[12] This apparently simple assertion turns out to be surprisingly complex in its implications. It does not imply (obviously) that all the footballers or football clubs under the FA's jurisdiction suddenly became 'professional' in 1974. Equally obviously it does not imply that they all became 'amateur'. It does not even imply that all footballers and football

---

12 See History of the Football Association http://www.thefa.com/about-football-association/what-we-do/history>. This decision also meant the end of "The Amateur Cup, the England Amateur Team and the Great Britain Olympic Team." *Ibid.*

clubs that were not 'professional' in 1974 suddenly became 'amateur' in that year. It simply means that, from 1974 onwards, in the eyes of the FA, all footballers were footballers and all football teams and clubs were football teams and clubs.

But why are these propositions not just tautologies? Because they both enshrine a crucial distinction, the distinction between playing football without remuneration *as a matter of fact* and doing so *as a matter of principle*. To say that 'all footballers are footballers' is to say that, even if they are not playing for remuneration, they are not 'amateurs' in the Victorian sense. At any given moment, all the players in a small town or village football club somewhere in England are playing for no monetary or other remuneration. However, among those players there are:

(1) Older players who once played for remuneration, but for one reason or another can no longer do so ('ex-professionals' playing on 'in retirement')

(2) Young players who want to play for remuneration and will go on to do so (they are 'good enough')

(3) Young players who want to play for remuneration but will *not* go on to do so (they are not 'good enough'). And – making up the overwhelming majority

(4) Younger and older players who dream, or have dreamed, of playing for remuneration but who know they have no chance of doing so. (They recognise, and have long recognised, that they are not 'good enough' but they still enjoy playing.)

In short, in abolishing the amateur/professional distinction, the FA implicitly said that all that differentiates Lionel Messi from Larry Massey (who plays as an attacking midfielder for a works team in Enfield) is that the former has realised his dreams and the latter has not. All that differentiates Christiano Ronaldo from little Ronnie Christie (who plays as a striker for a South Barnsley comprehensive school team) is that the former has realised his dreams and the latter has not (yet?). All that differentiates Gareth Bale from Karl Byrne (who plays as a semi-professional for Boston

United[13]) is that the former has realised his dreams much more than the latter. And therefore, all that differentiates Liverpool Football Club from Liverwart Football Club is that the former is full of young men who have realised their dreams and the latter is full of young men who haven't.

In effect then, in 1974 the FA said that a 'real' amateur would be someone with the skills of a Messi, or a Ronaldo, or a Matthews, (or a Bloomer or a Meredith), who, confronted with a would-be employer waving a massive wad of cash or a blank cheque, would say (his back half-turned, arm out-stretched behind him), 'get thee behind me Satan. I shall of course continue to play my brilliant best for Barcelona, Juventus, Blackpool, Derby County, Manchester City, etc., but I shall also continue to earn my living, as I always have, as an architect/school teacher/coal miner/turner/road sweeper.' Have there ever been any amateur footballers who behaved like that, or even roughly like that? Well possibly a few – but certainly a *tiny* few – in comparison with the millions of boys, men, girls and women who play, or ever have played, the game of football 'just' for the love of it. This, in essence, is what the FA officially and belatedly recognised in 1974, when it abolished the amateur status in football.

In doing so it also made William Spedding's statement to that meeting in Spennymoor in 1937 (Chapter 5) retrospectively inaccurate. He was right, no doubt, to say that 550 or so of Durham County's 'about 700' football clubs were 'minor clubs', with no professional or even 'shamateur' players. But he was wrong to say that therefore they were 'amateur clubs' composed of 'amateur players'. Because even if all their 5,500 players *were* 'playing for the love of the game', this did not mean that all of them always had, or that *any* of them would if they were 'good enough' to play for money as well as love.

And all that has another implication. Football became a commodity, and footballers' abilities became commodities, from the moment it was discovered that large numbers of people would pay to watch them, from the moment football became a spectacle and footballers the heroes of that spectacle. But from that moment, football as a spectacle (and thus as

---

13   He actually did at the time of writing.

a commodity) also began to colonise, not merely the activities and bank accounts of a few footballers, but the dreams and aspirations of all footballers. Football is not merely an individualised hierarchy of professional players, it is a vast individualised hierarchy of all players. And in that hierarchy the highest professional level is the focus of aspiration, dream and (in a few cases) memory, for an enormous pyramid below it, a pyramid whose base reaches right down into parks, schools and playgrounds as well as into – (what shall we call them?) – the mass of non-professional clubs.

In short then, there is little or no chance that the mass of amateur footballers would oppose or try to reverse the commoditisation of football, for, in an ideological sense, the vast majority of them are not, and never have been, amateurs. They are just football players whose abilities have ceased to be, or have never been, commodities. They are footballers who are not part of football as a commodity, although many (most?) of them would have liked to be or have dreamed of being.

Opposing Football Commodification? The Clubs?

Football clubs became commodities from the moment that they became limited liability companies, and the first clubs to convert to limited liability status (in the 1890s) did so mainly to fund ground improvements. The capital cost of such improvements required clubs to take on debts, and under pre-existing 'membership' structures, all club members became individually liable for those debts, a risk that very few 'ordinary' playing or non-playing members were willing to take.[14]

The very few studies of the origins and functioning of football clubs as limited companies have focused on two issues above all – the social composition of shareholding and shareholders, and the question of whether, in Wray Vamplew's words, football clubs were/are 'profit-maximising' or 'utility-maximising' businesses.[15] The latter question in particular is an

14   Vamplew, *op cit*, p. 86 and Taylor, *op cit*, p. 72.
15   Vamplew *op cit*, pp. 82–7.

interesting one, because, as Steven Tischler suggests, it may not be decidable simply by looking at the published profits figures of clubs or the dividends they paid to shareholders. It is possible that, in the Victorian and Edwardian periods and for a long time afterwards, the local businessmen who mainly bought and ran football clubs may have benefitted indirectly from club and/or fan *expenditure* as well as from dividends. This was particularly true if, for example, they owned breweries, or hotels, or construction or catering companies. In short, expenditures that appear, in their accounts, as deductions from club profits, may have converted into increased profits and earnings for club directors.[16]

However, as Wray Vamplew's impressive and still unique book shows, it is hard enough to research the formal accounts of clubs, it is effectively impossible to trace these more informal revenue flows and their effects. It is notable, for example, that, while Steven Tischler raises these 'indirect' ways for directors to make money from football as a logical possibility, he produces no direct evidence of it happening, and there are two major problems (at least) in doing so. If one is researching the issue historically (as Tischler is, his book is entirely concerned with the late Victorian and Edwardian periods) there is highly unlikely to be any surviving documentary evidence of such profits, and informants who might have known about them are usually dead. And if one is researching the issue contemporaneously, asking a football director or directors how much money they are making 'on the side' from their directorships (as against how much they make formally from fees and dividends) is unlikely to yield reliable answers or (therefore) evidence.

Moreover, and despite these problems, I am (like Vamplew, and most other people who have examined the issue) inclined to believe that most football clubs and directors were and are 'utility maximisers'[17] Their prime aim is indeed competitive success, with the level of profits they earn (if any) being a side effect of that success, rather than their central objective.[18] So

16   See Tischler, *op cit*, chapter 4.
17   Vamplew, *op cit*, pp. 82–7 and Taylor *op cit*, pp. 70–3.
18   See Vamplew, *op cit*, Table 8.3 for the average net profit figures of 22 English and 10 Scottish football clubs in the period 1906–14. As the table shows however, these averages meant very little, because deviations from the mean were so enormous

while there may be/ have been 'Tischler-type' exceptions to this general-isation for particular club directors at particular times, I accept the oft-repeated assertion that 'nobody ever got rich from owning a football club' and that 'prestige' and local community 'status', were, and are, the main motives leading people to become football directors.

The main reason I believe this is simple enough. If a club is successful and highly profitable (in gross terms) as a result, its aim is to remain so, which usually means spending large amounts of money on player wages and transfers, thus reducing gross profits (and dividends). And if it is *not* successful (and has low profits or even losses as a result) its aim is to become so, which usually means spending whatever money it can afford, or borrow, on player wages and transfer fees. Since at any one time only a small mi-nority of clubs can be successful, most clubs find themselves, most of the time, increasing 'success-seeking' expenditure to whatever level they can afford without going bankrupt, rather than maximising profits and divi-dends. In short then, although there may be/have been some exceptions, it is generally true that neither football clubs nor football directors get rich from football. It is football *players*, and a few other people (managers and coaches above all) who get rich from football. Football clubs are places where people who have got rich from other activities *spend* their riches in the pursuit of status and prestige. And that is as true now, when the own-ership of at least some British football clubs has been globalised, as it was when they were all domestically owned.[19]

(from a net loss of over 150% of share capital for Birmingham City to a net profit of 152% for Newcastle United.) These large variations were due to the playing suc-cesses and failures of individual clubs at the top level and to a generally lower level of club profitability in the lower leagues. For example, all four English non-league clubs and both the Scottish second division clubs in Vamplew's sample made net losses, as did half the English second division clubs. But this was because clubs with ambitions to enter their respective Football Leagues, or to gain promotion to their first divisions, spent money to improve their teams. This expenditure "lowered profits, increased debts and undermined their tangible assets ratio, but to such clubs expenditure was of less concern than footballing status." *ibid*, p. 87.

19   Until relatively recently football clubs were limited liability companies but *not* publicly listed companies – that is, their shares were not traded on stock ex-changes. As a result, there was little or no *speculative* dealing in football clubs or their shares. But that may now be changing. The purchase of SAFC by Stewart

It follows that it is football players, rather than directors, who have always been the primary beneficiaries of football as a commodity. They were the primary beneficiaries of the football 'business' before the maximum wage was introduced, and (as we saw from the Sunderland case – Chapter 4) even before clubs became limited liability companies Despite appearances, they were still its primary beneficiaries while the maximum wage (and the retain and transfer system) were in operation, and they have continued to be its primary beneficiaries since the maximum wage was abolished and the transfer system 'relaxed' in favour of players. The only thing that has changed is how rich some players, (and some managers and coaches) can now become as such beneficiaries. And that is mainly a function, not of clubs radically changing the way they spend their revenue. (It is mainly spent in the pursuit of success now, as it 'always' was.)[20] It is primarily a result of many clubs having far more revenue to spend in absolute terms (from media coverage above all) than they ever had before. In other words, when clubs had much less revenue (exclusively from gates) most of it found its way into players' pockets (despite the maximum wage, etc.) and professional football players were generally far better off than the average worker as a result. Now that clubs have much more revenue it still finds its way primarily into players' pockets (and bank accounts and share holdings) and now they are not merely well off in comparison with the

---

Donald's 'Madrox' company looks like a classically speculative transaction – the leveraged purchase of an 'undervalued' asset with the aim of rapidly 'restructuring' it and then reselling at a considerable profit. If it was, it badly misfired, mainly because the club failed to obtain the 'quick and cheap' promotion from League 1 to the Championship that would have immediately raised its resale value. Whether the purchase of NUFC by Mike Ashley/Sports Direct was a speculative transaction is less clear, but he/they have certainly been unwilling to sell the club at anything less than a considerable profit. Note also that shares in a number of major European football clubs *are* now listed on stock exchanges. (See https://uk.advfn.com/football> for details.)

20 Vamplew shows that, before 1914, nearly 65% of the expenditure of eight English football clubs was on player wages and transfer fees, while in the same period ten Scottish clubs spent over 62% on wages alone (they were probably net recipients of transfer revenue). He also suggests that the bulk of other expenditure was on ground improvements. Vamplew, *op cit*, pp. 84–7 and Table 8.2.

average worker, many of them are rich, and some of them incomparably rich, as a result. *Plus ça change ...*

Football clubs then are no more likely than football players to resist, or want to reverse, the commoditisation of football, but for a rather different reason. Football clubs exist to be competitively successful, and in a commoditised game the only way for them to do that is to buy, and retain, their most valuable commodities – their 'good' players. And the only way to do that, is to pay them the maximum possible wages affordable without the club going bankrupt. To put it brutally, it is true of *every* football club, (from the EPL down to League 2, and into the 'non-league' world) that it needs its best players more than they need it. And so long as that is true, so long is every football club on the same treadmill, put there by its players.

It follows that it is only if clubs are prepared to act collectively that they could even modify the commodisation of football (let alone end it). But, in Britain at least, they have tried that once (the maximum wage, etc.) and it never really worked. 'Player power' undermined it significantly while it was in operation and terminated it when the cost of retaining it became too high for the best players to tolerate. Moreover, the ownership of elite European, as well as British, football clubs has now become globalised. So any collective action by clubs now would have to be trans-national, and is surely even less likely as a result. Furthermore, collective action among clubs, just like collective action among footballers, is severely compromised by both the ceaseless competition among them, and the forms of hierarchy to which that competition leads. I now turn to this latter.

Competitive Hierarchy and Hierarchy of Place

In one of the notes to Chapter 3, I observed that when Mercutio joined *The Newcastle Daily Leader* in 1885, Sunderland FC and Newcastle East and West End were just three of a clutch of Durham and Northumberland football clubs that were broadly on a par in terms of support and playing strength. In the case of the two 'central Newcastle' clubs their serious rivals included three clubs from mining villages (Shankhouse,

Bedlington Burdon and Sleekburn), three 'suburban' Newcastle clubs (Elswick Rangers, Elswick Leather Works and Rendel) and a club from a small Northumberland market town (Morpeth Harriers). In the case of Sunderland, its serious County Durham rivals included six teams based in five Durham towns (Gateshead, Birtley, Darlington, Stockton and Bishop Auckland), a Durham University team, and two teams from suburban Sunderland (Whitburn and Southwick). Yet when Mercutio left the North-East, just seven years later, all this had changed. Sunderland was already a Football League team and enjoying support and revenue dwarfing not only all its 'old' County Durham rivals, but all the Newcastle and Northumberland clubs listed above.[21] By 1892 in Newcastle, the West End club had collapsed and East End was on the verge of becoming 'Newcastle United'. And by the late 1890s, even before the club's great Edwardian days, attendances at NUFC matches were beginning to exceed those at Sunderland. By that time too the St James' Park club had dwarfed all other Tyneside and Northumberland clubs which had once been able to challenge it. In short, in the space of a decade an intense, and broadly equal, competition of football 'minnows' on Tyneside and Wearside had been replaced by the NUFC/SAFC football 'duopoly' which has lasted, with various ups and downs, to this day.

There is no mystery as to how and why this happened, because it was happening all over the country in the 1880s and 1890s. Playing success depended on playing strength, playing strength depended on club revenue, and in this period (and for the first sixty or so years of the twentieth century) club revenue depended almost entirely on the size of 'gates'. And obviously clubs in large urban centres found it far easier to attract large crowds than clubs in villages, small towns and the satellite suburbs of cities. (And this was particularly true in the late Victorian period when poorer working people often went to matches on foot.)

Football club owners and administrators were clearly aware of this spatial dynamic, and its longer-term implications, from the 1880s onwards – that is, from the earliest years of professionalisation and commercialisation.[22]

21   See Chapter 3, note 9 above.
22   See Tischler, *op cit*, p. 81.

Indeed, the fear that club financial strength would become a simple function of spatial location was one of the factors making the maximum wage attractive to the pioneer professional clubs of Lancashire. Based in the smaller cotton towns of north-west Lancashire (Blackburn, Bolton, Preston, Accrington, etc.) the directors of these clubs feared that, in a market 'free-for-all' for football talent, they would ultimately lose out to clubs based in the 'rising' urban metropolises of Liverpool, Manchester, Birmingham, and (ultimately) London.

They feared this centralising dynamic, and its consequences, because they had already seen it operate *within* Lancashire to marginalise what had once been significant clubs like Darwen and Turton. Indeed, just as the dynamic had operated in the North-East to create a Sunderland-Newcastle duopoly out of what had been a broadly equal clutch of minnow Northumberland and Durham clubs, so it had operated in the Midlands to produce the domination of three Birmingham clubs (Aston Villa, Birmingham City and West Bromwich) out of a mass of smaller West Midlands rivals, and in south Yorkshire to produce the Sheffield 'duopoly' of Wednesday and United out of the clutch of South Yorkshire 'peri-urban' clubs that had once made up the 'Sheffield Association'. Therefore, if such a 'power concentrating' dynamic could operate regionally, why could it not operate nationally, and reduce what had once been regionally (even nationally) dominant clubs to comparative minnows?

The answer was that it could, and it did. As the twentieth century wore on British professional league football came to be dominated by clubs based in a handful of the country's largest urban centres – Glasgow,[23] Liverpool, Manchester, Birmingham and London above all. And as part of the same process, clubs based in the smaller urban conurbations – of north-west

---

23   Glasgow is anomalous though, because it was a major hub of commercialised football long before these other UK metropolises, and even before Lancashire and other English 'early adopter' regions. In fact, it was the first such hub in Britain, emerging as such in the second half of the 1870s. It was *not* anomalous however in its ultimate development, producing the Rangers/Celtic duopoly out of what had originally been a clutch of smaller Glaswegian and peri-Glaswegian clubs. For an excellent synthetic account, see Tony Collins, *How Football Began ... op cit*, chapter 7.

Lancashire, the east Midlands, south and west Yorkshire, and Tyne and Wear – were reduced to a kind of 'second tier' elite status, trying desperately (and mostly unsuccessfully) to retain their competitiveness against the metropolitan 'giants'.

And then, in the 1990s, came the 'globalisation' of British elite football, with the ownership of clubs slowly being detached from local capital and business, and passing into the hands of a number of 'super-rich' individuals, companies and conglomerates from the US, the Middle East and Asia. To date this globalisation of club ownership has not produced any really major shifts in British football power, because it is the already dominant metropolitan clubs produced by domestic concentrations of capital and support, which have proved the most attractive targets for the richest foreign buyers (Arsenal, Chelsea, Spurs, Manchester United, Manchester City, Liverpool, etc.)

But though this is true, it is also true that the globalisation of club ownership has brought into even sharper focus an uncomfortable truth about competitive power in a commodified sport – that since it can always be purchased by money, it can just as readily be lost to more money. And this becomes ever truer as professional football globalises and the competition for outstanding football talent becomes ever fiercer. In football, as in other areas of life, globalisation glaringly reveals what has always been true of life under capitalism, but not (perhaps) so obviously or blatantly – that however brightly and warmly the sun of success may be shining on you now, it may move on across the sky (the whole sky, the global sky) at any moment, leaving one in shadow, if not in total darkness.

So we can conclude that no attempt to rein in (let alone eliminate) the commoditisation of football is likely to come from players or clubs. In the case of players, a highly individualised pursuit of 'success' stretches all the way from the most obscure school, youth or local community team players, through non-league and lower league clubs, to the stars of the Premier League. All footballers share the same dreams and aspirations, even if only a tiny few realise them. And making money always plays a part in those dreams and aspirations, even if an apparently secondary one behind 'fame' and 'success'.

In the case of clubs, it is precisely the most powerful and successful clubs, whose support would be necessary for any even limited de-commoditisation of the game to occur, who benefit most from its continuance. It is true that the huge revenue flows which both enable and result from a club's playing success, are always potentially unstable. Playing success depends ultimately on attracting and holding 'the best' players, and as 'the beautiful game' becomes global, and ever more competitive as a result, there is always the danger, even for the richest of clubs, of being out-competed (which means out-monied), for the services of elite players by someone, or something, even richer.

But even though they all experience these fears and insecurities, all the football clubs of Britain (and of France, Spain, Italy, Germany and the Netherlands) are on this competitive treadmill and see no way of getting off it. And as things stand, they are right. In fact the only way in which this 'treadmill-producing' link between club income and playing success could be loosened (let alone broken) would be if it came to threaten professional football itself as a commodity – which means if people *en masse* ceased to watch or support it. What are the chances of this? That question immediately brings us to:

Opposing the Commodification of Football? The Fans?

The psychology and behaviour of the fans of professional football teams have defeated the expectations of observers from the very beginning. Writing in 1895 C. B. Fry opined that:

> The crowds who flock to see two football teams play in the North or Midlands like a good match, but their predominating desire is to see their own champions win, and this desire is made the more intense by the fact that the players are fellow-townsmen with whom they are in touch, or whom perhaps they know personally.[24]

---

24   C. B. Fry, 'Football', in *Badminton Magazine of Sports and Pastimes* (1895), p. 484, quoted in William J. Baker, 'The Making of a Working-Class Football Culture', *Journal of Social History* 13 (2), 1979, pp. 241–51. Quote is from p. 248.

From which one might infer that if the players were *not* 'fellow-townsmen' and *not* 'known personally' to those watching them, the desire of fans to see 'their own champions win' might become *less* 'intense'. But this inference, though logical, turned out to be false. It is true that, as we saw (Chapter 4) when Scottish players were first imported to SAFC, in the late 1880s, there was a 'backlash' against this within the club which led to James Allan's resignation. But it seems that this hostile reaction, and the attempted formation of an exclusively local Sunderland Rovers club, was more an expression of frustration and disappointment among the club's playing members (and of other members' suspicions of Allan's financial probity) than any popular movement among its nascent fan base. And the very categories of 'member' and 'playing member' became antique once SAFC became a limited company (in 1896).

Equally, there is no evidence that the supporters of any of the pioneer professional clubs in Lancashire had their ardour dampened, or their pride in their clubs' successes dented, by the knowledge that those successes owed a lot to Scottish players. And the same could be said of fan attitudes towards Sunderland's 'Team of all the Talents' of the 1890s or to Newcastle's great Edwardian team, both of which were strongly Scottish in composition. It is notable in fact that nearly *all* the disapproving comments about 'imported' players that football historians have turned up, come either from disgruntled devotees of amateurism, or from late Victorian and Edwardian sports journalists. (The overlap between these two categories being considerable until the inter-war period.) For example, Andrew Walker is clearly talking about men of this sort writing for the *Lincolnshire Echo* when he says:

> Whilst by the early twentieth century there seemed to be no expectation that professional footballers should be locally-based in order to receive positive reports within the local press, this had not been the case in the 1890s. During this decade, considerable concerns were expressed in the pages of the local papers about the proliferation of Scottish players employed by English league clubs.[25]

---

25   Andrew Walker, *op cit*, p. 458. Tischler, *op cit*, p. 46, quotes three highly critical comments on early Scottish imports to Lancashire clubs. But two of them are from editions of the *Athletic News* for 1882 and the other from an edition of *The Athlete* for 1884, precisely the kinds of 'amateurist' sources which are dubiously

It is also notable that while Steven Tischler instances a number of reasons why some Scottish players returned 'prematurely' to Scotland from Lancashire in the early 1890s (to be, as he says, 'whitewashed' back to amateur status) local fan hostility does not seem to have been one of them.[26]

So from the very beginning football fans have *not* required their heroes to be of local origin. They cheered them on (up to the 1960s), irrespective of where they came from in the UK and Ireland. And since the 1960s, they have continued to cheer them on irrespective of where they come from in the entire world.

But perhaps even more remarkably, football fans not only do not require (although they like) their team heroes to be locally born, they also do not require them to share (even roughly) their material standard of living. As we have noted, most professional players were paid wages well in excess of skilled (let alone unskilled or semi-skilled) working men and women from the very beginning. Up to the 1960s, these wages did not place professional footballers in a completely different economic realm to the majority of football fans. But especially when supplemented by bonuses and testimonial match revenues, they certainly enabled players (at least if they saved and had decent luck with injuries) to fund a lifestyle in retirement significantly more affluent than enjoyed by most of the people who watched them in their playing days.

---

typical of ordinary fan views. And as Tischler himself says, these "same 'imports' attracted a great deal more popular enthusiasm, measurable in the huge crowds that turned out to watch the better teams play." In fact, "teams signed 'imports' because they were good players and attracted good gates." *Ibid*. And to be fair to C. B. Fry, in the same piece in which he suggested that club 'champions' were often locally born, he also noted that Scottish "invaders from across the Border ... were soon identified with their new home, and became to all intents and purposes natives." Baker, *op cit*, p. 248.

26   "While relatively high wages lured many players great distances, monetary compensation was not always sufficient to induce professionals to work on distant soil. The separation from families and friends, the general uprooting of their lives, and the recognition of the realities of professional football work terms and conditions prompted many to return to their native districts." Tischler *op cit*, p. 100.

And since the 1960s the economic situation of professional footballers, not only in Britain, but all across Europe, has been qualitatively
transformed, and has taken many of them into an economic 'stratosphere'
bearing absolutely no relation to that of even better-off fans. In the UK
alone, wages at the very lowest professional levels allow for considerable
affluence, and at the higher levels they now make players rich by almost
any standards.

One has only to review the crude averages instanced above to have these
only-too-well-known truths rammed home. The 'average' Championship
player earns ten times the UK average male wage and over fourteen times
the female wage. Even an 'average' League 1 professional earns twice the
average male UK wage and over three times the female. As for the EPL,
even a player earning the 'average' Premier League salary earns 76 times
the average UK male wage, and no less than 111 times the female. But the
global stars of the Premier League are in another category entirely. In 2018
the highest paid players in the EPL earned wages which equalled more
than 550 times the average male wage in the UK and 813 times the female
wage. In other words, they earned more – far more – on every day of their
contracts than most of the people watching them earned in a year. Figures
like this are frequently quoted, in the tabloid press and elsewhere, and not
infrequently they are accompanied by words like 'greed', 'obscene', 'breath-
taking', 'unbelievable', etc.

And yet, not only do most football fans not speak in these terms, they
do not seem to begrudge even the most stupendously paid of their heroes
their riches, *provided that* (and it is a crucial proviso) they 'earn' this money
by making their club and team successful. One of the most extraordinary
revelations of reading the online 'fanzines' of NUFC and SAFC today,
is that the vast majority the fans of both clubs (and in this I am sure they
are entirely typical) not only do not begrudge the stars of 'their' club their
enormous wages, they are constantly pressing the directors of both clubs
to spend yet more money on transfers and (if necessary) wages, in order
to acquire, or retain, the services of some star player or other. In fact, one
has the strong sense that if their directors were to behave as many of their
fans want them to, both SAFC and NUFC would actually be bankrupt,

rather than continually skirting its margins.[27] One could say that this is at least in part because, being very far from rich themselves, most fans have no intuitive grasp on the magnitude of player wages, or indeed on the economics of football clubs as big, or even medium-sized, businesses. But even if that is true, it does not make their sentiments here any less economically generous, at least on the surface (see below).

Moreover, and as part of the same outlook, contemporary football fans, not only do not require 'their' club to be locally owned, they are often the most vociferous supporters of foreign takeovers, if the latter will enhance, or even holds out hope of enhancing, the club's competitive position. Our club is currently owned by a Uruguayan consortium which is putting in millions. But there is a rumour that a Russian consortium is interested and will put in hundreds of millions. Bring it on! Then perhaps 'next season' we will really be able to challenge for the league title! In other words, fans appear as sanguine about the commodification of football clubs as they are about the commodification of footballers.

In one sense all this is quite impressive. It seems that contemporary football fans are prepared to bestow their favour, and their enthusiasm, not only 'cosmopolitanly' across national, religious and even (these days) continental boundaries, they are equally prepared to bestow them across positively cavernous economic divides. As long as our brilliant young Cameroonian striker keeps on banging in the goals he will be honoured, and even loved, despite his black skin, his Islamic religion and the £250,000 per week he is earning. Because, despite all that, he is 'our' striker and banging in the goals for 'us'. And the same goes for 'our' Saudi or Thai chairperson so long, of course, as s/he keeps banging in the millions. Certainly, wherever that old Conservative *bête noire* – 'the politics of envy' – may operate, it is not in football!

---

27 This was as true of SAFC fanzines as of NUFC ones until SAFC plummeted into League 1 following two successive relegations from the EPL and the Championship in 2016 and 2017. The severely reduced revenue that followed meant that the club *had* to cut the wage bill savagely just to survive. But while SAFC fans reluctantly accepted that in general terms, it seems, from reading *A Love Supreme* and other sites, that wage cuts are still not acceptable if they lead to the loss of some favoured player or other.

The Football Club as Totem

Many academic observers have noted this (in other respects and contexts) 'extraordinary' and 'surprising' cosmopolitanism and socio-economic 'generosity of spirit' of football fans. But what explains it? For me the psychologically most plausible explanation riffs on Émile Durkheim's analysis of totemism in his *Elementary Forms of the Religious Life*.[28] On this account, football fans, like the Australian aboriginal people whose religious beliefs Durkheim was supposedly analysing, are ultimately worshipping themselves (but as a community, not as individuals) *through* worship of 'the totem'[29] And that explains why it is a matter of indifference to them whether the wearers of the totem are from England, Scotland, Ireland, the Ivory Coast, Argentina or Iraq, or whether they earn £5 a week, £250 a week,

---

28 Émile Durkheim, *The Elementary Forms of the Religious Life* (1912), translated from the French by J. W. Swain (New York: The Free Press, 1915). The analysis of totemism is found in Book 2, pp. 121–93.

29 Since I am now an Australian resident and citizen it especially behoves me to say that Durkheim's analysis of Aboriginal 'clan' totemism as a 'simple' or 'primitive' form of religion, was long ago debunked. His whole discussion relied on one source, which was probably inaccurate about the central Australian people it described, let alone about all Aboriginal people. In addition, wide-ranging criticisms have been made of *The Elementary Forms* …, as an 'sociological' explanation of religious belief in general. For a detailed discussion see Steven Lukes, *Émile Durkheim: His Life and Work: A Historical and Critical Study* (Harmondsworth: Penguin, 1975), especially 462–84 and 506–29. However, although profoundly problematic as an explanation of religious belief, Durkheim's analysis of totemism had greater plausibility (as many of those same critics said) as an account of crowd or collective *social psychology*, which is why it has been suggestively applied both to politics and sport. It appears that the earliest attempts to apply Durkheim's sociological account of religion to sport (though not specifically to football) date from the 1970s. For an overview, see Susan Birrell, 'Sport as Ritual: Interpretations from Durkheim to Goffmann', *Social Forces*, 60 (2), 1981, 354–76. See also Michael Serazio, 'The Elementary Forms of Sports Fandom: A Durkheimian Exploration of Team Myths, Kinship and Totemic Ritual', *Communication and Sport*, 1 (4), 2012, 303–25. I first came across the idea applied specifically to football fandom in Anthony King, 'The Lads: Masculinity and the new consumption of football' *Sociology*, 31 (2), 1997, 329–46.

or £250,000 a week. Because the players, whoever or whatever they are, are of significance only when, and for so long as, they wear the totemic shirt, and because their exertions are only a means to the psychic triumph of the community of fans. Apparent fan worship of club and players, is, in reality, simply a 'totem-mediated' form of *self*-worship. The 'cosmopolitanism' and 'economic generosity of spirit' of football fans turn out, dispiritingly, just to be disguised forms of self-love, but of collective, not individual, self-love.[30]

This neo-Durkheimian account seems to me the most psychologically and sociologically plausible explanation of the surprisingly tolerant attitude of football fans towards 'their' (but only 'their') players' nationalities, ethnicities, religions or incomes.[31] But whether it is or not, the behaviours themselves have the same implication. One can no more look to fan 'disgust' at the massive riches of footballers or the ever-narrowing competitiveness of professional football, to reverse, or even qualify, these trends, than one can look to the massive inequalities among players, or the 'competitive desperation' of football clubs, to do so. For on the one hand fans always see player riches through the most myopic of partisan lenses, that is, as perfectly acceptable for 'our lads', but 'disgusting' for theirs (which means, in effect, not morally disgusting at all). And on the other, as I have already noted, fans also have mechanisms for either ignoring, or psychologically

---

30   This also implies that the brilliant young Cameroonian striker is *not* loved at all. It is the totemic *shirt* he wears that is loved, so when he removes it permanently, all 'love' for him disappears. But this is not, it should be emphasised, because of his nationality, race or religion. Fan 'love' for him would disappear just as quickly and completely if he were English, white, Protestant and paid £350,000 a week. The point is that the worshippers of the club totem are race, religion *and* economic-blind, but *only* for strictly defined purposes and periods.

31   Plausible but difficult to prove. Its plausibility lies in its accounting for the 'cosmopolitanism' and 'economic generosity of spirit', of people who, in other contexts, may not manifest much of either. It also very plausibly explains why fan tolerance of a player's ethnicity, religion or massive earnings collapses as soon as he transfers to another club. But how could one prove or disprove it? Clearly *not* by asking any football fan whether s/he worships the club shirt as a totem; or by asking fans *en masse* whether, when they cheer for their team, they are 'really' cheering themselves as a community or collective. Durkheim's theory manifests the same difficulty as all 'unconscious' or 'sub-conscious' explanations of human behaviour.

compensating for, professional football's ever-narrowing competitiveness and relegation of the majority of clubs to 'also-ran' status.

Football and Class: The Past

But even if everything above is true, why is it important for football history and historians? Because a great deal of football history, and certainly some of the best, has been written from a neo-Marxist class and cultural perspective drawn from the work of E. P. Thompson above all. In this perspective (of which Steven Tischler's fine book is a classical and self-conscious case)[32] football is seen as a major aspect of something called 'working-class culture', football players and football fans share a 'working-class' identity, and (in Tischler certainly) the relationship of footballers to the clubs that employ them is seen as directly analogous to the relationship of any other group of 'workers' to their capitalist employers, that is, it always involves the exploitation of the former for the benefit of the latter.

Tischler's book is not historically inaccurate, and nor are the many other football histories with the same class perspective. From the last two decades of the nineteenth century to at least the 1960s, association football *was* an overwhelmingly 'working-class' game in two senses – the bulk of its fans were working class, and the bulk of its players (professional and 'amateur') were also, at least in background.[33]

But while this is true, and one should always be wary of rewriting history through hindsight, one cannot help being struck by certain tensions in Tischler's account, if one is reading it in the second decade of the twenty-first century. For example, his close analysis of professional football

---

32   Tischler, *op cit*, pp. 1, 8 and 12.
33   There is widespread agreement on this, despite the fact that, though there is a mass of impressionistic observation of the sort I quoted in Chapter 3, there is very little or no 'hard data' on the social composition of football crowds for this early period, and only slightly less sketchy information on the occupational backgrounds of players. For a discussion, see Taylor, *op cit*, pp. 91–2.

in 1890s Lancashire brings out clearly that, even in these earliest days, the wages (and more informal rewards) earned by Bolton Wanderers or Preston North End or Blackburn Rovers players, were already far greater than those earned by the vast bulk of the working-class spectators watching them. As he stresses, this is precisely why increasingly worried club owners were attracted, often despite their own ideological predilections, to the idea of a maximum wage and the tighter 'tying' of players to clubs.[34] Despite these insights however, Tischler unquestioningly aligns the formation of a football players' union in 1907 with other expressions of Edwardian union militancy (on the docks, mines and railways, etc.). And he does so despite the fact that, on his own account, the enthusiasm of many players for abolishing the maximum wage, let alone for strike action to do so, was distinctly lukewarm.[35]

In short then Tischler's book, sets out, in a traditional 'Marxist' way, to present the relationship of football players to football clubs as simply a relationship of 'labour' to 'capital'. But he understands that, in the traditional 'social history' manner, as a relationship between classes, that is, between football 'workers' and the club-owning 'capitalists' or 'bourgeois' who employ and exploit them.[36] But it is clear now that, at the top echelons of the game at least, the sale of rare football ability can actually turn workers *into* bourgeois, (if one still wants to use those terms). It can turn young men who, initially, have 'only their football abilities to sell' into

34   Tischler, *op cit*, pp. 42–8, 60–5.

35   *ibid*, pp. 105–20. Tischler makes clear that the formation of a Players Union in 1907 was primarily intended to "restore free market relationships in football" and that the failure to strike in 1909 was due, at least in part, to "the satisfaction of some footballers with a relatively high wage" under the maximum wage regulations (pp. 110 and 118).

36   Tischler supports this view of Victorian and Edwardian footballers – as being exploited just like other workers – by reference to their vulnerability to injury, the general shortness of their careers, and their often-poor employment prospects once their footballing days were over, and there is undoubtedly much to these arguments historically. *Ibid*, pp. 95–9. But radical improvements in sports medicine over the twentieth century, and the sharp rises in footballers' wages since the 1960s have seriously weakened them, at least for players in full-time professional football (i.e. from the League 2 level upwards.)

owners of their own businesses, and even (these days) into controllers of large share and real estate portfolios. And it does so because the very rarity of those abilities when they are commodified actually puts those players in a power position (an 'exploitative' position?) *vis-à-vis* their employers.

In short, we can see now, in the twenty-first century, that there are relations of labour to capital that are commodity but *not* class relations. Those relations continue, in the vast majority of cases, to benefit employers far more than workers, but there are also a few cases, of which football is one, where they benefit the latter more than the former. In fact it is both trends operating simultaneously that produces ever-increasing inequality in modern service economies. I want now to explain the broader social and political importance of all this. Doing so will require me to make some explicitly theoretical observations, not only about contemporary football but about contemporary capitalist societies generally.

Commoditisation and Class: A Hypothesis

To put the matter simply, the history of football is just one example and demonstration of a much broader truth – viz. that if commodification of labour is maintained for long enough and spreads widely enough, *it dissolves social classes and class divisions themselves*, at least where 'classes' are understood as groups of people having a shared relation to Capital.

I should be clear what I mean and do not mean by this assertion. I do *not* mean that the dissolution of classes means the reduction of economic inequality. On the contrary, it is part of a process whereby economic inequalities become *more* extreme but are individualised. I do *not* mean that when classes dissolve workers cease to be exploited by those who employ them. On the contrary, such exploitation may become far worse, because collective forms of resistance to it are markedly weakened. I *do* mean however, that the commoditisation of labour in modern 'service' economies gradually dissolves social classes, because the level of remuneration of labour in those economies depends entirely on the rarity of and the demand for that labour.

Both dimensions are important. A form of service labour may be rare but poorly remunerated if there is little or no effective demand for it (the labour of archaeologists or of brilliant Latin teachers comes to mind.) Conversely a form of service labour may be comparatively abundant but well remunerated if demand for it is buoyant (e.g. the labour of plumbers or electricians, or computer technicians) But clearly the people who do best in a world of service labour are those whose labour is rare *and* in massive effective demand (elite footballers of course, but also other sports stars, and some kinds of musicians, artists, scientists, engineers and technical experts). Those who do worst are those whose form of labour is abundant and in low effective demand (cleaners, waiters, check-out chicks and fellas, pizza delivery riders, unskilled manual labourers of all kinds.)

But within each of these categories of service labour (rare but undemanded, rare and demanded, common but demanded, common but undemanded) there will be individual variations or gradations of remuneration, depending on precisely *how* rare a form of labour is, and *how* demand varies for it both from place to place and from time to time.

To take the example central to this book, the ability to play football well is rare, the ability to play it at Premier League level is rarer, and the ability to score goals regularly at that level rarer still. So nearly all professional footballers are (comparative-speaking) well remunerated, premier league footballers are incredibly well remunerated, and good premier league strikers earn an absolute fortune.

Conversely, the ability to wait table is common, but if you are practising it in (say) a luxury hotel in Nice, you are likely to do better (at least from tips) than if you are practising it in a high street café in Workington. And even within the luxury hotel in Nice and the café in Workington, there may be significant differences in individual waiter earnings, depending on the attitudes and policies of owners or manager, the relationship of an individual waiter to those owners or managers, as well as differences in levels of waiting skill.

So the world of commodified service labour is a world of vast, but finely graded and individuated inequality – a huge statistical spread made up of innumerable tiny increments from poorest to richest, not only in football, but in every occupation. But while the professional football spectrum stretches from the well off at the bottom to the extraordinarily rich at the top, the table-waiting spectrum stretches from the barely surviving at the bottom to the 'just about managing' at the top. And in between the 'plumber spectrum' (say) will have lowest incomes well above the bottom of the waiter spectrum, (and perhaps even above the poorest end of the football spectrum) but even its highest incomes will be far below those of football's peak earners.

Economists can draw horizontal lines through these spectra and identify 'income groups' or 'wealth groups' or 'income share group's and 'wealth share groups' made up of people from all occupations. Sociologists can draw other horizontal lines through them and identify 'status groups', or 'blue collar' or 'white collar' workers and their different levels of 'home ownership', or differing holiday and leisure preferences. And feminist scholars can draw yet other lines showing major 'gender inequalities' running across virtually all occupations. But none of these statistical groupings or 'strata' are social classes in the traditional sense of the term. They are just statistical creations of observers. The people 'in' them have no sense of collective identity or community, in the way social classes are – or were – supposed to have.

But if the above hypothesis is true then the two most problematic aspects of football history are (a) its presentation of football as an aspect of something called 'working-class culture' and (b) its tendency to see football clubs as in some way representing working-class 'communities'. I shall take these two topics in order.

Football History Revisited and Revised

(a) 'Working-Class Culture'

At the end of his extraordinary book, *The Uses of Literacy*, Richard Hoggart said:

> The fact that illiteracy as it is normally measured has been largely removed only points toward the next and ... more difficult problem. A new word is needed to describe the nature of the response invited by the popular material I have discussed, a word indicating a social change which ... thrives on basic literacy ...

We may now see that in at least one sense we are becoming classless – that is the majority of us are being merged into one class. We are becoming culturally classless …

It is possible to say that the new mass audience is roughly formed of twenty million or so adults who read the popular daily newspapers … they can loosely be called either working class or lower middle-to middle class … But … it is plain that their differences are largely superficial … the kinds of culture which each paper embodies, the assumptions and appeals, are largely the same. The emerging classless society is likely to be a compound of these two audiences; at present it is held in a separation which is becoming less meaningful from year to year … it is probably easier to merge working-class people into a larger, culturally characterless class when they no longer have such strong economic pressure as makes them feel the great importance of loyal membership of their known groups. No doubt many of the old barriers of class should be broken down. But at present the older, the more narrow but also the more genuine class culture is being eroded in favour of the mass opinion, the mass recreational product and the generalized emotional response … The uniform national type which the popular papers help to produce is writ even larger in the uniform international type which the film studios of Hollywood present. The old forms of class culture are in danger of being replaced by a poorer kind of classless, or by what I was led earlier to describe as a 'faceless' culture, and this is to be regretted.[37]

Hoggart wrote that sixty-three years ago, when terrestrial TV had barely arrived in the UK, let alone satellite subscription services or 'social media'. So it is absolutely clear now, as it was not (quite) to him, that anything that one might wish to call 'working-class' culture has disappeared, as has anything distinctive that we might call 'middle class culture'. Both have been merged into what is called, accurately enough, 'popular culture', of which football playing, spectating and supporting is an integral part. However, this popular culture is more than the compound or dilution of pre-existing 'middle' and 'working-class' cultures that Hoggart describes. It is just one result of the actual disappearance of both classes into a deeply hierarchised *mass* of economic individuals. It is the dominant 'mass' culture of a society which *is* indeed 'classless', in an economic as well as cultural sense (but not, needless to say, in any egalitarian sense.)

37   Richard Hoggart, *The Uses of Literacy: Aspects of Working-Class Life with Special Reference to Publications and Entertainments (1957)* (Harmondsworth: Penguin, 1977), 341–3.

Whether this disappearance 'is to be regretted' is a matter of opinion. As his entire book shows, Hoggart was profoundly ambiguous about the 'de-classing' processes he described. On the one hand he recognised that they had involved significant educational and economic improvements in the lives of working-class people. On the other hand, he feared and disliked the intellectually bland, sensationalistic and (in the deepest sense) uncritical 'mass' culture which he saw emerging as the prime expression of that 'classlessness'. And it was *that* which he (tentatively) 'regretted'.

I think though that he may have exaggerated this trend, at least to a certain extent. I think that, in 2020, we can see that it is the education levels of individuals, rather than class, gender or even ethnic differences, that produce the deepest social and political divisions in contemporary capitalist societies.[38] And that is precisely because education (especially higher education) seems to result in more and more people being critical of, or at least sceptical about, popular or conventional wisdoms of all kinds, whether in regard to material consumption and aspiration, or to sexuality, ethnicity, religion or nationality. So if Hoggart was worrying that the disappearance of a working-class culture meant the disappearance of intellectually reflective criticality, he may have been worrying too much. He may in fact have been eliding two separate and separable phenomena. To be culturally or politically critical you do not have to be working class, middle class or any other class. You just have to be an individual with the necessary intellectual tools and training, and as part of the continuation and deepening of the very same trends which Hoggart described, many more people have had that training and possess those tools.

But whether Hoggart was over-pessimistic more generally, he was certainly right about 'working-class culture'. What he feared was happening to it *has* happened to it. It has disappeared.

Therefore, writing about football as an expression of 'working-class culture' is now an anachronism which should be abandoned by everybody but students of (certain periods of) football *history*. Football's crowds are now almost as occupationally and socio-economically diverse as the general

---

38   For some thought-provoking observations on this, see David Runciman, 'How the education gap is tearing politics apart', https://www.theguardian.com/politics/2016/oct/05/trump-brexit-education-gap-tearing-politics-apart>.

population of Britain, and football's TV viewers absolutely so.[39] Football players (meaning soccer players) are still, it is true, not recruited in large numbers from two particular sections of British society – public school boys and girls and young men and women from the 'rugby league' areas of northern England. But in neither case are these 'class' exceptions, not even in the 'public school' case. They are both simply 'playing tradition' exceptions, and now that elite rugby union is itself a professional sport, they do not even prevent outstanding public school 'rugger' players becoming professional sportsmen.

For good or ill then, football is now just one part of a highly commercialised popular or mass culture, and its strengths and weaknesses are the strengths and weaknesses of that culture. But that is just to say that the strengths and weaknesses of commodified football are the strengths and weaknesses of capitalist society as a whole.

(b) 'Community': Real and Imagined

Seeing football clubs and teams as representing working-class communities, is, again, not historically problematic. In the late Victorian and Edwardian periods, and for at least sixty years afterwards, football clubs often *did* 'represent' regions (or parts of regions), towns and cities, (or parts of cities), that were also occupationally based working-class communities. Their supporters came from adjacent areas dominated by single industries, or closely related groups of industries – coal-mining, iron and steel making, ship building, dock working, textile and related factories, the engineering works of the Midlands, etc. Thus the men who came to

---

39   See Taylor, *op cit*, pp. 366–8 and 372–5. Again it is difficult to substantiate long run changes in the social composition of football crowds and fans because of the lack of systematic (as against impressionistic) data. Taylor's discussion of the 1990s suggests that the degree of change may have been exaggerated. But even if that is true, is tells us nothing about changes before that or since. For what it is worth, my feeling is that, since the 1990s, the social, gender and racial composition of support for elite English clubs has changed far more than that for clubs at lower levels. Indeed Taylor cites two studies that suggest just this. (*ibid*, p. 368).

support their team on a Saturday afternoon often knew each other personally as workmates or neighbours, and they often came to the match in work or locality groups. Historically then football clubs did not present themselves as 'communities', they represented and symbolised pre-existing economic and social communities, and indeed gained a great deal of their passionate fan loyalty (or so it was said) from doing so.

But when football crowds come (gradually) to be made up of economic individuals it becomes essential for clubs to present *themselves* as communities. Football grounds became places where people who seldom if ever felt themselves part of a collective (whether occupational or residential) could feel precisely that, and intensely. This club 'community' is certainly 'imagined' rather than face-to-face. (But so are nations, and the intensity of attachment to them is not the less for that.[40]) It could be said that the community of the football crowd, unlike the nation, is fleeting – beginning at kick off and ending at the final whistle. But the crowd is just a part of the community of *the club*, which, like the nation, can exist 'in the mind' of each individual far more continuously. For as she or he follows their club's doings on mass and social media, looks back and analyses victories and defeats, looks forward to forthcoming fixtures and hoped-for triumphs, s/he is all the while expressing and deepening a psychological and emotional attachment to the beloved 'totem'.

Football clubs themselves supplying the need for collective belonging also explains, at least in part, why, at the elite end of the game, these 'imagined football communities' can happily embrace multi-millionaires on

---

40   "I propose the following definition of the nation: it is an imagined political community – and imagined as both inherently limited and sovereign ... It is *imagined* because the members of even the smallest nation will never know most of their fellow-members, meet them, or even hear of them, yet in the minds of each lives the image of their communion ... it is imagined as a *community*, because, regardless of the inequality and exploitation that may prevail in each, the nation is always conceived as a deep, horizontal comradeship." Benedict Anderson, *Imagined Communities: Reflections on the Origins and Spread of Nationalism* (London: Verso, 1983), 15–16. If one omits the word 'sovereignty' and the adjective 'political' from this passage it is as true of football clubs as of nations. Neither are face-to-face communities and both are conceived in "deep horizontal comradeship" irrespective of their internal inequalities.

the pitch and renters of damp, cockroach-infested apartments in the stands. One should say, though, that these contemporary football communities of individuals are more gender, ethnic and occupationally diverse than were the working-class football crowds of old. They are more socially inclusive than the older crowds were, but no less purblindly partisan for that. In fact, if anything, the need of atomised individuals for an intense sense of belonging (no matter how fleeting) has made football crowds and fans even more myopically partisan than ever.

Conclusions: Football, Beauty and My Father

These observations about 'community' or the lack of it,[41] bring this book back to where it began, to my father and the real, face-to-face, coal-mining community of Fencehouses.

I sometimes think that my dad's capacity to distance himself psychologically from the fetid 'imagined community' of football fandom, derived, at least in part, from his belonging to a real one. Because he had the latter, he simply did not need the former, psychologically or emotionally, or certainly not as contemporary 'community-less' individuals do. But perhaps that is just wrong. Perhaps he would have been like that whether he'd been a coal miner in Fencehouses or an investment banker in Frankfurt. Perhaps it was just the way he was.

However that may be, it was contemplating all these implications of the commoditisation of the game I love, and that my father loved, that

41 "Never was the word 'community' used more indiscriminately and emptily than in the decades when communities in the sociological sense became hard to find in real life." Eric Hobsbawm, *Age of Extremes: The Short Twentieth Century 1914–1991* (London: Abacus, 1995), 428. Hobsbawm went on to instance 'the intelligence community', 'the public relations community' and 'the gay community' as examples. He also claimed that this linguistic cult of 'community' began in "the late 1960s", as part of that "extraordinary dissolution of traditional norms, textures and values, which left so many inhabitants of the developed world orphaned and bereft." *Ibid*

undermined my taste for further research on north-eastern football history. Because it seemed to me that this money-obsessed, competition-strangling fate of the contemporary game was – like the 'telos' of some ancient Greek tragedy – 'built in' to that initial moment of its professionalisation; that the short, swirling period of invention, adaptation and improvisation that saw the creation of professional soccer *was* also a kind of Fall from Grace, albeit an exhilarating one.

And even if its 'seeming' that way to me was just another example of the dubious determinism of hindsight, it underpinned both my deep fascination with the commercialisation and professionalisation of football as a short-period historical process, and my general lack of interest in it, (even in the North-East), once it had occurred. In short, distaste for some aspects of present-day elite football came to undermine my enthusiasm for researching my local monograph as soon as even the outlines of that present-day came into view.

Let me therefore end this book, by expressing the hope that, despite my fears, and against all odds, those who run 'the beautiful game' *will* embrace reform, (which means enacting its at least partial de-commodification) before that process fatally compromises and undermines, not football's beauty (for that is, if anything, more a feature of football play at the elite level now than it has ever been) but the capacity of the vast majority of fans to take pleasure in it. For in the case of football, just as in the case of the arts generally, beauty too sullied by money becomes beauty that simply cannot be enjoyed.

Appendix: Restraining the Commodification of Football (If Anyone Wants to)

If – despite everything said above – one is a football fan, or a club director, or a player, who *is* agonised about the commodification of football and its long-term effects, is there any model of football professionalism which might even moderate this seemingly ineluctable trend?

Four possible suggestions have occurred to me and to other people. These are:

(1) probably the most frequently canvassed – *applying some version of the NBA's 'draft pick' system to football.*[1] In this model, the names of the most talented young players from club academies are put into a hierarchically organised 'pot' for each league. Clubs in the league are then allocated priority in choosing from 'the pot' in inverse relation to their performance in the previous season. Club X, having finished just one place above relegation, is given the first chance to obtain outstandingly talented young player Y – the first-ranked player in the 'pot' – or, in basketball terminology, 'the first draft pick'. If, for some reason, Club X does not want player Y, it is then offered first choice of player Z, the 'second draft pick', etc. Conversely, the clubs performing best in the previous league season have the lowest priority in drafting players. This often means that they do not get a 'pick' at all, or, if they do, do not want any of the players still available. (Both things happen in the NBA).

This model would clearly do something to widen competition and to at least weaken the tendency of the 'highest bidder' transfer system to concentrate all the playing talent in a few clubs. It would also act as a disincentive for rich clubs to simply 'stack up' young talent in academies, as happens at the moment. The problem however is that such a system would immediately be open to legal challenge under 'restraint of trade' laws. And even if not challenged, it might only have a very limited effect if it

---

[1]   As it is already in Australian Rules Football.

coexisted with the present transfer system. For of course a young player 'draft picked' to a less successful and less-well-off club, could, at the end of his contract, simply transfer to a richer one. For that reason a second reform has been suggested:

(2) *reinforcing the 'draft pick' system by altering the transfer rules for young players*, so that they could not be transferred from the club that had nurtured them until a set period (three years? five years?) after their 'first team' debuts. This would at least impede the now familiar pattern in which the rise of a club through producing home-grown talent is first arrested, and then aborted, by that talent being 'siphoned off' to richer clubs.

But this reform too would require player unions not to bring 'restraint of trade' actions against it. Its logic is also partly in conflict with the 'draft pick' model. For clearly if clubs in a league are required to put their best young players in a draft 'pot' every close season, then they risk quickly losing the talent they have nurtured, especially if they have been successful in the previous season. One possible way of removing this inconsistency would be to use the 'draft pick' only for young players in a country's *top* league, with all the lower leagues using the 'restricted transfer' system. That is, an outstanding young player nurtured by a League 2 club in England (for example), would not, for a minimum period, be available for transfer either within that league, or 'out' to League 1, The Championship *or* the EPL. Undoubtedly the crucial question for negotiation in this system would be the length of this 'transfer ban' period, given the relative shortness of playing careers.

(3) *Operating a 'salary cap' for every club in a league or division.*[2] Under this system clubs can negotiate any salary they wish with an *individual* player, but their total wage bill for *all* players must not exceed an agreed maximum. Since player salaries tend to rise over the period

---

2   At the beginning of August 2020, the clubs in Leagues 1 and 2 actually voted to introduce a salary cap, against the objections of the PFA. This was, however, a response to the projected sharp fall in club revenues from Covid-19 crowd restrictions, rather than a move to enhance competition. It is also unclear how long the measure will last.

of their contracts, the effect of this ceiling, at least as it operates in the National Rugby League (NRL) in Australia, is to force clubs to part with some of their players on a regular basis to avoid exceeding their 'cap'. Judging by the NRL experience, this does have some 'competition equalising' effect, although, as always, ways can be found of diluting or circumventing it. The most common way of doing so, in the NRL at least, is the use of various kinds of 'external' commercial player 'sponsorships'. Such sponsorships have the effect of maintaining or raising player incomes – in cash or kind – while not being counted as part of a club 'cap'. Nonetheless, since the 'salary cap' system does not directly impact *individual* salary negotiations with players, it does have the advantage of being less open to 'restraint of trade' challenges.

Finally, there is a fourth, more radical, and much-less-canvassed, possibility.

(4) *Developing a modernised 'contract' form of the old 'retainer' system of professional sport for football.*[3] Footballers would be transferred between leagues as well as between clubs. The bulk of professional

---

3   Eighteenth and early nineteenth century jockeys, boxers and cricket players, were not paid employees of clubs, but lifetime 'retainers', or servants, of aristocratic or gentry patrons. Hence, unless they were released from their servitude, these first professional sportsmen never changed the stables for which they rode, or the cricket team for which they played, or the patron for whom they boxed in prize fights. This is indentured sports labour. It certainly should not be simply resuscitated, but it could be modernised and modified. It is notable in this context that resuscitating the 'retainer' model in a modified form also has appeal in another context – the arts in general and the fine arts in particular. In a market economy, artists, just like everyone else, require a monetary income to survive. Hence, if it is not thought desirable that they obtain this income through selling their skills and their products "on the open market", the only alternative is for them – or some selected group of them – to become retainers, not of aristocrats, but of the state or of state institutions (e.g. the UK Arts Council.). This idea has all kinds of problems and issues – the danger of censorship, the always controversial issues of the criteria used to choose the artists supported and of the people to apply them, and the proprietorial rights to art products (paintings, sculptures, poems, novels, plays, film scripts, etc.) accruing to the state in return for their producers' upkeep. But nonetheless, just as in the case of footballers, 'modified retainerism' is the only alternative to artists becoming *de facto* clients of the rich. That this is so may be significant. For if extraordinary

footballers would continue to be employed by clubs, but leagues would also be legally empowered to employ them and to pay transfer fees and wages. In every season a minority of players in any league (25%? 30%?) would be such league 'retainers'. For the period of their contract they would then be 'distributed' and 'redistributed' amongst a league's clubs in accord with some 'competition-expanding' formula.[4]

This reform would allow national and global markets in players to continue, and with them (no doubt) astronomic transfer fees and player wages, but, like the 'salary cap' system, it would have the advantage of not being open to 'restraint of trade' challenges. For players would be able to play for any club *or* any league which bid the most for their services and paid them the highest wage. This implies of course that clubs and leagues could, and would, bid against each other for players.

Finance could be a significant impediment to this reform however. In order to fund this system, leagues would have to receive a significant proportion of the attendance, sponsorship and media revenue which currently accrues to clubs, a change which would certainly be resisted by the richest clubs. Nonetheless, if their resistance could be overcome, this reform could bring 'the return of hope' to a lot of clubs and fans.

---

football skill is itself a kind of art, and, like all other kinds, productive of beauty, then the argument that it should be as widely available as possible and not entirely subordinate to the ability to pay, will appeal for essentially the same reasons as it does in the other arts.

4   If applied to a league, such a formula must specify a proportion of clubs to win its title over a specified period of time. In a league of 20 clubs, a formula operating over 20 seasons could, in logic, vary between absolute equality (each club to win once over twenty seasons) and a more unequal 'percentage' target (50% or 40% or 30% of clubs to win at least once in the twenty seasons.)'Absolute' competitive equality makes any league competition pointless, so only a 'percentage' formula could operate and would be further complicated by promotion and relegation. But so long as the 'planned' winning percentage of clubs was greater than the current 'free market' percentage (12% in the case of the EPL) there would be an increase in competitiveness. Whether such an increase would be a popularly accepted or endorsed however is another matter. (See discussion below.)

However, the main objection to this suggestion might be to its sheer artificiality rather than its financing. Imagine, for example, that it is the beginning of the 2013–14 EPL season and Leicester City have just avoided relegation. The 'plan period' for the EPL's 'win formula' is nearing its end (see note 3 above) and Leicester are one of the clubs who have yet to win the title. In accord therefore with its 'competition widening' formula, the EPL instructs six of its best 'retainer' players to play for Leicester City from the beginning of the season. City duly improve in 2014–15 but still finish well short of the title. So the EPL adds another four outstanding 'retainers' to the club's ranks. In the next season Leicester City duly win the title. Would that victory have been hailed as the 'fairy tale' that Leicester City's actual victory was? Would it have induced Hollywood movie speculations in the way the actual victory did? Or would it, on the contrary, have been seen as far too much of a contrived 'fit up', even by Leicester fans, for any real joy to be taken in it?

These questions raise some much wider issues about the political or administrative regulation of market relations, and the forms of such regulation that will be popularly deemed 'fair' or 'unfair'. They have, for example, important implications for all policies aimed at rendering capitalism 'socially just'. But that broader discussion does not belong here. Suffice to say that, in sport, the popular acceptability of administrative reforms to competitions – even ones that are widely recognised as being deeply 'distorted' or 'unfair' – depends on their maintaining the 'spirit of competition'. Reforms have to be compatible with maintaining a sense that success has been 'earned' by a football club, not 'gifted' to it. And buying success with money still seems, to many people, to earn it in a way that obtaining it through the bureaucratic application of a formula would not.

That said though, the sense of an administrative 'fit up' above is certainly enhanced by the way 'competition-widening' is described – league officials hurrying to meet some rigidly defined 'planned-win' target and pouring players into a 'laggard' team, etc. But one could imagine the whole thing being approached more flexibly than this, with team-strengthening being done in close coordination with the club involved. Also the 'win percentage' goal (be it '25% of clubs winning at least once in a 20 year period' or whatever) could be used as a broad guideline rather than a rigid 'target'.

Approached in this more flexible way, some such system *could* significantly broaden competition in elite soccer while also being acceptable to fans.

However, as may be implied from the tone of all this, I have little confidence that *any* of this will actually happen. On the contrary, the only change in twenty-first century elite football I think likely is a further development of its elitism. I think that a 'European Super League' (ESL) of the continent's very richest clubs may well be founded within the next few years, bringing yet further escalation of transfer fees and player wages. The ultimate implication of that could be that the winning of this 'ESL' (or of a Chinese Super League, say) would require a club 'war chest' exceeding the Chinese or Saudi Arabian national exchequers. But in such a situation, surely growing fan distaste *would* turn into widespread disgust, waning enthusiasm for 'the beautiful game' *would* turn into mass boycotts of TV sets as well as football grounds? Surely?

I don't know, but I fervently hope so.

Bibliography

I. Books and Journal Articles

Anderson, B. (1983). *Imagined Communities: Reflections on the Origins and Spread of Nationalism*. London: Verso.

Appleton, A. (1961). *Hotbed of Soccer: The Story of Football in the North-East*. London: The Sportsmans Book Club.

Baker, W. J. (1979). 'The Making of a Working-Class Football Culture', *Journal of Social History*, 13 (2), 241–51.

Berridge, V. (1986). 'Content Analysis and Historical Research on Newspapers' in M. Harris and A. Lee (eds) *The Press in English Society from the Seventeenth to Nineteenth Centuries*, pp. 201–18 London: Associated University Presses.

Birrell, S. (1981). 'Sport as Ritual: Interpretations from Durkheim to Goffmann', *Social Forces*, 60, (2), 354–76.

Brake, L. and Demoor, M. (eds) (2009). *Dictionary of Nineteenth Century Journalism in Britain and Ireland*. Gent: Academia Press.

Collins, T. (2015). 'Early Football and the Emergence of Modern Soccer, c.1840–1880', *International Journal of the History of Sport [IJHS]*, 32 (9), 1127–42.

Collins, T. (2017). 'Review of Curry and Dunning's *Association Football: A Study in Figurational Sociology* (2015)', *Sport in History*, 37 (4), 529–66.

Collins, T. (2019). *How Football Began; A Global History of How the World's Football Codes Were Born*. London: Routledge.

Cox R., Russell D. and Vamplew, W. (eds) (2002). *Encyclopaedia of British Football*. London: Frank Cass.

Curry, G. and Dunning, E. (2015). 'The Power Game: Continued Reflections on the Early Development of Modern Football', *IJHS*, 33 (3), 239–50.

Curry, G. and Dunning, E. (2017). 'The Origins of Football Debate and the Early Development of the Game in Nottinghamshire', *Soccer and Society*, 18 (7), 866–79.

Days, P. (2011). *The Battle for a Town: Sunderland AFC v Sunderland Albion*. Sunderland: Blue House Field.

Dobbs, B. (1973). *Edwardians at Play: Sport 1890–1914*. London: Pelham.

Durkheim, E. (1915). *The Elementary Forms of the Religious Life* (1912) translated from the French by J. W. Swain. New York: The Free Press.

Fishwick, N. (1989). *English Football and Society 1910–1950*. Manchester: Manchester University Press.

Garnham, N. (2002). 'Patronage, Politics and the Modernization of Leisure in Northern England: The Case of Alnwick's Shrove Tuesday Football Match', *English Historical Review*, 117 (474), 1228–46.

Garside, W. R. (1971). *The Durham Miners 1919–1960*. London: Allen & Unwin.

Gramsci, A. (1971). *Selections from the Prison Notebooks*, edited and translated by Quintin Hoare and Geoffrey Nowell Smith. London: Lawrence & Wishart.

Harris, M. and Lee, A. (eds) (1986). *The Press in English Society from the Seventeenth to Nineteenth Centuries*. London: Associated University Presses.

Harvey, A. (2005). *Football: The First Hundred Years. The Untold Story*. London: Routledge.

Hobsbawm, E. (1995). *Age of Extremes: The Short Twentieth Century 1914–1991*. London: Abacus.

Hoggart, R. (1957). *The Uses of Literacy: Aspects of Working-Class Life with Special Reference to Publications and Entertainments*. Harmondsworth: Penguin.

Holt, R. (1989). *Sport and the British: A Modern History*. Oxford: Clarendon.

Huggins, M. (1989). 'The Spread of Association Football in North-East England, 1876–90. The Pattern of Diffusion', *IJHS*, 6 (3), 299–318.

Hunt, B. (compiler) and Amos, M. (ed.) (2000). *Northern Goalfields Revisited* (privately published and printed). Shildon, Co.Durham.

Johnson, D. (2009). *A Storm in a Teacup: The Durham Sham-Amateur Affair of 1928*. Beeston: SoccerData.

Jouannou, P. and Candlish, A. (2009). *Pioneers of the North: The Origins and Development of Football in North-East England and Tyneside 1870–93*. Derby: Breedon Books.

King, A. (1997). 'The Lads: Masculinity and the new consumption of football', *Sociology*, 31 (2) 329–46.

Kitching, G. (1988). *Karl Marx and the Philosophy of Praxis*. London: Routledge.

Kitching, G. (2011a). 'From Time Immemorial: The Alnwick Shrovetide Match and the Continuous Remaking of Tradition 1828–1890', *IJHS*, 28 (6), 831-52.

Kitching, G. (2011b). 'What's in a Name? Playing "Football" in Mid-Victorian North-Eastern England', *Ethnologie Française*, XLI (4), 601-14.

Kitching, G. (2015). 'The Origins of Football: History, Ideology and the Making of the People's Game', *History Workshop Journal*, 79 (1), 127–53.

Lee, A. J. (1980). *The Origins of the Popular Press in England, 1855–1914*. London: Croom Helm.

Lukes, S. (1975). *Émile Durkheim: His Life and Work: A Historical and Critical Study*. Harmondsworth: Penguin.

Magoun Jr., F. P. (1938). *A History of Football from the Beginnings to 1871*. Cologne: Bochum-Langendreer.

Mangan, J. A. (1981). *Athleticism in the Victorian and Edwardian Public School: The Emergence and Consolidation of an Educational Ideology*. Cambridge: Cambridge University Press.

Mangan, J. A. and Huggins, M. (eds) (2004). *Disreputable Pleasures: Less Virtuous Victorians at Play*. London: Frank Cass.

Mason, T. (1980). *Association Football and English Society, 1863–1915*. Brighton: Harvester.

Mason, T. (1986). 'Sporting News 1860–1914' in Harris, M. and Lee, A. J. (eds) *The Press in English Society from the Seventeenth to Nineteenth Centuries*. London: Associated University Presses.

Metcalfe, A. (1988). 'Football in the Mining Communities of Northumberland, 1882–1914', *IJHS*, 5 (3), 284–95.

Milne, M. (1971). *Newspapers of Northumberland and Durham: A Study of their Progress during the 'Golden Age' of the Provincial Press*. Newcastle: Frank Graham.

O'Leary, L. (2017) *Employment and Labour Relations Law in the Premier League, NBA and International Rugby Union*. Dordrecht: Springer.

Pearson, H. (1994). *The Far Corner: A Mazy Dribble through North-East Football*. London: Warner Books.

Phelan, J., Manuel, M. and Stewart, A. (2001). *The Story of Crook Town Football Club*. Crook: Linton Printers.

Russell, D. (1997). *Football and the English: A Social History of Association Football in England 1863–1995*. Preston: Carnegie.

Serazio, M. (2012). 'The Elementary Forms of Sports Fandom: A Durkheimian Exploration of Team Myths, Kinship and Totemic Ritual', *Communication and Sport*, 1 (4), 303–25.

Shearman, M. (1887). *Athletics and Football*. London: Longmans Green & Co.

Swain, P. (2015a). 'The Origins of Football Debate: The Evidence Mounts 1841–51', *IJHS*, 32 (2), 219–317.

Swain, P. (2015b). 'The Origins of Football Debate: Football and Cultural Continuity 1857–1859', *IJHS*, 32 (5), 631–49.

Tate, S. (2005). 'James Catton, "Tityrus" of the Athletic News (1860 to 1936): A Biographical Study', *Sport in History*, 25 (1), 98–115.

Taylor, M. (2008). *The Association Game: A History of Football*. Harlow: Pearson Education.

Tischler, S. (1981). *Footballers and Businessmen: The Origins of Professional Soccer in England*. New York: Holmes and Meier.

Tranter, N. (1998). *Sport, Economy and Society in Britain*. Cambridge: Cambridge University Press.

Vamplew, W. (1988). *Pay Up and Play the Game: Professional Sport in Britain 1875–1914*. Cambridge: Cambridge University Press.

Voltaire, (1756). 'Essai sur l'histoire generale at sur les Moeurs et l'espirit des nations', ch. 70.

Walker, A. (2006). 'Reporting Play: The Local Newspaper and Sports Journalism c.1870–1914', *Journalism Studies*, 7 (3) 452–62.

Young, P. M. (1973). *A History of British Football*. London: Arrow Books.

II. Internet Sources

'Against Modern Football', <https://www.goal.com/en-au/news/against-modern-football-what-grassroots-campaign/1s6qqrxn1xv7013v4z208i5vr6 and https://www.facebook.com/Against-Modern-Football-247030311967/>.

'Average salary for a female clerk in England in 1925?' <http://www.rootschat.com/forum/index.php?topic=679283.0>.

Burnton, Simon, 'The forgotten story of Manchester City flouting finance rules in 1906'<https://www.theguardian.com/football/2020/feb/26/manchester-city-falling-foul-of-ffp-in-1906-forgotten-story>.

Daily Telegraph, 'A taste of Life in Britain in 1925' <http://www.telegraph.co.uk/news/uknews/1491140/A-taste-of-life-in-Britain-in-1925.html>.

Days, Paul *Sunderland Echo* article of February 18, 2016 <http://www.sunderlandecho.com/news/sunderland-afc-were-formed-a-year-later-than-believed-says-author-1-7739198>.

'Football clubs you can buy shares in' <https://uk.advfn.com/football>.

Hansard, July 30, 1925, (answer of Sir W.de Freece, Minister of Labour, to a question about average rates of wages in twelve chief industries) <http://hansard.millbanksystems.com/written_answers/1925/jul/30/average-weekly-wages>.

History of the Football Association <http://www.thefa.com/about-football-association/what-we-do/history>.

'List of FA Amateur Cup Finals' <https://en.wikipedia.org/wiki/List_of_FA_Amateur_Cup_finals>.

'Lower league footballers' salaries', <www.sportrac.com>.

'Measuring Worth' <https://www.measuringworth.com/calculators/ukcompare/relativevalue.php>.

Northern Football League, <https://en.wikipedia.org/wiki/Northern_Football_League>.

Premier League seasons, <https://en.wikipedia.org/wiki/List_of_Premier_League_seasons>.

Ronay, B. 'European finalists deliver a very English great moment forged overseas' <https://www.theguardian.com/football/blog/2019/may/10/great-english-football-moment-champions-league-forged-overseas>.

Runciman, D. 'How the education gap is tearing politics apart' <https://www.theguardian.com/politics/2016/oct/05/trump-brexit-education-gap-tearing-politics-apart>.

'Ryehill Football' <http://ryehillfootball.co.uk/>.

Sporting Intelligence, Global Sports Salaries Survey, 2019 <https://globalsportssalaries.com/>.

'Tyneside Tyzacks', <http://www.tyzack.net/>.

Watson, Tom ('The greatest football manager you've probably never heard of') <http://www.victorianfootball.co.uk/>.

III. Newspaper Sources Cited

Alnwick Journal (AJ) 1862
Alnwick Mercury (AM) 1856–66
Athletic News 1928
Durham Chronicle (DC) 1879
Durham County Advertiser (DCA), 1880
Hexham Courant (HC) 1865–78
Newcastle Weekly Chronicle (NCh) 1884–86
Newcastle Courant (NC) 1856–76
Newcastle Daily Chronicle (NDC) 1875–92
Newcastle Daily Leader (NDL) 1885–1900
Newcastle Evening Chronicle (EC) 1888–92
North-Eastern Daily Gazette (Middlesbrough) *(DG)* 1887 and 1892
North Mail (Newcastle) *(NM)* 1927–37

Northern Athlete (Newcastle) *(NA)* 1883–4
Northern Daily Mail (Hartlepool) *(NDM)* 1927–28
Northern Echo (Darlington) *(NE)* 1892 and 1929
Northumberland Gazette (Alnwick) *(NG)* 1888
Nottingham Daily Express (NDE) 1905
Shields Daily Gazette (SDG) 1892
Shields Daily News (SDN) 1927
Sunderland Daily Echo (SDE) 1881–94
Sunderland Daily Post (SDP) 1881
The Sportsman 1905

IV. Other Archival Sources Cited

Alnwick Castle Archive: (Documents ACC 107; DNP MS 187A/118 and 'Dukes of Northumberland Scrapbook', vol. X, 'Fourth Duke').
Bailiffgate Museum, Alnwick: 'Alnwick Shrove Tuesday Minute Book 1871–1953'.
Football Association Archive, National Football Museum, Manchester:
    (1) Football Association, *Report and Recommendations of the Commission appointed to enquire into alleged Breaches of the Rules of the Association by Officials and Players of certain Clubs in the County of Durham*, London: 42, Russell Square, June 18, 1928.
    (2) Football Association, *Council Minutes*, October 5, 1928 and January 29, 1929.
    (3) Football Association, *Emergency Committee Minutes*, October 9 – December 3, 1928.
Northumberland Record Office, Woodhorn: 'Alnwick Shrove Tuesday Minute Book 1871–1953' (NRO 3851).
Tyne and Wear Archive, Discovery Museum, Newcastle: Documents S/RFC4/14/29-35.

Index

Sport, History and Culture

This series publishes monographs, edited collections and reprints of classic studies on the history and the contemporary role of sport, primarily in Britain and Europe but including other parts of the world. The editors wish to make available the very best of recent doctoral and post-doctoral work in the subject area whilst also looking to established scholars for major new books or collections of articles.

Although the focus of the series is historical, it also embraces more contemporary interdisciplinary studies of the role of sport as a local, national and global phenomenon. The series includes both new and established areas of research into the class, age and gender dimensions of sport as well as its political and ideological aspects, including nationalism, imperialism and post-colonialism. The editors wish to encourage economic and transnational studies of sport as well as new work on ethnicity, sports literature and material culture. The series will also reflect on the significance for the writing of sports history of new cultural and theoretical debates.

Genuinely international in approach, the series also seeks to publish English translations of some of the most outstanding scholarship on the history and culture of sport in Europe, South America and beyond. The series aims to act as a focus for the historical study of sport internationally and facilitate interdisciplinary debate on the subject.

Lightning Source UK Ltd.
Milton Keynes UK
UKHW021249030621
384868UK00011B/70

9 781789 978346